How To
PAINT YOUR Car
ON A BUDGET

PAT GANAHL

S-A DESIGN

CarTech®

Edited by: Kris Palmer and Josh Brown

ISBN-13 978-1-932494-22-8
ISBN-10 1-932494-22-7

Printed in China

CarTech®

39966 Grand Avenue
North Branch, MN 55056
Telephone (651) 277-1200 • (800) 551-4754 • Fax: (651) 277-1203
www.cartechbooks.com

OVERSEAS DISTRIBUTION BY:

Brooklands Books Ltd.
P.O. Box 146, Cobham, Surrey, KT11 1LG, England
Telephone 01932 865051 • Fax 01932 868803
www.brooklands-books.com

Brooklands Books Aus.
3/37-39 Green Street, Banksmeadow, NSW 2019, Australia
Telephone 2 9695 7055 • Fax 2 9695 7355

Cover:
This prize-winning Corvette gets a complete paint job in Chapter 9.

Title Page:
This 1953 Chevy was painted by author Pat Ganahl. He did most of the work himself, including the three-stage pearl paint with clear.

Back cover main:
Right before you start spraying paint, it's best to open a fresh tack rag and use it, with your blow gun, to remove any remaining lint, dust, or dirt specs from the surface.

Inset:
Keeping your spray gun clean is paramount to proper spraying. Especially important is keeping the inside of the nozzle area free of any dried paint.

CONTENTS

I've been planning and thinking about this book for quite a while. That's why my '52 Chevy has been driving around in spotted-in factory original paint with some chrome strips missing for so long.

But finally sitting down to write this has given me pause. The one thing I have never really considered is: Where did I learn to paint cars?

There weren't any books like this around at the time. The closest thing to it were George Barris's little "Spotlite Books" and his frequent articles in the various car magazines showing how to make a scoop, French an aerial, roll a pan, and so on. I read and absorbed all that stuff. But it told more about how to cut, weld, grind, hammer, and dolly sheetmetal (and round rod) than how to spray paint. Teaching how to spray paint in printed words and photos is quite difficult. You learn much more by actually doing it. That's what I did. And that's what you will do.

I learned about welding, grinding, and metal fabrication as a young teen in metal shop classes in school, and got further experience when my father bought an acetylene welding outfit for use on the family ranch, and made me the primary welder. Again, you learn by doing—burning and cutting your fingers as well as burning holes in metal.

However—and this is a theme repeated throughout this book—I was learning these things at a point of major transition in the entire bodywork/welding/painting industry. For generations, bodywork was done with hammers and dollies, welding was done with torches, filling was done with lead, and painting was done with lacquer. That's the way it was done from the 1920s through the early 1960s. Those are the methods Barris showed readers in his how-to articles.

But paddling lead was way beyond me (and most) young beginners. On the other hand, resin-based "plastic" fillers, which were just coming on the market at that time, afforded an alternative. Unfortunately, typical of pioneering products, many weren't quite perfected, nor were their methods of application. This gave plastic fillers a bad name they definitely no longer deserve, but still find hard to shake. The real problem with plastic fillers is the same today as it was then—and it's a fault in technique, not the product. Filler is very easy to apply, with no special tools or talents, and was and is therefore often spread too thickly over poorly prepared surfaces. The latter was also true of lead; it just took a bit more training and equipment to do it.

We're getting ahead of ourselves, but let me give you one example from my early experience that gives a hint of dealing with changing technology. Brazing is simpler, faster, and causes less warpage than gas welding sheetmetal. It's not as strong or permanent as welding for joining pieces of metal, but it's great for things like filling holes. It's also perfectly compatible with lead. Most of those early articles showing Barris, Starbird, and others doing custom bodywork showed them brazing on sheetmetal,

and then covering it with lead. It's what Barris said to do. So that's what I did in several cases, but then I covered it with filler instead of lead. But filler, no matter how good, is not compatible with brazing. I don't know the chemical specifics, but they just won't stick to each other. I learned this the hard way, after my carefully sanded, primed, and painted bodywork produced bulges or bubbles wherever I had brazed the surface and filled over it. The only way to fix it was to cut out the brazed area, weld in sheetmetal patches, and start over. Today, as I am finding lots of small brazed areas from long-ago bodymen as I prepare my original '32 Ford body for paint, I am glad to learn that certain high-adhesion sealers (such as PPG DP40, or similar) can be applied over brazing and then coated with sanding primers or even plastic fillers.

Continuing the theme of early experience and changing technology, spray paint cans didn't become prevalent until the early '60s. So when I wanted to customize my first bicycle (riser handlebars, bobbed rear fender, and so on), I took it all apart, carefully hand-sanded the frame and other parts, then brush-painted them with some sort of gloss enamel—purple, I believe. About the same time (the late '50s), my friends and I switched from model airplanes to model cars, which we also customized (this soon became a national fad). These we also brush painted, painstakingly, to get them as smooth and glossy as possible. But we also spent considerable time prepping the plastic bodies: sanding down mold lines, filling depressions (or customizing the body) with putties, priming, and then doing lots more sanding with increasingly fine grits of paper, before we thinned down the "enamel for plastics" paint and flowed it on with carefully chosen brushes. Then, especially as the kits became more complete, we learned to use different and realistic colors to hand-paint engines, chassis parts, chrome trim, and so on. What this early model building taught us was careful and thorough preparation, color selection, detailing, and patience. These are all requisites of a good paint job on a real car.

Then came spray paint. This wasn't an entirely new learning curve, because the prep, patience, detailing, and so on didn't change. But we had to learn a new technique that wasn't easy, at first, to master. It took a lot of practice and experimentation: making jigs or props to hold the various parts, getting all the dust off, spraying tack coats, warming the paint under hot water in the sink, then trying to keep all dust, dirt, or bugs off until it dried. But the real talent was learning how to wield that spray can so you could get an even—and the glossiest possible—coat in that seemingly very narrow window between orange peel and runs. We also learned that switching from one type of paint to another (enamel to lacquer, for instance), or even changing brands, usually required some testing and adjustment. Moving from spray cans to spray guns was a bigger step, but it still takes the same talent and the same feel. The best way—the only way, really—to learn how to paint with a spray gun is to do it. Spray cans are an excellent (and cheap) place to start. But whether you are painting model cars, the kids' bikes, or the back porch furniture, go out and paint stuff. Start practicing. Right now.

Most of my friends were older and got cars before I did. They were also smarter, and got cars that didn't need any real bodywork, just new, better, sharper or cooler paints jobs. In our small town, there were only a couple of "paint shops." One guy built a cinder-block spray booth in his backyard and the other had an old building downtown that I'm not sure even had a booth. But both were glad to spray cars for a minimal fee if we did all the prep and bought the materials. See, if you know how to spray paint—and if you do it regularly—that's the easiest part of the job, by far. And we were young and eager (especially me), so doing the grunt work not only saved money, it was even fun. The only cost was several sheets of wet-or-dry sandpaper and rolls of masking tape. Disassembling the cars (removing bumpers, lights, emblems, and so on) was intuitive. Removing things like doors handles and certain chrome trim was more mysterious. We either figured it out, or left them on and masked them. Sometimes getting them back on was more difficult.

Again, I don't know how we learned to start wet-sanding with 220 paper, how to fold it, how to featheredge chips, how not to use our fingertips, and how to finish with 360 or 400 grit—probably from the magazines. But there was also some sort of common knowledge among us teens who worked on our cars, which we all shared. In fact, I remember a few "paint parties," wherein the car owner would buy the beer and invite everybody over to sand the car in an afternoon. You wouldn't always get the best quality, but you'd get the grunt work done, and you could touch up the rough spots later. I also remember some bloody fingers.

For my own first car I wasn't nearly so smart. I inherited a sound, but exceedingly beat-up old Chevy sedan. It needed a whole lot of bodywork, and about all I knew was beating out big dents with a heavy rubber mallet that my dad used for similar purposes. Using blocks of wood as dollies, I tried doing what it showed in the magazines, but of course it wasn't nearly

When it came to body and paint, my first car gave me plenty to learn. But I couldn't hurt it. The good part was that it didn't have any rust. But it was really beat up and abandoned in a field when I got it. In this photo, I'd already been working on it six months, including taking the fenders off and pounding them flat against the ground. Of course I got the car for free.

I found a parts car for $10 with good sheetmetal and swapped the fenders, trunk, and other parts. I sanded the car down and removed most trim in preparation for paint, but that's as far as I got, so I drove it like this through high school.

After several years of daily driving with this first enamel paint, the car had some dings and dents. I fixed those and started refurbishing it in preparation for a better lacquer paint job.

During my first summer home from college I rented a small sprayer and primed, re-sanded, and masked the car. Then I bought three quarts of enamel ('62 Corvette Fawn Beige and Cordovan Brown), one of sealer, and got a local painter to spray it in his backyard booth for $25. This was the next day, mostly reassembled (the front bumper was at the chrome shop).

was as easy as it looked (and I didn't have the proper equipment). Finally I figured out I could remove the fenders, lay them on the driveway, and beat them flat against the pavement. I don't recommend this today, but "whatever works" is still a rule of bodywork in my garage. Fortunately, by pure luck, I happened across a $10 dead identical parts car that had excellent sheetmetal that I could simply swap for my bent

and broken parts. Thus I learned a new lesson in bodywork: It's often much easier and ultimately cheaper to bolt on a new, decent fender (or other body part) than it is to try to straighten out a mashed one.

However, my old bomb was 2-tone to start, and the replacement fenders and trunk were a third color, all of which I eagerly sanded down. But I had no painting equipment (nor money to pay someone else to paint it), so I touched up a few bare spots with spray-can primer and drove this laughable coat-of-many-colors all through high school. It wasn't until about a year later that I rented a cheap little compressor and gun, primed the car in my dad's garage (got in trouble for that), bought two shades of metallic enamel (and a quart of "aircraft sealer" that the painter wisely recommended), and got one of the local guys to spray it in his backyard booth for $25. Wow, what a difference! I waxed it about once a week through college to keep it that way (dorms didn't have garages and car covers were unheard of). But I finally

started wearing through the enamel, and tiring of people asking me "Did you paint that yourself?" and having to reply, "No." What I really wanted was a "custom" lacquer finish, anyway.

I should admit right now that I obviously have a hot rod/custom car bent that derives partly from my generation, but probably more so from a personal and financial do-it-yourself mentality. For me, hot rodding is 70% about fixing up old cars—taking something cheap that no one else wants and making it look good, then using some traditional tricks and my own ingenuity or creativity to make it look better than good (that's the other 30% of rodding and customizing). But this book is not about "custom painting." Plenty of books talk about that already. We won't even talk much about custom paints or products, because they are changing constantly. We talk about the basics of stripping down, straightening out, fixing up, prepping, and repainting any vehicle that you think (1) needs it, or (2) will look better in a different

That paint job didn't happen, as other projects took precedence (family, job, pickup, etc.). But by then I had a garage to paint in, my own compressor, and so on. Since it basically only had one paint job over factory paint, I never stripped any of it. Nor did I fully disassemble it. I just sanded it thoroughly, sprayed it with lacquer primer, sanded some more, then sprayed it in the same colors in lacquer (no clear), and hand-rubbed it out, as seen here in 1981.

Since this car had finally been promoted from daily driver to fun car (not show car), I decided it was time to detail the underside, as well. Other than the gas tank, which was painted with leftover lacquer from the body, the rest of this was done with spray cans (and one piece of chrome). This cost virtually nothing other than cleaning and sanding time, and was surprisingly easy to maintain.

Here's the same car, same paint, in 2005. People say straight lacquer won't last that long, but it will if you take care of it. A garage, a car cover, and plenty of careful wax jobs help.

color. We also proceed on the premise that you want to do this because (a) you don't want to pay thousands of dollars for someone else to do it, or (b) you think you can do the job better yourself, without paying someone else thousands of dollars to do it less well. Just being of that mind makes you something of a hot rodder in my book (and a bit of a rebel, at that). But no matter. This book is for anyone who wants to repaint a car at home, for whatever reason. An added bonus is that once you have the equipment and know how to use it, you can paint all sorts of things.

Since I'm talking about my own experience and self-teaching here, before we get to yours, let me give you a couple more instructive examples.

Somehow I acquired a '49 Chevy pickup, late on a dark night, for free. I wanted it because it had the five-wndow cab. When I saw it the next morning in daylight, I knew I was nuts. But I kept it

While a starving student (with no garage to work in), I came across this '47 Chevy pickup abandoned in a very dark canyon one night. I'd always wanted a "fat cab" Chevy, especially the "5-window" version. The property owner said I could have it if I hauled it out right then. When I saw it in bright light the next morning, I realized how foolish I was. Free is free, but find something better than this to start with. It obviously had no driveline, but I had a running 6-cylinder, 3-speed '62 sedan that donated engine, transmission, wiring/electricals/ radiator, and so on.

Since these old Chevy pickups are (still) quite plentiful, I swapped much of the sheetmetal, including the entire bed, but still did a lot of hammer/dolly/filler bodywork, before spraying (with rented/borrowed equipment, in my driveway) my first full paint job, in black lacquer. It's truly easy to paint and maintain. Got some chips? Spot it in and rub some more. A daily driver, it had made several cross-country trips when these photos were taken. The camper was metallic silver catalyzed enamel, color sanded and buffed out (my first try at that). Ed "Big Daddy" Roth added the pinstriping (red on the camper, blue on the body).

Besides, I'd always heard that "hand-rubbed" lacquer was best. So I rubbed out that whole paint job, with paste compound and rags, by hand, until it had that deep gloss that only black lacquer can have. It took a couple of days. My hands were blistered. But it was beautiful! What did I know? With a little camper on the back, my wife and I drove that truck all over the country, several times. When the paint got chipped or dinged I just spotted it in and rubbed it out some more. Black lacquer is probably the easiest-to-maintain paint there is (or was; I can't get it where I live any longer). You don't have to color-match it. It doesn't need clear. Simple.

About this time catalyzed paints were coming on the scene. Trickier

and started fixing it up. First I transplanted everything possible (from driveline to gauges, radio, wiring, radiator, etc.) from a beat-up but good-running '62 Chevy 4-door I had. I found a new bed, rear fenders, and running boards. Somebody gave me some seats. It took a couple years before it was ready for paint. The single-car garage at the triplex we were living in then wasn't big enough to paint a car in (besides, my first Chevy was stored in it), so I did it in the open driveway. I decided to paint it black lacquer, and got the proper materials from a nearby auto paint store. A friend loaned me a good spray gun, and I rented a decent-size 110-volt compressor that kept blowing the circuit breaker during the job. But it didn't matter because straight-color (non-metallic) lacquer is really easy to spray. You can start

and stop. If something screws up or a bug lands in it, wait 15 minutes, scuff it down, and spray that part again. I never stripped this truck to bare metal, and I can't remember if I ever primed the whole thing, but whatever (little) paint was still on it was old enough that nothing lifted or wrinkled. I was lucky.

But here's the funny part—nobody told me anything about color sanding. And I didn't have any kind of buffer.

ones, like Imron (or urethanes, or whatever they were calling them) really needed to be sprayed in a booth, and were very susceptible to fisheyeing, running, and other problems. But there were also new catalysts that could be added to regular automotive enamels, so I tried some of that on the truck's camper—silver metallic. The first thing I learned is that if you got runs or sags, you could sand them out the next morning

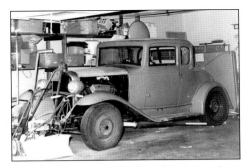

There were a lot of misguided trends during the '70s, one being a brief flirtation with "un-Ford" street rods. The main attraction? They were cheap! I got this Olds-powered, orange, ex-drag '32 Chevy for $500 with a busted Hydromatic transmission.

By then I had a one-car garage to work in—not big enough for painting, though. After the Olds Tri-Power caught fire, I decided to put a hot little Chevy six in it and paint it two-tone metallic blue (two-tone "resto rods" were another '70s fad). Here I'd prepped and painted the firewall before installing the new engine.

This was my first metallic lacquer paint job. I should have stripped the existing paint, but fortunately it was old enough that I could just sand it down, spray several coats of lacquer primer over it, and block sand. I also should have sprayed some clear coats, especially over the lighter blue, before rubbing it out, but I didn't know about that yet.

After more than a decade, I made a few minor changes. But the only parts I repainted were the front fenders. That old lacquer paint job held up pretty well.

and respray them. I also learned, some-how, about color sanding. But no amount of hand rubbing would bring it up to its as-sprayed high gloss. It wasn't until much later that I discovered that these catalyzed enamels (or urethanes, acrylics, or whatever they're calling "two-part" paints) need to be power-buffed with proper cutting pads and com-pounds, and then re-buffed with glazing compound to get a gloss anywhere near as good as old hand-rubbed lacquer.

One further example: Given that these new catalyzed paints went on really smooth and glossy, without rub out, I decided to try a new catalyzed clear coat over a Porsche light green metallic lacquer on a VW bug for a friend. I figured it would be simple and quick, and these clears were compatible over lacquer (most of today's aren't). Everything went fine as I finished laying on a good, wet, glossy coat of the clear. It looked beautiful until it suddenly broke

When my wife and I got married we bought a near-new '69 VW Bug that mechanically self-destructed. So we found this cherry, one-owner '65 on a car lot going for something like $600 because it had faded red paint and a couple primer spots. All it needed was a good paint job. VWs have lots of painted metal inside. Since this car was red to start with, I sanded down the outside and sprayed it with Porsche India (or Guards—same color) Red in lacquer, rubbed out. In subsequent years I painted it twice more; same color, but in single-stage urethane, which didn't need rubbing.

out in a case of fisheyes worse than any teenager's zits—all over the whole car. I called my paint store to ask what might have gone wrong, and he called the Ditzler regional rep, who actually came over to my house to see. His first question was, "Did you wait 20 minutes and spray a second coat of clear, as the label says?" Of course I didn't. I sprayed it like I'd always sprayed enamels—a light tack coat followed by a heavy gloss coat a few minutes later. It flowed out great, and I wasn't planning to color-sand or rub it, so I didn't want to push my luck spraying it again. Plus the thing about "second coat after 20 minutes" was buried in the fine print on the label, and I never saw it. After asking lots of questions about my prep, and looking at my equipment, he couldn't come up with any reason why it fisheyed; but he assured me that, since I hadn't added the second coat after a 20-minute interval as the directions said, the whole thing would wrinkle up if I added a second coat now. Something about "chemical cross-linking." My only recourse was to very carefully color-sand the clear down until the fisheyes just disappeared, and then buff it out, both without going through the clear coat. It was very painstaking and time consuming, but in the end my friend thought it was a beautiful paint job (which it was) and got lots of compliments. But it was way more work than I had planned

I can't remember how we figured out the problem, but it took a while. I think someone suggested I double-check my old compressor, which I had bought used. Sure enough, it was worn out, just like a smoking engine, and was pumping minute amounts of oil from its crankcase, with the air. While it doesn't affect lacquer, any oil, either on the surface to be painted or in the air supply, causes fisheyes—or worse—with modern two-part paints. I rebuilt the compressor with new rings to solve the problem. Further, someone who knew told me to also get a new hose, because my old one was contaminated with oil (the same problem occurs if you have ever used an oil-vaporizer on your compressor to lubricate air tools). Clean air and an oil-free hose are musts for painting.

While the red VW became Anna's driver, I picked up this '60 for $100 and started fixing it up for mine. In its first form, as seen here, I painted it inside and out (under hood, under deck, interior) in lacquer in Porsche Metallic Salmon. Still no clear. But as I drove it over 15 years, I kept repainting parts that needed it, finally using a lacquer-compatible clear urethane on the fenders and hood. One point I'm hopefully making here is that if you take care of your car, use a cover if it sits outside, and maintain the paint, it will last for years—even decades. And if you painted it yourself in the first place, you can touch it up when it needs it, right?

It may be typical of do-it-yourselfers, but I'm a slow learner. This was my lesson in "paint cars only for yourself." I bought this '40 Ford sedan, with a non-running Olds engine and blown (out the bottom) early Ford trans, at a swap meet for $1,200. I figured I'd do the bodywork, get it running, paint it black lacquer, and sell it for a tidy profit. Being a California car, it was sounder than it looked, with no body rot and only minor dents. The part I didn't figure was that someone had sanded much of the body (including the whole roof and one side) to bare metal with a grinder, then let it sit out 14 years. The surface rust was impenetrable, and I didn't dare grind the metal any further. So I finally resorted to some icky, yellow, spray-on "rust converter" that chemically changes rust into…something else.

After getting the engine running, installing a new trans, doing other mechanical work, killing the rust, hammer-and-dollying, filling, block sanding, and lacquer priming, the car didn't look much better, but it was progressing. A cheap repro grille, lights, and bumpers helped.

Once the mechanicals were redone, the body and paint were really the easy part. But when it came to all new upholstery, interior/dash trim, new glass, running boards, wheels/tires, and so on, it got to be a losing proposition in a hurry. I forget what I sold it for, but it wasn't nearly enough to cover my costs and labor. That's the last time I tried that.

Okay, this introduction is getting lengthy, but I hope instructive. Besides the lessons already taught, I just want to stress that whatever else I have to teach in this book, I have learned by doing, making mistakes, and asking lots of questions.

Many books of this type are written by (or with) professional painters or shops that have perfected a specific system that works for them. That doesn't help much if something goes wrong, and it's very hard to preach one system in today's ever-changing world of paint products and equipment. This is especially true if you're painting at home in your garage, not in professional shop conditions. On the other hand, some books are written by people who work

Continued on page 14

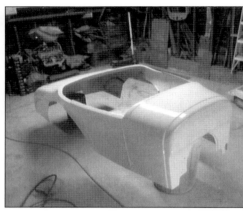

This one was pure fun. About the time nostalgia drag racing got started, I found this old Altered sitting ignored in someone's backyard. The owner obviously didn't want it, letting me have what you see here for $300. Honest.

Other than adding an extra hoop to the roll cage and rebuilding the brakes, I didn't have to do anything but clean and paint it. I used "Urethane Black" spray cans on the frame, which were excellent (but no longer available), and sprayed things like the axle, spring, and radius rods with a Mercedes silver. Several other parts I had cad plated, which is really cheap.

The fiberglass body and grille shell had never been painted, so I sanded off mold lines, primed them, and sprayed them Corvette Yellow in single stage, glossy, catalyzed enamel. No rub out needed.

The injected Chrysler Hemi was an extra $500 and needed a couple of new parts. The very talented Steve Stanford added the turned gold-leaf "Low Buck Special" and "Pure Purgatory" lettering, along with painted-on teardrop taillights and license reading "Cheap." And, no, that's not me in the driver's seat. I like the building part, not the scary part.

Let's end with this '53 Chevy, which became my most involved car project. I wanted to promote '50s rods at Rod & Custom magazine, and my cousin's inherited coupe looked like a cherry-pie prospect—until we stripped it down and bead-blasted it to bare metal. Since it was a magazine project, I got some expert help repairing the worst sheetmetal and filling/peaking the hood.

I painted the dash and window frames charcoal gray to match the upholstery. But note the quality of paint and detailing in the door-jambs. It was easy to paint these when all the interior and glass were out of the car. But this sort of detail is what makes the difference between a regular and really high-quality paint job. It just takes time and effort.

I still did the vast majority of the car in my own garage. I didn't remove the doors because they fit well and the bead blasting cleaned the jambs thoroughly. But the entire interior was stripped, all glass but the rear window was removed, and all the front sheet metal came off (a few times). With some bodywork and custom modifications, here is the car coated in PPG K200 (an excellent high-fill primer that is no longer available), prior to a lot of block and board sanding.

Since it was a magazine project car, that meant it was the first time I didn't have to work within my own personal budget, so it's, by far, the nicest car I've built. I just had to do most of the work myself, which included filling, smoothing, and painting the firewall, inner fender panels, under the hood, splash aprons, and lots of other parts, all in the 3-stage pearl with clear.

This paint color sort of came about as a mistake, or a compromise. This was the '80s period when pastels were briefly popular on street rods. I would have painted the car competition orange (or black), but we went for a custom mix somewhere between cantaloupe and watermelon—just a solid-color lacquer (non-metallic). But after I painted the car this color, it looked like an atomic-reactive pumpkin. It glowed in the dark. So I decided to soften and tone it down with a lighter pearl coat, which became known as "Peach Pearl." It might not be the color I'd choose today (I'd go with the black), but I have to say it's probably the best paint job I've done. And it's the first pearl I did on a big, full-size vehicle. Nobody told me to spray it like a candy, so I'm lucky it came out even.

for, or are "sponsored by," a particular paint (or polish) company, and therefore push a single brand of products. Not only are such books skewed, but today they are out of date as quickly as they are printed. More on this later, but I avoid specifying products by name and number in this book because (1) as soon as I named them, they'd be superceeded, and (2) I'm not sponsored by anybody.

I'm not a professional painter. I've never done a paint job for money. But I have painted all or parts of every car I've ever owned, as well as plenty for friends and relatives, since my early teens. I'm sure I haven't discovered all mistakes yet, but I've made—and figured out how to correct—plenty. I have done paint jobs that have won awards and made magazine covers—all from my garage at home. That's how I learned. And that's what I am passing along in this book. Best of luck to you.

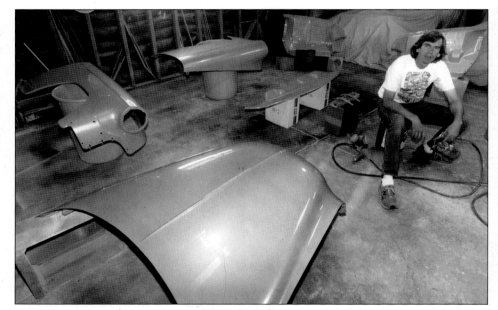

In the first chapter I ask why you want to paint your own car, and point out that it's a lot of hard work, which I think this photo exemplifies. I have just sprayed the final clear coat on some front-end sheetmetal, and I look a little tired. But the real point of this photo—and this whole introduction—is to show that I painted this car, and the others shown here, by myself, in my garage (or driveway), with regular home equipment and no training. You can do the same. Reading this book gives you many pointers. Doing it—trying it—teaches you how.

TO PAINT OR NOT TO PAINT

If you have a choice, find a good car to fix up that mainly needs a new paint job. This '55 Chevy 2-door has been sitting in my SoCal neighborhood more than a decade. It even used to be shiny. But there are no rust bubbles showing anywhere on it, it's straight, it's complete, and the fact it's a Bel Air makes it even more desirable. You could strip it to bare metal to satisfy your curiosity, but all this car probably needs is a good sanding and new paint—besides other usual restoration. But, of course, the owner plans to do that "soon" and won't sell.

Why Do *YOU* Want to Paint this Car?

A car body is very much like a human body. In the first place, unless it's new or near new, it's probably not going to be perfect any more. Secondly, it's inevitably going to further deteriorate with age. But there's bad news and good news.

First the good; relatively speaking, it's easier to keep your body in good shape than it is to get it back into that shape once you've let it go for a while. Like your own body, your car's body can be kept in pretty good shape fairly easily if you care for it. If you house it properly, keep it out of bad elements as much as possible, and treat it kindly, it will stay in good condition for a long time. The problem is, unlike our bodies, our cars often come to us from other owners who have not treated them well over the years. Such cars might have suffered anything from chafed, spotted, or wrinkled skin, to scrapes, bruises, and scars, or much worse maladies such as sick internal organs or the dreaded cancer (rust that's more than skin-deep). In this book we won't treat any mechanical problems whatsoever, or matters of couture (interior/upholstery). We discuss minor to even moderate bodywork, because that's integral to any good paint job. But we won't get into the serious cut-it-out-and-replace-it type of metal transplant that serious rust requires, or body realignment that necessitates frame-pullers or Porta-Powers.

The simple and obvious point is that if you protect your car as much as possible (not just from dents and scrapes, but especially from the sun), and take good care of it (wash and wax it regularly), its paint job will look good and can continue looking that way for years. If it was a good paint job to begin with, it will look even better; but with some work and upkeep, you can revive an ailing paint job or make a poor one look better than it was. We cover that fully later.

That advice is useful to know, but since you've bought this book, you've likely concluded that your car's finish is beyond reviving. So on to our main point: Why do *you* want to paint this car? If you just want to change the color, or put a higher-quality paint job on it than the one it has now, that's fine. It is a lot of work, but hopefully you have the right intentions. On the other hand, if it *needs*

You're not supposed to teach with bad examples, but this is classic. I came across this little dented sedan (I can't even tell what it is) in northern British Columbia, Canada. Even though it's been recently sprayed with silver spray-can paint, rust is popping out all over it. The owner said he was a certified welder and he was going to fix it. Why? The rust on this car is growing from the inside out. A paint job won't fix it. Some major metal surgery could—but this car just isn't worth it.

a new paint job, how did it get that way? Assuming that you got this car in this condition (probably for a good price because of it), and now, being a do-it-yourself type person, you want to fix it up to enjoy for yourself or to eventually sell it for more than you paid for it. Two things here, second one first—don't even think about counting your time and labor as part of the profit made from selling a car you painted yourself. Painting a car is a big job. It's very labor-intensive. It is not a good way to make money. The point of this book is to teach you how to do a job well; to get the quality of paint job you want and might not be able to get readily elsewhere; to save a considerable amount of money doing so (particularly if you count your time doing this as hobby time); and to have the satisfaction of knowing and being able to say, "I did this myself."

Now, let's get back to that question: "How did this car get this way?" If you let your own car fade, craze, crack, peel—or worse—I think you're deluding yourself if you really think you're going to immerse yourself in a repaint project, and then keep the car nice and shiny afterward. I've seen a whole lot of at-home paint projects that got as far as some chrome stripped off, some filler applied, the body sanded, and maybe even a whole coat of primer applied before the project stalled and surface rust started showing through. Most of the owners of such projects really had no idea how much work the whole job would be. On the other hand, I've seen a lot of hobby cars make it to shiny paint and fresh chrome, only to naturally revert to their former state within a few years. I'm saying this partly to forewarn you, and partly to (hopefully) shame you into full follow-through. If you do it right and maintain it well, you have accomplished something you can take justifiable pride and satisfaction in.

However, I mentioned "two things." In addition to dismissing the notion that this is a big money maker for you, the other point to consider is that maybe you really shouldn't paint this car yourself. If all you really want is to make a faded and fatigued car look better (and probably didn't realize how much work a full-on paint job is), we give you several alternatives in this book. The days of the "Any Car, Any Color—$19.95" paint job are long gone. But you can get a decent "one-day" paint job, and we show you how here. We also show how to spiff up an otherwise ho-hum factory paint job, or re-coat a faded or spotted car in its original color, easily and inexpensively. There are several stages of home paint jobs, between a quick "scuff and squirt" and the full-on show-winning deal that we cover here. Take your pick. Choose your personal level of involvement and intensity.

In fact, your faded car might not need painting at all. You might be surprised how even long-neglected paint can be brought back to life, and how some touch-up or spotting-in can save a paint job you thought needed complete refinishing. That later, but first…

Why Do You Want to Paint *THIS* Car?

If you're going to spend some major time and effort painting a car at home, you'd probably like to have something you can be proud of when you're done, and it certainly wouldn't hurt if it had decent resale value if and when you might get tired of it or you find a new project you want to tackle. Don't put your sweat and elbow grease, let alone your heart and soul, into fixing up or rebuilding a car just because it's free, it's there (and you drove it through high school, or whatever), or because it was your uncle the priest's, your father-in-law's, or your grandfather's. I'm guilty on every one of those counts. I know what I'm talking about. And I still have my grandfather's free, 4-door sedan (that I drove through high school) to prove it. I put way too much work into it. And I've tried every way I can think of to sell it, with no results whatsoever. It wasn't what I wanted in the first place. I don't

Here are some examples of ones that should have been fixed up, starting with some close to home. When I was in high school, my dad bought this '47 Chevy convertible from a co-worker, in decent shape, for $50 because he wanted the wheels and tires. I gave him $50 for the rebuilt engine. Then he parked it on our ranch (as seen). A few years later he sold it to someone for $50, and I spotted it at a swap meet going for $350. No rust, no dents, all there—but we weren't into convertibles in the '60s. Sigh.

I nabbed this '32 Tudor sedan for $900 because it was too good to pass up. It had lots of surface rust, inside and out, but no real cancer; it was surprisingly straight; and it came with rear fenders and an extra floor (behind car). This was a very restorable car but, again, I had no place to keep it. A friend let me store it on his property, and I collected swap meets parts when I found them, cheap. After several years I hadn't touched it, and someone made a ridiculous (low) offer and took it to Sweden. I won't admit the price, but the grille, hood, firewall, and gas tank were worth much more than he paid (not counting the quickchange rear axle). I just hope it finally got built.

like it now. I don't want it. But it's too nice to donate to the Salvation Army. And I wouldn't get much of a tax break for it, anyway. It's got a beautiful, show-winning paint job. But it's a hundred dollar saddle on a ten-dollar horse. You're not listening are you? I can tell you're not.

Hey, it'd be great if your grandfather—or uncle the priest—drove a '57 T-Bird and willed it to you, even a clapped-out one. That's definitely worth fixing up. But not aunt Meg's 4-door

Corvair, or the family '75 Suburban, or much of anything else made in the '70s or '80s, for that matter. There are exceptions, of course, which price guides can help you understand. But if you want to put a whole bunch of hours into fixing up some 4-wheeled stray dog primarily because it has "personal attachment" (or, worse, just because it followed you home), fine. Just plan on being personally attached to it for a long time. If you really do love the car, for whatever reason, and you really do plan on keeping it

I got this '62 Grand Prix convertible from a college friend for $100. I rebuilt the radiator and heads, and did the little bodywork it needed. It had the good wheels and all the trim. But I had nowhere to keep it. So I rented a little compressor, painted it light blue primer, and tried to sell it. No luck. So I gave it away. Ugh.

This is a '36 or '37 Ford Tudor body I saw at a swap meet in Kansas. Even if it were a '32, I'd question trying to save this one. As it was, I didn't even ask the price.

I saw this convertible at a swap meet. If it were just a '67 Fairlane 'vert, even apparently complete and running, it probably wouldn't justify the $4,500 asking price. But this is a GTA with a "numbers correct" 330-hp 390 big block. Yet, that's Midwest road-salt rust showing in the wheelwells, so you know there's plenty more you can't see underneath.

For example, here's a '55 Olds that looks straight, with only surface rust...until you start poking around down under the chassis, where the road salt has been eating it away. Not only do you have to deal with rust rot on such cars, but every nut and bolt down there has to be removed with a cutting torch.

Even on relatively new cars, like this Honda, this is the stuff to watch out for: big bubbles in the paint and holes through the sheetmetal, especially around wheel openings. This isn't surface rust. It can't be fixed by a paint job. It's coming from the inside out, and like cancer, it will grow back if you don't cut it all out and replace it with new metal. Is the car worth it?

indefinitely—go for it. Give it the personal attention and loving care only you can.

More important and more serious is trying to assess the true condition of the vehicle you plan to spend some real time fixing up and painting. Since we're concerned with the exterior surface here, we have to leave it to other sources (and your trusted mechanic) to determine its mechanical well being, but that of course should be taken into strong consideration. In the case of straight restorations, you must consider the rarity of the vehicle and the consequent availability (or unavailability) of replacement parts. In other cases, where originality doesn't matter,

one good option is to transplant newer mechanical components that are fresher or rebuilt, are readily available, and fit the chassis directly or reasonably easily.

Our concern is the exterior of the car. Check two things first: the original-

ity and completeness of the vehicle, especially an older one. If the car still has its original paint job, even if it's faded, chipped, cracked, or peeling, good. The worse the paint, the less the car costs. That's a big part of the point here. But look closely to make sure it's really the original color (there's usually a "color code" number on an I.D. tag on a doorpost, but that's hard to verify on the spot). If the car's been repainted, you can usually see where masking wasn't perfect, overspray got on non-painted parts, or areas didn't get fully resprayed, such as under the hood, trunk, or wheel-wells and rockers. Next look for areas that might have been touched up or spotted-in. If the paint is old, these areas might be shinier or a slightly different color. This is an indication that body-work has been done. Then the question is: how much, and how well? If the panel looks straight (not wavy or bumpy) and

We look at this one again next chapter, but here's another perfect example from my neighborhood. The '57 Nomad is a highly desirable, collectible car, and it looks like all this one needs is a new paint job. We know the paint isn't original, and there's been some less-than-perfect bodywork done (the sides are wavy). But the fact that the top is crazed tells us this paint has been on the car a long time, and no rust, filler cracks, or peeling have occurred. If it were for sale, the need for a full paint job should lower the price substantially. And if you painted it yourself... but, of course, it's not for sale.

Another good example, this little Mustang project is following our Chapter 2 "How to Build a Car" sidebar well. It has a new EFI V-8, 4-speed, and 4-wheel disc brakes already installed, along with new performance wheels and tires. The primer spots tell you some minor bodywork has been done. Now all it needs is a good sanding through the peeling clear coat, and a fresh home paint job.

On the subject of red Mustangs, here's exactly what you don't want. This car looks fairly good and straight at first glance. But all it's had is a quickie "resale" paint job, covering who-knows-what bodywork and prep. In fact, the close-up shows not only a poor fast-mask job, but the recent paint is already starting to peel and flake. Very bad. Worse, close inspection shows much of the car is missing. Bottom line: don't pay for a paint job you don't want, especially a recent one. Buy a car that needs a paint job, to save on the price, then paint it yourself—partly to know that it's done right.

fits properly, you can at least assume the job was done well. If so, such areas can be sanded and repainted without further work. If you can see ripples, waves, pin-holes, bubbles, or grinder marks—or worse, if it's already cracking or even falling out, you know it's a problem area that has to be stripped of filler, cleaned, straightened, and re-worked. Also check the gaps and fit between body panels and parts such as doors, hood, and trunk. If

any of these are uneven or don't fit prop-erly, some part of the car has probably been crunched and replaced. That's no big problem as long as the replacement part or panel is good, and can be realigned properly, and the frame is straight. But beware of things such as doors or windows that don't open and close smoothly.

Completeness is another concern, especially on older or rare vehicles. Make sure that all chrome trim, handles, latches, lights, grille pieces, and so on are on the car and are not bent or broken

beyond simple repair. Even though we're talking about painting the outside, this is a good thing to check in the interior, too. For newer cars, such pieces can be ordered from the dealer, but can be expensive (and ask yourself, why are they missing or broken?). For popular older cars (including foreign ones), a surpris-ing number of these parts are available as reproductions. Others aren't. For one example, as this was written the chrome "eyebrows" over the headlights on '55 Chevy Nomad station wagons—unique to this year and model—were not avail-

Here's our last bad example. Even though I saw this one stored in SoCal, the snow tires and severe rust tell me it came from some snowy clime. Sure, it could be fixed, at great effort. But plenty of similar examples abound, in much better condition. Even at free, this car isn't worth it. Been there, done that.

Here's another real-life example close to home. As a magazine project to prove that there's plenty of good '50s car material out there, in decent condition, for good prices, I found 30-some cars, and selected this one-owner, never hit, all-original '52 Chevy 2-door sedan as the one to buy ($1,200) and bring home. I wish I had a picture of it sitting, crusty, on four flat tires in the yard where I found it. But this is after I'd cleaned it up and was rebuilding the brakes. As you can see, the original dark green metallic paint is not only very faded, but also had surface rust all over.

I love to poke fun at '58 Buicks and similar huge, overchromed '50s cars. Who knows how much restoration this 2-door hardtop took—but it's basically a smooth, shiny, bright red paint job, lowering, and new wheels and tires that make it a standout. There's no customizing or other tricks. This car shows how much impact a good new paint job can have, even on a big, otherwise ugly old car. Well, it's not ugly anymore.

In proper order, I fixed all the mechanicals first, including brakes, suspension, steering, wiring, and eventually added a V-8, automatic trans, stereo, and even air conditioning. I had the bumpers and grille rechromed and removed and filled emblems on the hood, trunk, and elsewhere. Then my upholsterer talked me into adding white tuck-and-roll inside (out of order). So I had Stan Betz mix a little color-matched green lacquer so I could spot-in the few places I'd primed where chrome was removed and a ding or two were filled. Then I tried a little 3M rubbing compound with a buffer. Wow! It not only took all the surface rust right off, but it polished that old nitrocellulose lacquer to a high sheen, as you can plainly see in this photo. Believe it or not, this is mostly the factory original paint, just power-buffed and waxed. It looked so good; I drove it this way for several years before starting this book. Now it's finally getting the full-bore bodywork/repaint.

able in reproduction. Originals (if you could find any) cost upwards of $2,000. Check these things before buying a new project vehicle.

Bad Filler and Dreaded Rust

If a car has one or more new paint jobs over the original, you really have no idea what might be under them. We talk about this more in the next chapter on stripping paint. Fortunately, filler—especially bad filler—is usually pretty easy to see. If it's not immediately obvious from bulges or waves, sight carefully down the sides of the car, from front to rear and vice-versa. Besides front- and rear-end damage (which is relatively easy to replace), cars most often get hit in the sides (as opposed to the roof or tops of the trunk or hood), and this can be more serious. If you don't see waves or ripples as you look down the sides of the car, open the doors and check the jambs. Bodymen usually don't spend a lot of time in these areas, and damage is easier to spot here. If you do see bent or twisted metal, or poorly sanded filler, especially in the middle pillar of a 4-door, I'd probably pass and look for a better car.

Another way to find filler is to look and feel inside body panels that you can access, such as inside the trunk or the wheelwells. If a panel is bumpy on the inside and straight on the outside, you know it has filler in it. If you can feel both sides with two hands at the same time, you can probably tell how thick it is. But, especially on newer cars, many areas are inaccessible. The owner isn't going to let you pull off the door panels or other parts to see (or feel) inside.

I have seen several types of "filler finders." Most work magnetically, some with batteries and beepers or lights. Look in auto accessory catalogs to find them. But with a little practice and something

Since we're discussing rust in this chapter, here are a couple examples from my Chevy that are of the fixable type. About the only place I found exterior rust was under the chrome trim, where water collected. But this was primarily surface rust. I used a small, air-drive grinder to remove most of it, but this area had a hole in the lower right about the size of a 50-cent piece that needed a patch welded in.

With the rust ground off, weld ground smooth, one coat of high-fill primer, and a little catalyzed spot putty, sanded smooth, this is how the same area looked after a final coat of primer.

But you never know where you might find rust in a car. When I removed the interior panels, I discovered the left rear window channel drain tube had been plugged up, and the inner side of the trough was rusted completely through. Note the drain tube in the lower right, which had to be unclogged to start with.

like a refrigerator magnet, you can get pretty adept at judging whether—and how much—filler is under the paint. Any type of magnet works; just make sure it has something over the surface (such as masking tape) so it doesn't scratch the paint on the car.

Rust is either easier or harder to find, but, unless it's simple surface rust, it's badder than filler any day. If you can actually see rust bubbles—or worse, holes—in the paint, be warned that it's the tip of the iceberg. Such body rust is coming from the inside out. If you can see any on the outside, it has to be worse on the inside...probably much worse.

The rusted area then had to be cut out with a cutting wheel on a die grinder. I scraped and wire-brushed as much as possible inside to remove more rust, but it was pretty inaccessible. So I resorted to liberally spraying the inside areas with a spray-can "rust converter" made by Permatex.

Then I cut and welded patches to fill the cutout portions of the inner panel. If you have rust holes on the outside of the body, the process is similar, but that's really beyond the scope of this book.

But, once again, many under-the-surface areas of car bodies are hard to access and these are the places where rust breeds and grows. Start by checking logical places for water to collect: the trunk floor, the interior floors (if you can lift the carpets), around exterior window channels (especially at the bottom corners). Open the doors and check the bottoms. If you can't check interior floors from the top, crawl under the car and look at the floorboards from the bottom. This is especially important for cars that have ever lived in a cold climate where roads are salted (regardless of where the car might be right now).

Here's an instructive example. My son was looking for a 1950 Ford to build. He found one in Ohio, and the owner proudly stated, "All new patch panels have already been installed, all around the car." Being a Californian, this sounded good to me. All the body rust had been cut out and replaced with new sheetmetal. But a friend who grew up there said, "Whoa! If the car was so rusty that it needed full patch panels, you can bet everything under the car is rusted tight. You won't get a nut or bolt off of it without a cutting torch. And you'll find more rust in areas you never thought of." Good lesson. My son bought a '50 Ford from Arizona, and he's still driving it. The cost of a trip to a drier, warmer area to look for a car could be well worth it in the long run.

Finally, there's one phenomenon about buying hobby cars—or any cars—that I've never been able to understand, but it really is central to this book. Why buy a paint job you don't want or aren't going to keep? Especially in the rod and custom field, I see people pay the big bucks for a nice, finished car and then, a year or so later, decide they'd rather change the color, and the upholstery, and maybe the wheels and tires, to make it more "their car." Well, they're paying twice for all that stuff that was fine to begin with.

The point of this is to find a sound well-priced car with good potential that needs a paint job. You add your own paint and finish the car however you like it. That way you can pay about half instead of double, have the car look the way you really want, and have the satisfaction of doing it yourself. Somehow that sounds more sensible to me.

Further, the first thing that you should be suspicious about on any car you're looking to buy is a fresh paint job. You've heard of "resale red," and with any experience you can spot quickie cover-up paint that very likely hides a multitude of sins. But I've seen far too

many high-dollar cars, of all types, with beautiful-looking—even show-winning—paint jobs that turn out to have a ton of filler under that shiny, smooth surface. They're not all that way, of course. But production body shops, and even busy custom shops, know they have to get cars in and out quickly, and sanding filler smooth is a lot easier and faster than properly straightening, forming, or replacing sheetmetal. If you buy something with new paint (even a full, fresh coat of primer), you really don't know what's under it. If you buy something that needs paint, or still has all its factory finish on it, you have a much better idea what you're getting.

Save an Old Paint Job

You'd be surprised how dead a paint job you can bring back to life. I'm not talking about making the car show-winning perfect. I'm talking about a car that someone has let go—left out to fade and oxidize—and all you want to do is make

it shiny and nice once again. On the other hand, at concours shows you see old, original classics that have been meticulously taken apart, cleaned, and polished—both old painted and bare-metal parts—until they look just like new. You can do much the same thing to any old car, for nearly no investment other than time and elbow grease.

In the old days I heard of people oiling or waxing primer to make it shiny. If you ever intend to paint over it, don't do that. Also, I'd see guys (especially lowriders) wax whatever paint was on the car, repeatedly, until it got real shiny. If they went through the paint down to the factory primer, that was okay. It'd be shiny, too. With the abrasive paste waxes of the day, you could shine up most any old paint job pretty quickly; the more you waxed, the shinier the car got. Here, we'll do something similar, with more modern polishing products, and hope we don't hit primer.

Another option, with the variety of catalyzed clears available today, is to

We show more on spotting-in paint in following chapters, but let's consider a vehicle that looks like it needs a new paint job, but might not. The car in question is a '93 Honda Accord wagon that my wife bought, new. She took very good care of it for 200,000+ miles, including several cross-country trips (seen here somewhere east or west of Laramie), but it never once spent a night or day under cover—nor got waxed. The clear coat was getting chalky in places, but the metallic red hadn't visibly faded—a testament to today's factory paint jobs. When Anna got a low-mileage white Camry (which you see in Chapter 8), she willed this one to me, and I decided to see what I could do to fix it up without a full new paint job.

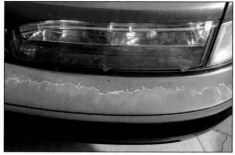

Oftentimes, new cars get damaged in shipment and repaired at the dealer before they're sold. Apparently that happened with the front bumper. We crunched the rear gate and had to have it repaired and repainted. These were the only two places the clear coat had actually peeled off. In such cases neither buffing nor recoating with clear works; you have to sand it down, repaint the base coat, and reclear it.

Try to sand off as much of the peeling clear coat as possible, but also try not to sand through the factory primer coats. Also note the peeling black-rubber roof strips had stainless steel underneath. I removed the remaining rubber with a razor blade and buffed the stainless.

Being the rodder I am, my first job was to peel off what trim I could, remove the washer and wiper, and weld up holes where the emblem and washer had been.

Next I wet-sanded the areas to be repainted with 360-grit, taping off other areas to protect them.

Before spot-painting the bumpers and tailgate, I tried buffing a portion of the weathered paint to make sure it would "come up," which it did nicely.

If you can repaint full body panels separated by seams, it's not the same as "spotting in" and matching the color exactly isn't nearly as important. Here I have masked off the entire sanded tailgate, plus the rear bumper, which got some dings and scratches erased with high-fill primer.

scuff down and clear coat whatever you've got. That's a possibility (even over primer), but we won't delve into it here because it isn't common; any scratches, blotches, or other irregularities in the underlying paint (including sanding scratches) not only show but are usually magnified. On the other hand, the big

craze among the rod and custom crowd now is "patina." Not only are worn, faded and flaking paint jobs prized (partly to prove that the car has old, original sheetmetal), but some people are actually "weatherizng" paint jobs to create fake (or "faux") patina. Whatever. You'll have to find some other book or magazine to teach you that.

What we show here, instead, is how to buff and polish a tired old paint job until it looks, maybe not as good as new, but a heck of a lot better than it did. It still takes some effort, but we can make

---

the vehicle look presentable without all the preparation, labor, materials, equipment, and expense of a full-on paint job. We rely primarily on wax and polishing compounds, with some minor spot painting, if necessary.

First off—this needs to be discussed somewhere in this book, and this is as good a place as any—automotive wax products are mostly snake oil, in my opinion. Somebody comes up with a new "Wonder Wax" that does everything short of curing cancer and pimples seemingly every month, and advertises it aggressively until a new one takes its place. Car magazines are full of ads for them. Barkers at car shows and county fairs hawk products that polish anything from beer cans to leather seats. To a certain extent they all work. I suppose some might do more harm than good. I don't know. I don't use them.

I've got a whole slew of wax and polishing products in my garage cupboard, ranging from basic 3M rubbing compound in a big jug to pure carnauba wax in a bottle. As with paints, I'm not going to recommend any specific products here. But I have relied on the Meguiar's line of glazes and polishes, 3M compounds, Mother's wax, and certain items from a place called The Wax Shop (that may not be around any more). I'd say: (1) lean toward name-brand products that have been, and will be, around a while; but (2) try out various products to see what works best for you; because (3) ultimately, it's much more important *that* you wax your car than *what* you wax it with. You can quote me on that.

Buff it Out

Assuming that the paint in question is simply faded and oxidized—it's not cracked, peeling, discolored, or otherwise damaged—the trick is to rub or polish it evenly until it all shines again. The paint's condition determines what products and procedures you have to use to revive it. A good hand wax job, or two or three, might be all it takes. For others, many "de-oxydizer" or "fine rub" liquids are available. You can hand rub or machine buff these. For bad cases, you need to resort to real rubbing compound and a buffing wheel. If you're not sure what it's going to take, try these products in the order mentioned. If you have to go to the rubbing compound, follow it with a sealer (polishing compound), and then a coat of wax.

Although I have seen magazine articles and other sources suggesting it, I do not recommend color sanding a factory paint job, particularly those with clear coats, especially if it's old and worn. The factory doesn't put enough paint on to warrant sanding, and if it's partly eroded, you're asking for trouble. Even using a power buffer and rubbing compound is iffy. Start with finer polishes first.

I wouldn't use any wax that has silicone in it because it is very difficult to clean off if you ever need to repaint or touch-up the finish later (silicone causes fisheyes in new paint). Pure carnauba (or a similar "gloss wax" product) is a great finish wax; it gives a high-gloss and a protective coat that should last a while. But it doesn't clean any grit, grime, road

After similarly masking off the front bumper areas needing repainting, I sealed the entire rest of the car with plastic sheeting, available from paint stores for this purpose. Base coat is little problem, but overspray from the urethane clear sticks to everything.

I've seen other painters recently using 1,000-grit or finer paper for "scuffing" a surface for repainting, but on this older finish I used 360-grit, dry. Never wet-sand a masked area; you don't want to get the tape or paper wet. On the other hand, after dry sanding, be sure to wipe and air-blow all sanding dust not only off the surface to be painted, but also out of all folds in the paper or other masking materials.

I had the base coat mixed to the original color code. If I were spotting-in the paint, I'd have to have it "color-matched" to the existing, slightly faded paint, either by computer or experienced eye. But in this case a perfect match was not so important. A pint of base coat was plenty for this job, and I'm using a graduated beaker to measure the proper amount of reducer/catalyst.

tar, or oxidation that doesn't wash off. So, in the old days, you'd precede the wax coat with a cleaner, which usually had a fine abrasive in it. It was a two-step process that required plenty of elbow work, but was effective. Today we have all kinds of good cleaner-waxes that do pretty much the same job in one step. The "super gloss" final-finish waxes (or glazes) are for show cars that spend most of their time indoors, covered. For any car that sees regular outdoor driving duty, I highly recommend a good cleaner-wax, used often. Some of these use fine abrasives as a cleaner, others use chemical cleaners. My favorite, and standby for years, is Meguiar's "red bottle." It goes on quickly and relatively easily (even in the sun), it cleans well (especially if you rub hard), it wipes off very easily, and it doesn't streak at all. Mother's makes a similar product that

Numerous "paint rejuvenators," "de-oxidizers," or even "swirl removers" are available from the wax purveyors. Try them out to see what works best for you. For this job you don't want a "non-abrasive" formula; you need a mild abrasive, if not more.

Spraying base coat is like spraying lacquer. It goes on easily and smoothly and dries quickly to a dull sheen. After it dries, follow with a couple of coats of clear. Do not sand either the base or clear between coats.

After all the masking is removed, the painted and cleared area looks glossy like this, requiring no rub out unless you want to. But now it's time to rub out the old paint on the rest of the car.

has carnauba wax in it. It's not quite as easy to put on and take off, but I think it lasts longer. The point is, try different wax products (perhaps not on your favorite car first) until you find one that works well for you.

On our test car, I started with a couple different kinds of cleaner-waxes, but they weren't strong enough. So I tried

Depending on your paint's condition, you could hand-rub it out with a mild abrasive.

using a couple different brands, and different strengths (super fine, fine, then mild abrasive) of "de-oxidizer" or "finish renewer" liquids, by hand. It was getting better, but I still wasn't getting through the old hazy tarnish. Trying these products with a buffer and wool pad still didn't cut it. So I got out the 3M rubbing compound with a "cutting" buffer pad, and that did it, surprisingly without going through the clear. Obviously (as we see in the rub-out chapter) this had to be

If the clear is starting to craze or check, it's usually impossible to fix without repainting. But this case responded pretty well to some hand rubbing and waxing, as seen in the second photo.

followed with sealer/glaze and then a good coat of hand wax.

Now here's my big caveat—or rationalization—for this section: It's a can't-lose deal. Of course you want to buff out the paint to a like-new finish without breaking through the clear coat, or what-

ever the top layer is. If you can, great. You're lucky, and you've saved a lot of work and expense. But if you do buff right through—so what? Now you have to repaint the car, which is what we really started out to do, anyway, right? You haven't really lost anything. The car only needs minor sanding at this point, and then you can mask it and shoot it. Or maybe you can get by just spotting it in.

Spot it in

Speaking of clear coats, most new cars of the past couple of decades came with them, even over solid colors, like black (which seems strange to me). If the paint is crazing or peeling, obviously the clear coat is first to go. You've seen it. It looks like your skin when it's peeling after a bad sunburn. When the paint is in this condition, no amount of polishing or rubbing is going to save it. If it's bad enough, sand down (or strip) the whole car and repaint it, including a new base coat and clear coat. You can't just spray a new clear coat over a peeled one. The edges where it peeled will show.

However, on our test car for this chapter, the peeled clear was confined to panels separated from the rest of the car (the tailgate and the front and rear bumpers). Therefore, they could be sanded down, masked off and sprayed with a new base coat, and then cleared,

without having to "blend" the paint into any of the rest on the body. Given this, I simply ordered the color by code at the paint store, rather than having it "matched" to the now-slightly-faded original paint elsewhere on the car. They were close enough in color and separated by body lines.

Incidentally, you may not realize it, but many brand new cars (more so in the past; they try to protect them better these days) get damaged in shipping, or even on the lot, and get spot-repainted at the dealer's before they are sold new. I don't know exactly how the factory cures its paint jobs, but factory paint is invariably more durable than any kind of repaint. That was the case with our sample car. The front bumper was apparently repainted by the dealer and the tailgate was repaired and repainted by a bodyshop. These were the first areas to peel. The rest of the factory finish, even after 12-plus years outside, took plenty of rubbing and polished up nicely.

When you're spotting-in a paint job with a clear coat, it is relatively easy. If most of the clear coat is lifting, sand it all down, repaint the entire panel for full and even coverage with new base coat, and then clear coat the entire panel. If only a small portion of the clear coat is bad, or if the area has scrapes or other small damage, you can sand down the affected area (into the good clear coat), spot-in new base coat to cover the damage (again, spraying

You also might be surprised how many scrapes and abrasions on your car are less than skin deep, and can be removed or significantly repaired by some rubbing with compound.

On this car I decided to try 3M Super Duty compound to start, which is about as coarse as you'd want to use on anything. Since it comes in a jug, it helps to put some in a squirt bottle for ease of application. Then I used a cutting pad on my power buffer to do the whole car. This is extreme; you might want to start with something less abrasive. See Chapter 11 for more details on rubbing out paint, old or new.

over at least a small portion of the good clear coat), then clear coat the entire panel. This works fine even if you have to do a little bodywork and priming in the damaged area to start—as long as you fully cover all primer, and any of its overspray, with base coat. You can even try spotting-in the clear coat—again, spraying beyond the base-coated area and any of its overspray—and rubbing out the junction of the old and new clear coats. Sometimes this works, sometimes it doesn't. But, hey, if it doesn't (if you can see a line or edge between the new and old clear coats once it's buffed out), simply scuff down and reshoot the whole panel with a full clear coat. Depending on the type of car you're restoring, your proclivities, and how well you can get the clear coat to lay down and gloss out, you can either leave

it as-sprayed and start waxing it regularly along with the rest of the car, or you can color-sand and rub it out.

If your car doesn't have a clear coat, spotting-in is more difficult. With metallics or modern paints with pearl added, it is nearly impossible to spot-in a portion of a body panel, rub it out, and have it blend in with the former finish so you can't tell. About the only recourse here is to repaint a full panel separated from the rest of the body by seams or trim. Another possibility here is to spot-in areas that need it, and then clear coat the whole car. This is unusual, but certainly possible.

If your vehicle is painted in a one-step, non-metallic color such as red, yellow, or black, spotting it in and rubbing out the area is usually easy, particularly if the paint is fresh (i.e., you got a run while you were doing the paint job, a bug landed in it, some paint pulled off with the tape, whatever). Just sand the area with 360-grit until the dirt, bug, or rough edge is gone, repaint the area, and

rub it out. If you saved some of the original paint, this also works on an older paint job if you've kept it in good shape. Of course I'm talking about some sort of catalyzed, hardened paint (both the original and the spot paint), or lacquer.

Now, if you're dealing with older paint that's spent any time in the sun, it's going to be faded to some extent. Reds and lighter colors are especially susceptible. So even if you carefully saved some of the original paint, it's probably not going to match anymore. On the other hand, if the paint is new, but you didn't paint it, and you don't have any of the exact same paint that was used, don't expect new paint to match just because you ordered the same color code that's on the car. Nearly all automotive paint is mixed by the can, as it is ordered. Some minor differences usually show in the shade of the color, the cast of the metallic, or the intensity of the pearl, from one new can of paint to another. This doesn't matter

As I say in the text, the best thing about trying to restore old paint (factory or otherwise) is that, if you rub through it, you can then repaint it. We show how elsewhere in this book. But for 12-year-old paint that had never been waxed or spent a night in a garage, this one really came back to life with a little rubbing and waxing. No new paint job needed here.

if you're painting a whole car, and it usually doesn't matter if you're painting a whole panel—the colors are close enough that you can't tell.

If the old paint is perceptibly faded, or you're trying to blend spot paint in the middle of a panel, you need the paint "color-matched." Experts—and these are few—can do it by eye. Many shops these days have electronic equipment (spectrometers or spectrographs) to do it. Neither method is perfect.

Ultimately, it depends on how picky—and perceptive—you are. I notice mis-matched paint jobs all the time, usually on cars with metallic or pearl paints repaired at collision shops. The owners apparently don't notice or don't care. Probably both.

Then there are the super-picky. A friend won't finish his beautiful silver metallic '54 Chevy because the paint shop messed something up and had to repaint the front fenders. They've redone them three times now, and he still sees a slight difference in the hue. Silver is about the hardest color to match, and this one has pearl in it, which is worse. Just adding a second or third coat, especially of a light color, changes its shade

Once you have touch-up paint for the car, use it straight from the can (unthinned), with a small brush, to fill-in any small chips, scratches, or nicks that don't require spraying. For any car you paint, save a little extra for this sort of touch-up.

slightly. So will painting it over different colors of primer. Spot painting, or partial repainting—even with the same paint you started with—is hardly ever going to be perfect or seamless, especially to a very picky eye. If you're that type of person, I'd suggest you sand down the whole car, coat it evenly with an opaque sealer close in shade to the final color, then respray the entire car, preferably all at the same time, and definitely with the same number of coats on each part. Remember, it's your car, you're the only one you really have to please, and you're doing all the work yourself. How perfect do you want it?

The Stages of Paint

We keep talking about different processes that apply to different "stages" or levels of paint jobs, so we should run down a quick list of them here. Automotive paint jobs vary vastly from whatever a one-day "in-and-out" special costs these days, to a 5-figure (at least) professional show finish. We even start with an option that doesn't require any painting at all. The one-day special might include some quickie bodywork, but it doesn't include any vehicle disassembly, or (usually) any rub out. We assume that nearly all paint jobs done today, even at home, use two-part (and possibly two-stage) hardened (i.e., catalyzed) paint—of whatever specific variety is available when you read this—that can be color-sanded and rubbed out, and also dries to a high gloss that doesn't necessitate a rub out.

Since most of the stages employ basically the same kinds of paints and spraying processes, the differences lie primarily in the amount of prep work done, the lengths to which the vehicle is disassembled before paint, and whether the finish is color-sanded and rubbed out. To be honest, most people on the street can't see the differences between these stages of paint jobs, though they vary enormously either in cost or (your) labor to do them. And we've already talked about putting a $5,000 paint job on a $500 car. It's all up to you. This book assumes you're going to do the work yourself (in most cases), and that you know the differences in these stages of paint jobs. You should select the level of job that (1) befits the car you're planning to paint, (2) matches your level of expectation and commitment, and (3) you will be satisfied with, and can be proud of when it's done…and for a good while afterwards.

1: The No-Paint Buff-Out. Also known as the "Save-a-Paint Job," we've already covered this in this chapter. It requires no actual painting, and therefore no special equipment (or talent), other than possibly a power buffer (but this is optional). The only cost is for polishing products, which is minimal. The investment is your muscle power and elbow grease. Of course this

stage assumes paint that is old and faded, but still stable and savable. An extension of this step, shown in our later example, would include spot painting or touch-up, but this requires some painting equipment and ability.

2: The Scuff-and-Squirt. Also known as the "Sand-and-Shoot" or the "Mask-and-Spray," this can be done at least three ways. In choosing one of these methods, you are assuming that the body is in good shape and the existing paint, even if it's peeling or discolored, is basically stable. In the first, most basic, case, this means masking everything on the car, sanding the paint smooth, then shooting a new coat of the same color over the exterior, leaving the doors, hood, and trunk shut. This also works with our later example of spraying a pearl coat over a similar-shade existing, plain color. The second step involves removing as much trim as possible before sanding and spraying, with a further option of sanding, masking, and painting the doorjambs and under the hood and trunk. This, of course, requires masking off the whole interior, engine, and so on. The third step of this stage is similar—you remove trim and (probably) sand the car yourself—but then take it to your local one-day paint shop to let them mask and spray it. These latter two steps would allow a color change, if you want.

3: Bodywork and Paint. This is obviously for cars that have some dings and dents. We're not covering major bodywork here; you can have a shop do that and leave repaired spots in primer. Or you can do minor work yourself, where needed, as shown in the next chapter. After applying primer, block-sand these areas, along with existing paint. Or, maybe what this car needs is a full coat of high-fill primer over a good preliminary sanding, some spot putty in places, and then a good block-sanding, a little more primer, and then new paint. Since you're not stripping off all

Continued on page 30

The Stages of Paint CONTINUED

old paint, a good sealer is strongly recommended before the final color coat.

4: Strip and Paint. We cover several levels of stripping in this chapter, but for this paint stage we're talking about either hand stripping the body at home, or having it media blasted, primarily on the outside surfaces. Going further, it could include stripping doorjambs (even removing door glass and other door internals), and maybe under the hood and trunk. But it wouldn't include removing the windshield, back glass, interior (other than possibly door panels), or other major components, such as the engine.

5: Gut It. Okay, we're getting serious. Get all the glass out. Remove all body rubber (window moldings, weather strip, etc.). Assuming you're going to have the car reupholstered, rip the entire interior out—but talk to your upholsterer first. There may be things you need to note or to save, especially if this is an older or unusual vehicle. (If not, carefully remove everything you can, probably leaving the headliner in place and masking it off. Same for plastic dash panels and similar interior components.) Of course you've removed everything detachable from the outside, including bumpers, grille, lights, handles, trim, and so on. For this stage we recommend removing the hood, trunk, and front fenders, because they are relatively easy. The doors are your call, because they are much harder to replace and realign. Same with things like the

engine and wiring (it depends on how much you want to detail and paint the firewall and engine compartment). And, though it's highly recommended, paint stripping is also optional in this stage. If existing paint is new or original, you can just sand it all down (thus retaining factory-applied rust-inhibitors and undercoats). In this step it's more important to get new paint everywhere (i.e., under window seals, in doorjambs) that the factory originally put it.

6. Body-Off-Frame. This is the whole enchilada. There's no point doing it unless the car really needs it and is worth it. But if you're going this far, you might as well start (once you've got everything torn apart) by stripping the body either by immersion or by media blasting (if available—by hand, if not), inside and out. Might as well have the frame and chassis components sandblasted, too. Paint or powder coat the frame and suspension parts before reassembly, and paint driveline components as you rebuild them. Do whatever rust repair and bodywork is needed, and then paint all sheetmetal, top and bottom, inside and out. Then start reassembling the whole car with all new rubber, wiring, glass, upholstery, plating, and so on. This can all be done at home, with the possible exceptions of plating, upholstery, and probably glass. It is still exponentially cheaper than having a pro shop do it all. But don't expect to do this during your two-week summer vacation.

TO STRIP OR NOT TO STRIP

This car is for sale at a swap meet, and some sellers can be cagey (this one appears to have waxed the car to make it shiny); but we see no rust, no dents, no cracks, and no flakes. It looks like a candidate for a good sanding and a new paint job. You can get such a car for a much lower price and do the paint yourself.

Of all the cars I've painted, the only ones I've had no problems with, either immediately or later, were the ones I stripped to bare metal to begin with. This could be coincidence. But more likely it has to do with what lay below the surface of the dragged-home derelict vehicles that I didn't strip. Lord knows where they had been and how many times they had been painted.

When you're starting a paint project you once again have a few options. First, let's assume you know, or are pretty confident, that the paint on the car is either factory original or a respray that was done properly in the past, and there is no evidence of cracking, checking, peeling, bubbling, or so on. If this is the case, you can usually sand down the paint on the car, smoothly and evenly, and paint over it using most of today's modern paints. If the existing finish is still relatively new and in good shape, and you just want to change the color or put something like a pearl coat over it (as we show later), then sanding down the existing paint and recovering it should be fine. Don't forget that some new cars get damaged and spot-painted—sometimes even body-worked—at the dealer before being sold. Hopefully such work has been done properly, with good catalyzed paints, primers, and sealers. If so, it can be painted over like the rest of the car. If not, you probably won't know it until it wrinkles or lifts while you're painting the car. Similarly, if the original paint, or a good repaint, is just faded, or possibly the clear is peeling in places, you can sand it down and repaint it the same color (including a base coat and a clear coat), without having to repaint the doorjambs, under the hood, and so on. Further, when the car is built at the factory, the body and other sheet-metal components are dipped, electrostatically sprayed, or otherwise treated with rust-protective coats and other primers that are tougher and better-bonded than anything you can buy and spray at home (it's the same for bodyshops or custom painters). So some painters suggest not stripping the vehicle to bare metal (especially inside-and-out, as in immersion stripping), so that you don't remove these tough factory undercoats. It's a debatable point.

The second—and usually better—option is to thoroughly sand whatever

Here's a similar car that has been sanded and partly stripped, ready for new paint. Assuming it's all straight and smooth, I'd spray some sealer on any bare metal spots (if not the whole car, just to be sure), and then mask and spray color. This is exactly what we did with several cars as teens (short of taking glass out). We then had them sprayed by a local painter, with never any problems. With your own garage and equipment, you can do the painting yourself.

Here's that Nomad again. As we say in the text, there's no point stripping or grinding out someone else's filler (undoing work already done) if it's done relatively well. You can see from the waves in the reflection in the side of this car that (1) it has filler in it, and (2) it needs further block/board sanding to get it as straight as it should be. But the paint's been on the car a good while, and there's no rust coming through, no cracks, and none of the filler is falling out (which does happen). We'd recommend sanding with 80-grit on a long board until it's pretty straight, then spraying with high-fill primer and blocking again with 180-grit.

paint is on the car, then cover it with a good sealer followed by a modern catalyzed primer. Actually, if the existing surface sands down nice and smooth, you could spray a coat of catalyzed sealer over it (preferably a colored sealer of a shade close to the final paint color, if the sanded surface ends up multi-colored), followed by the new paint. However, most cars needing a paint job also have dings, door dents, scrapes, or other surface problems that won't simply sand out. So most often, if you're going to paint over existing paint, we suggest sanding it down with relatively coarse paper (180 to 220 grit), and then either shooting the whole body (preferably), or just any rough, dinged, or bodyworked areas, with a good, catalyzed, high-fill primer. If the paint on the car is multi-layer, old, or otherwise edgy, give yourself extra insurance and add a coat of sealer before the primer. Then you can use some catalyzed spot putty where necessary over the primer and start block

sanding, as we detail in following chapters. Most of my early paint problems, when painting over existing finishes without stripping, occurred because I was using lacquer primer and lacquer paint. We talk more about this later, but lacquer solvents are extremely aggressive, and lift or wrinkle all kinds of underlying paints, especially older non-catalyzed ones, including old lacquer. For both of these reasons, modern paints really are better, especially if you're spraying it over existing paint.

The third option is iffy and always debatable. It pertains to older vehicles, or ones that you know have been damaged and bodyworked. But in this case the exterior surface, whether it's fresh and shiny, old and faded, or maybe in a coat of primer, looks relatively smooth and straight and shows no evidence of cracking, bubbling, rust, or other badness. If the surface is shiny and fresh, and you want to repaint it, I can only assume you just bought the car and paid

for a paint job you didn't want. Don't compound the issue (in my opinion) by immediately stripping this paint off only to find what you consider to be an excessive amount of filler underneath. Lots of good paint jobs, even by big-name builders, have filler under them. It's the most expedient way to get a super-straight show-winning body and paint job. But the majority of these cars are stripped to bare metal to begin with, metal-worked pretty close, and then the filler and other undercoats are added properly. If you strip all this off, you're just erasing several man-hours of work that have to be repeated, either by you or someone you'll have to pay big bucks by the hour. If somebody has already spent a lot of time bodyworking, priming, and sanding the car, you'd be nuts to strip all that out and do it over again, right? Now, if there's rust under there, or the filler's an inch thick, it's a different story. The body needs stripping to start, and more work after that.

On the roof of this car, however, we see that the paint is crazed and checked. Assuming only the top coat of paint is so affected, it either has to be completely sanded off (down to stable undercoats), or strip just the roof of the car, either by media-blasting or liquid hand-stripping. If the checking isn't too bad, you might be able to sand it smooth and coat it with today's catalyzed high-fill primer. But often such checking will "telegraph" (through shrinkage) back to the surface, especially after new paint is rubbed out.

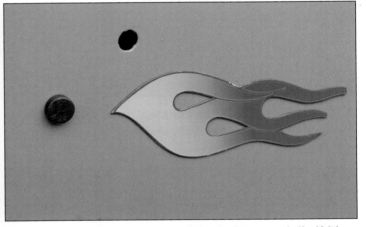

How can you tell if a car has filler in it, especially if it's painted and looks smooth? The first clue is to check the backsides of any panels accessible to see (or feel) if they're wrinkly or wobbly. Some people can "hear" filler just by rapping their knuckle along the outer body. Otherwise, I have seen numerous "filler finder" devices that use spring-loaded magnets, or are battery-powered with lights or beepers. However, a simple, small refrigerator magnet, like the two shown here, can work just as well, especially if you use the same one regularly and get to know its "feel."

Let's use my '52 Chevy as an example of how you can use high-fill primer. We know this car only has factory paint, except where I've spotted it in with lacquer, such as here on the trunk, where I removed the handle/emblem, welded up the holes, ground them, then added a thin coat of filler and sanded it smooth before priming, spot painting, and rubbing it out. It looks okay here, but I could still see ripples in it after a few months' shrinkage.

But this option we're discussing pertains to vehicles that you know or suspect have had some bodywork done, and you assume it has been done properly because nothing indicates otherwise. In such cases I suggest not stripping the car because most types of stripping either remove existing filler, or "infect" it with chemicals so it must be removed. Opinions differ on this issue, but I think it's smarter to be an optimist. Given that you've checked carefully for any real gremlins, and the body looks good the way it is, sand it down and repaint it. Even if it's a little wavy, do your block sanding on what's already there, if it's a stable surface. Add some high-fill primer or spot putty, as needed. But consider yourself lucky you didn't have to go through the major job of stripping and a bunch of arduous bodywork. If you keep this car for years and it starts showing signs

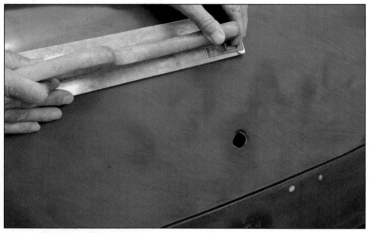

Some sanding with 180-grit paper on a long board quickly revealed low areas. But they're not deep enough to require new filler. In the lower panel you can see two small high (bare) spots that uncovered themselves from this block sanding. I tapped them down level with a body hammer and dolly; they won't require filler either.

Since I know this paint surface is stable, I sprayed it with a few coats of catalyzed, high-fill primer.

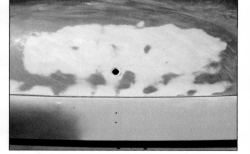

Again using the long board with 180-grit and sanding at 45-degree angles, both left-to-right and right-to-left on this curved surface, it didn't take long to level the area, using only the primer and existing paint as "filler." If you hit bare metal during this process, it's best to spray these spots with an etching sealer, or at least more primer, before spraying base color.

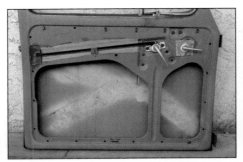

Here's another good example of metal that doesn't need stripping. This is a '56 VW door, but it could be a whole car. Amazingly, after 50 years, it still has factory-original paint on it—the fact the inside matches the outside is a good clue—with virtually no dents, and very complete.

Let's look at some examples that do need stripping. In this case the car obviously has been repainted, probably fairly recently. It's shiny and even rubbed out. However, both the top layer and one or more underlying layers are split and peeling up. We don't know exactly why, but something was not done properly during some stage of the preparation for this paint job, and that stage—filler, primer, whatever—is not adhering. I would strip this car to bare metal, by any method, before repainting it.

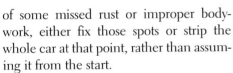

My son purchased a pair of these for $100 each for an early Bug he's rebuilding (much simpler and cheaper than fixing the ones on the car). They were shipped from Australia, and what minor surface rust is on them appears to have occurred on the boat trip.

The first place to check for serious rust on any car is at the bottom edge of the doors, which should have unclogged drain holes to let water out. These have minor surface rust, but no nasty rust coming from inside out.

You never know what's under paint. If this weren't peeling, it might look like a factory job. But who knows? It appears to have no primer under the paint—so of course it is peeling, as well as starting to rust. This one looks like a candidate for sand/media blasting. Don't just fix this area. If it's peeling here now, it will peel everywhere eventually, even with new paint over it.

of some missed rust or improper bodywork, either fix those spots or strip the whole car at that point, rather than assuming it from the start.

On the other hand, if you're a true pessimist or Doubting Thomas, and you don't know what lies under the painted or primed surface of your vehicle, there's only one way to find out—strip it to bare metal. This is the final option, and it's the only viable one if you know the body has too many layers of paint already, has obvious problems with existing paint not adhering to the body, has bodywork you can tell is bad (including excessive filler), or shows visible signs of rust. The only question, given this fourth option, is how to strip the body.

So Strip It

First the don'ts—please don't take a grinder, or any kind of rotary sander, to the body to try to strip all the paint off. Not only does a grinder not reach into lots of areas that need to be stripped, but it scars the surface and actually removes metal, which you do not want to do during the stripping process. If you use a big body grinder, it not only gouges the surface, but it can also heat and warp the sheetmetal. During the stripping process, you want to remove everything *except* metal from the body.

A note about fiberglass-bodied cars: If you're working on a fiberglass body, most all of the other paint processes

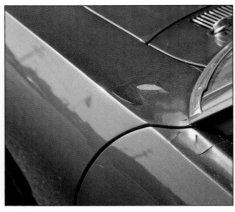

In the prior examples the existing or underlying paint was unstable. In this case a painter for a local bodyshop added a smooth, glossy—and very expensive—coat of "flip-flop" custom paint to his otherwise original Nova. There was nothing wrong with the existing pea green factory paint (except the color), but he failed to sand it sufficiently or use any primer or sealer to make the new paint stick, with apparent results. Given that it's already peeling, you could probably remove the top layer only, using liquid stripper.

Another area where rust often forms is around window rubber, especially at the lower corners of rear windows. This, at first, appears to be the case on this '50 Ford, but a closer look shows that the custom 'flake paint on the roof is peeling because of poor prep and lack of sanding—which is also common around rubber window moldings.

Here's an interesting case. This shoebox Ford was a famous custom, first built in a simpler, red form by well-known Valley Custom in the early '50s, then rebuilt by them in this version later in the decade. It hasn't been touched since, but has been left outside and surface rust is forming. Should a restorer try to "save" as much as possible, as is, or disassemble and strip the car to bare metal for full restoration? This surface rust looks pretty serious, and I think the latter is probably necessary (if it ever gets restored).

covered in this book apply, but not most of the options for stripping—and definitely not anything like a body grinder. Some media blasters say they can carefully strip fiberglass bodies, and I've seen it done. But fiberglass doesn't rust or dent, so most bodies of that type should need nothing more than a good block sanding and typical prep before repaint.

Trying to sand layers of paint off a whole body, by any means, is usually a waste of time compared to stripping. All kinds of sanders, strippers, strappers, flappers, and whatnot are advertised for removing paint, either self-powered or for use with an electric drill. Given enough time, patience, and maybe a burned-out drill or two, you could strip a whole car with one,

but I wouldn't recommend it. The same goes for any sandblasting attachments for a home air compressor that I've ever tried.

I once saw someone with a bag of quarters strip a whole paint job off a car with the wash jet at the 50-cent car wash. That was obviously a while ago, and it was a $29.95 paint job. If you can strip the paint off your car with any kind of pressure washer, at least you know it needed stripping.

Typical, acceptable forms of automotive paint stripping fall into two categories: chemical stripping and compressed air blasting with some form of abrasive particles.

Dunk It

Let's start with the most serious and most thorough. It's generally known as "immersion." Simply put, it's a giant vat or open tank of an acid solution (usually muriatic acid, just like you put in your swimming pool) big enough to dunk a whole car body in (actually, such strippers often have their own "secret formulas" for stripping and derusting metals that include an acid bath preceded or followed by a caustic, or alkaline, bath so that they neutralize each other; but we don't need to get into the chemistry here). Such a process obviously requires complete disassembly of the vehicle to do it properly. I have seen one example where a '40 sedan was immersed with its frame, suspension, and even wheels and tires still attached. I don't know why. Maybe its chassis was so rusty nothing would come apart until they did this. But for chemical dipping to do its job, you really need to take the body off the frame, take the glass out, take the doors and trunk off—remove everything. Then the bare body is dipped and stripped and parts like the fenders, hood, and so on, are dipped separately. This is obviously a major deal for a full-on rebuild or restoration. If all you want is a new paint job, don't do this.

But if it's an older car that comes apart easily, if the body has lots of paint and crud on it, or—and this is probably the most serious—if this car has some real rust problems, this is your best way to go. Immersion/acid stipping is the only method that attacks and removes rust. It not only chemically removes all rust from the surface, but it also eliminates rust from the inner surfaces—even inside enclosed body areas that you can't reach any other way. A good immersion-stripping job leaves your body and other sheet-metal parts looking like they just came out of the stamping presses, brand new. In fact, immersion stripping works very well on frames, chassis parts, and is a real hot tip for engine builders—it actually cleans out rust build-up in water jacket passages inside old engine blocks (it's not perfect at this, but better than any other process). The only question here is what the stripper lets in his tanks—usually not a bunch of grease and oil.

Immersion/acid-bath stripping is the most thorough and easiest way to remove paint, assuming you're doing a full tear down and rebuild of the vehicle in question (which, we realize, is only a small percentage of our audience). But, like anything, there are drawbacks. The first is trying to find one of these places. There aren't many in the first place, and given tightening environmental regulations, the few that do exist seem to be disappearing as quickly as chrome shops. To find one, I'd suggest you search the Internet (if your phone book fails). The few that I've dealt with in Southern California say they have customers shipping them bodies and parts from all over the country. This diminishes the "easy" part.

Another problem with dip-stripping that seemed to be more prevalent in the past than it is now, is getting all the stripping chemicals out of body seams, joints, and other nooks and crannies, so that nothing seeps out later to ruin your paint job. Adequate neutralizing and thorough pressure washing of all parts with water after they've been dunked solves this problem. I haven't heard of it happening in several years—just be aware of it, and be assured by your stripper that it won't happen. Secondly, because dip-stripped steel parts tend to mildly surface rust very quickly, some strippers coat

Paint stripping by immersion in a caustic bath is usually the most thorough and removes rust, but it requires full vehicle disassembly (this '50 Chevy hardtop also has temporary braces welded inside the bare body), is usually the most expensive, and requires complete rinsing to remove all caustic residue. A further hurdle today is to find places that still do this operation.

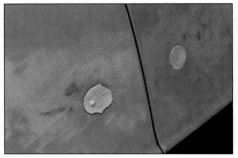

If you have a dip stripping facility available, it can be an excellent way to strip and clean certain parts, such as the hood from my '52, which had surface rust on the inside that didn't want to come off with a wire wheel.

The acid bath won't remove plastic fillers, but ruins them so they must be ground out afterward. I should have filled these areas with metal the first time, anyway.

Dip stripping won't warp, harden, or pit the metal like sand-blasting can, and it not only removes paint, but dirt and rust as well. The expense (about $75 at the time) was well worth it.

Blast It

Once again, there are several options in this category. Sandblasting is by far the most common. Sandblasters can be found in most any industrial, agricultural, or urban area. They can quickly—and cheaply—blast paint (and other grunge) off everything from tractors, trucks, and heavy machinery to the stucco, bricks, or wood on your house, let alone the yellow lines down the middle of your street. Such places are usually not equipped or experienced to strip paint off sheetmetal on cars (even if they tell you they can). Industrial-strength sandblasting is great for frames and similar hard parts, but warps sheetmetal and also surface-hardens it (like shot-peening), which makes it harder to bodywork and more susceptible to cracking from fatigue.

Glass beading is essentially the same as sandblasting (glass is made from sand), though it's usually confined to a blasting cabinet and used on small parts, such as cylinder heads, primarily for cleaning rather than paint stripping. Sandblasting and glass beading are both primarily high-pressure methods of stripping otherwise hard-to-remove crud off hard surfaces quickly and inexpensively.

That said, some sandblasters do know how to delicately strip paint off of automotive sheetmetal without warping or otherwise damaging it. However, I

them with a phosphate, or other rust-preventive, as a final step. Generally, you don't want this, because such coatings must be completely removed before painting. Either way, your first step before painting should be to use a metal-etching conditioner (i.e., Metal-prep), which also removes any minor surface rust, followed by a good etching primer. Don't let stripped metal parts sit and rust. Don't strip your car until you're ready to do the rest of the job. Got that?

The final point on immersion stripping is not really a problem as much as it can be a big surprise. You may have

heard of drag race cars that had "acid dipped" bodies to lighten them. The paint-and-rust removal process doesn't remove parent metal that way, if done properly. On the other hand, your body may have had significantly more rust on it than your realized, hidden from view. If so, what comes out of the tank might be a lot less than what went in. This isn't the stripper's fault. That rust had to come out, one way or another. And this way, even if the body now has gaping holes in it, at least you know where the rust was. You can feel assured you got it all out and you know where you have to cut out and weld in new sheetmetal to make it right.

One problem with any stripped, bare sheetmetal, especially if it has been rinsed with water or touched with hands, is that it tends to mildly surface rust again quickly if not painted immediately. In the old days, "Metalprep" (PPG DX 579 shown here) was recommended on bare metal (1) to remove any minor rust, (2) to clean any oils or other contaminants, and (3) to etch the surface for improved paint adhesion. Today 2-part etching primer/sealers (such as PPG's DP series) are so good they are usually applied directly to bare metal, first thing.

would not trust such a sandblaster unless I had a recommendation from prior customers, I could see samples of his work (if he does automotive stripping, there should be some around the shop), and he can assure that he has dry, clean sand for this purpose. Further, just because he can do a fine job on Model A fenders doesn't mean he can do Volkswagen or (worse) new Honda or Toyota doors, which are considerably thinner metal, without ruining them. The same even holds true for many media blasters who specialize in automotive work. Several haven't discovered yet how thin-tinned most of the new cars (and some of the older foreign ones, let alone any aluminum body parts) are. Be careful. Possibly have some "test parts" stripped first.

What you want is a "media" blaster who specifically does automotive paint removal. This can refer to most anything (in small, granular form) which, when propelled in pressurized air, is abrasive

and erodes softer surfaces (such as paint) off of harder ones (such as sheetmetal). Plastic media is the most common, but "plastic" is a very nebulous word that can refer to several types of chemically derived substances. Acrylic is one you would recognize. But a good "plastic media blasting" paint stripper I interviewed said he used various substances including urea-formaldehyde (a synthetic resin), melamine, and even wheat starch. I've heard of cars being blasted with such things as talcum powder, baking soda, or anything resembling household scouring powder like Bon Ami. It makes sense. As opposed to softening or dissolving the paint with chemicals, media blasting is the same thing as sanding the paint off, except you have the sand (or other abrasive) blown on with

Media-blast paint strippers use compressed air and a hose/nozzle to shoot anything from sand or plastic granules to crushed walnut shells to clean paint, dirt, rust, grease, or filler off sheetmetal (or other painted surfaces). Paint strippers who specialize in, or know how to, strip automotive sheetmetal without ruining it are getting scarce. We found these recent examples at Hambro Sandblasting in San Fernando, California.

While other media are easier on sheetmetal (even aluminum or fiberglass, in some cases), a good sandblaster can remove rust, along with the paint, as shown in the tailgate corner of this '59 El Camino...

...And still leave factory lead over body seams. However, sandblasting leaves the surface rough and lightly pitted, as you can see. Many consider this good for paint (or filler) adhesion.

We don't know what this looked like before it was blasted, but you definitely want to uncover this sort of rust. It has to be cut out and replaced with welded-in new metal to be cured.

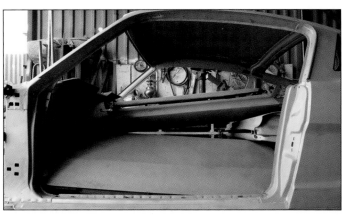

A good thing about media blasting is that it can be used selectively, and the car can be disassembled (or not) as much as you want. This one got the whole interior blasted, including the dash, roof, and even the steering column. A good blaster can also leave plastic fillers in place, if you want, as seen around the doorjambs.

pressurized air. In fact, I had one car walnut-shell blasted. It worked fine for taking off the paint, and even existing filler, but I wouldn't recommend it. First, such organic substances can have oils in them that they can deposit on the surface. I had no problem with that. But this one also filled the car, in every crack, crevice, and inaccessible cubbyhole inside, with a fine brown dust that seemed impossible to get completely out by blowing with compressed air, or any other means.

All media blasting leaves behind some sort of dust residue—some obviously worse than others—that has to be thoroughly cleaned out of the car before you start painting (otherwise it can blow out into the wet paint as you're spraying). Discuss this with your media blaster. Hopefully he can use something that isn't too "dusty," and can get it all out when he's done.

Another drawback to media blasting is that, while it can remove any old plastic filler, it does not remove rust. You have to do that by other means, either by grinding surface rust off, or cutting out and replacing more seriously rusted metal.

The big plus of media blasting is that it works at lower pressures (usually 30 to 35 psi for steel). Some media is said to "chip" the paint off, while being

The same goes for bad filler. Actually, this is bad bodywork, uncovered when all the filler was blasted away. A really good metalman could fix it, but since they're available, both rear quarters will be replaced on this Mustang fastback.

blown at an angle, rather than just abrading the paint away. Done properly, it strips paint and plastic filler off sheetmetal relatively cleanly without warping it or hardening it. In the hands of a good operator, at a lower pressure (20 to 25 psi) it can strip paint off aluminum and even off fiberglass bodies without attacking the parent surface. It doesn't really require removing the body from the frame, or even taking off things like doors, hood, and trunk. The blaster can do an effective job in doorjambs, around hinges, and so on. And, though we would strongly suggest

Sandblasting is also very good for cleaning greasy/rusty areas such as engine compartments and suspension components. Once clean, these parts can be disassembled for further detailing before being painted and reassembled. Note that some surface rust is beginning to grow in here because the owner has let them sit a couple of months. Bare metal does that.

removing such things if you're going so far as full paint stripping, the media doesn't attack rubber, so you can mask off windows and other parts and leave them in place. One car I had media stripped I actually drove there and drove home; I just had to remove and replace the headlights and taillights.

Finally, such media blasters aren't on every street corner. I think they're more common than chemical immersion strip-

The only practical way to strip layers of paint off your car at home is by using a brush-on/scrape off liquid stripper. Don't get the kind at the hardware store; go to your automotive paint dealer and get the very strong type made for cars, which is usually called "aircraft stripper." The job is tedious, very messy, and potentially dangerous. It also helps to have friends pitch in, as Jim McNeil is doing here while they begin to scrape 40 years' worth of paint off the famous Hirohata Merc Barris custom in Jim's garage. Note paper, cardboard, and boxes to collect the noxious drips and scrapings.

Jim should be wearing gloves, safety glasses, and probably a long-sleeve shirt. This stuff eats anything it gets on—including you! Note the piece of cardboard to protect the interior. The trick with this type of stripper is to brush on a thick coat (indoors or under cover, so the sun won't bake it on), let it sit until it wrinkles up the paint, and then remove what's loose with a scraper. Don't try to scrape the paint off; let the stripper do the work. It might take several applications and scrapings to remove several layers of paint (as in this case).

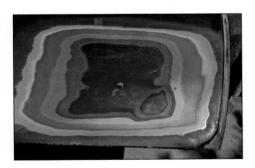

Before stripping the car, Jim sanded through all the previous paint layers so he could keep a record of all the colors that had been on it. This graphically shows how much paint was on the car (and this was all old, crinkly lacquer); it all had to be stripped off before a good, new paint job could be done.

pers, but you have to look for one that really knows automotive work. The one I've used in the past just closed because of environmental and city regulations, and I can't find a substitute anywhere nearby.

Scrape It

So this brings us to the type of paint stripping that you can do at home, anywhere. It's also the least expensive, by far. You can do portions of the body, strip the whole outside, or disassemble everything and do it all, inside and out. But, as you've probably guessed, it is also by far the most labor-intensive—your labor. And we're not just talking a lot of hard work; we're talking messy, stinky, and potentially body-harming hard work. You've probably used it before on something like old furniture—liquid paint stripper, the stuff that comes in a can. You spread it on with a brush, and you scrape it back off with a putty knife once it has wrinkled up the paint. But we're

This custom car had lots of leadwork, especially in the areas shown, which is soft and can be gouged by a metal scraper. Steel wool or Scotchbrite pads are best for removing final paint layers, once they're soft, and then for scrubbing the surface with plain water. As you can see, the stripper won't hurt well-applied lead filler. It eats into plastic filler, however, which should be ground out and replaced.

After the car was washed with water, which neutralizes the stripper, Jim went over the body with a Metalprep-type wash, followed by a coat of VeriPrime etching primer, and then a layer of K200 high-fill primer, as shown here. We show the rest of the paint job on this car in Chapter 10.

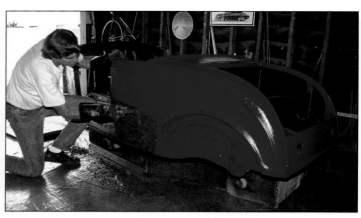

I have used aircraft stripper on a few projects in my garage, this one being my '32 Ford roadster body. Fortunately it only had one layer of red lacquer over primer (lacquers are the easiest to strip; new catalyzed paints are much harder to remove). Note that I'm wearing big, thick rubber gloves, and I have the floor covered with thick plastic to catch the corrosive droppings.

not talking hardware-store variety paint stripper, here. We're talking the meanest, nastiest stuff—usually called something like "aircraft stripper"—you can get at your automotive paint supplier.

If you're painting your car at home—hello, that's what this book is about—and it needs the paint stripped for any of the reasons outlined above, this is most likely the method you're going to use, because (1) you can do it at home, anywhere, any time (no appointments, no waiting time, no transportation); (2) the only cost is a gallon or two of the stripper itself, and it's not very expensive; (3) you can do it yourself, using your own time and labor rather than paying big bucks to someone else (again, what this book is about); and (4) the results, if you do it properly, are nearly as good as the other methods. It's just a big, long, sweaty, messy, even potentially danger-ous job. Be forewarned. If you ask friends or family to help with this, warn them. And this is one of those procedures where you really do need to wear big, long, thick rubber gloves, full-shield eye goggles, and preferably a long-sleeved shirt. Even if you live somewhere with a warm climate, don't attempt this in

shorts and sandals. Keep a hose, with ready-running water, at hand.

Further, wherever you do this, we sug-gest you spread out plastic sheeting, taped to the ground, around the vehicle, or some-thing like sheets of cardboard. Then be advised that once you start, you will get this stuff on the soles of your shoes and track it wherever you walk, so don't go far. In fact, if you're at all sloppy, I suggest you wear clothes, and possibly shoes, that you can simply throw directly in a big trash can when you're done. I hope I'm making my point. I've done this job many times. I'm not messy. But I know exactly what it feels like when you get a spot of this stuff on your skin. It feels the same as when a welding spark burns through your shirt or falls in your shoe. Fortunately, in this case, it goes away if you quickly douse it with water. You *do not* want to get this stuff in your eyes. These are not idle precautions. No lawyer made me say this. I speak from experience.

All that being said, get the strongest, gnarliest stripper you can get from your automotive paint store (not the hardware store), because this job does take time—inevitably more than one application, maybe two or three—and you want the stripper to work as quickly and deeply as

possible. *But let the stripper do the work.* Be patient. Pour some stripper into something like a big coffee can. Brush on a good, thick coat of this stuff (with about a 3-inch, bristle-type, old—or dis-posable—paint brush). Then have a lemonade; do a load of laundry; make some phone calls. Let the stripper wrin-kle, bubble, and lift the paint. Give it time. Don't start scraping until it does.

If you've gutted the car, you don't have to worry much about masking things. A big plus of this stripper is that, though it can run a bit, it basically goes where you brush it. It won't leave dust or other residue, and it won't get into places you can't see to wash it out. It does not attack rubber or chrome, just as it does not attack the metal you're cleaning. While we, of course, suggest removing everything practical from the body before this type of stripping, you can leave the windows in place and mask them off (with good masking tape and paper), and leave the doors (and hood and trunk, if applicable) shut, and strip the car that way. Then, if you're going to paint the doorjambs and so on, remove rubber weatherstrip and hand-sand those areas. Or, if the jambs have as much paint build-up as the rest of the car, you can mask off the interior and the insides of the windows to strip them, too (actually, the stripper won't hurt glass or rubber, so you don't really have to mask off windows; but you don't want stripper running onto wires, power window motors, etc.). If you want to do the best-quality repaint, however, remove all glass, handles, and so on, so you can remove all paint under them and their seals. To keep stripper from running inside the body, tape any holes from the inside with masking tape.

Further tips for "hand liquid stripping": Do not apply this stuff in the sun on a hot day. You don't want it to dry out before it does its work; in fact, you don't want to let it dry out at all. If you see any areas drying, possibly because you put the stripper on too thin, just brush on some more, then wait for the paint to wrinkle. Conversely, like most chemicals (including paint), it works slower the colder the ambient temperature is. I don't suggest doing this in winter in Detroit, even if you do the stripping inside a warm garage. The final step is washing all traces of the stripper and old paint off the body with running water and scouring pads. You probably don't want to do this inside the garage, and you don't want the water freezing on the car in the driveway.

One trick I've heard of for warmer climates (but have not tried) is to brush the stripper onto the whole car, then cover it with a layer of clear plastic sheeting (like Visqueen). This keeps the stripper from drying out, but allows it to get hotter and work faster.

When you've given the stripper plenty of time to work, and at least one or two layers of paint have wrinkled up, it's time to start scraping. Assuming you're working on a metal body (steel or aluminum, it doesn't matter), I suggest using a long-handled putty knife or flat-blade scraper to start removing the now-softened paint. Just remove the paint that's ready to go. Don't try to force or gouge it with the scraper. If you get down to bare metal in one application, you're really lucky. Otherwise, brush on another thick layer of stripper and let it go to work again.

Once you do get down to some bare metal, there will still be lots of traces of paint on the surface. For getting into corners and crevices, I'd suggest using a short-bristled wire brush. Do not use a rotary wire wheel, or anything like that; even a regular wire brush with inch-long bristles inevitably flings some stripper on you (or something else nearby you don't want it on). This stuff is nasty. Be careful.

Finally, to get the last specks and streaks of paint off the body, give it one more coat of stripper, let it sit a while, then start scrubbing it off with steel wool or, preferably, a coarse 3M Scotchbrite pad.

When you've got all the paint off, continue with the Scotchbrite pad with a hose dribbling water, which not only washes off all remaining liquid stripper, but also neutralizes it. Dry or air-blow the car down before it surface rusts, and you're done. Carefully roll up and dispose of the plastic or cardboard you put down to catch the scraped paint and drippings. Thoroughly spray the work area with water from a hose to wash off and neutralize any stripper that may remain on the ground. If any small spots of paint were missed, they should easily hand-sand off. And if you didn't strip areas such as the doorjambs, hand-sand them, being sure to feather any edges to bare, stripped metal.

Of course you want to prep the bare metal before painting, starting with Metalprep or an etching primer/sealer. One final caution: if you see streaks or splotches in your first coat of primer that appear not to dry, that means some of your stripper remains on the metal. You don't want that under your paint. So you have to restrip those areas or, preferably, sand them back down to bare metal. The sanding will probably remove any vestiges of stripper, but a rescouring with Scotchbrite and water wouldn't hurt. Better yet, give the car a double scour/wash with water when you're done stripping to be sure you've got all the stripper off before you start the paint process.

At this point I've added one more coat of stripper (from a big coffee can, with an old paint brush), to wrinkle and lift the last of the stubborn paint.

Then, after one more scraping, I moved the body outside and used a coarse Scotchbrite pad, with plain water, to clean the metal fully and neutralize any remaining stripper.

How to Build a Car

You would think the process should be obvious, or intuitive, to those who build cars, but apparently it isn't. You don't paint a new house before you shingle the roof, and you don't lay carpets until all the interior painting is done, right? Well, the process for building a car is similar, but with some exceptions.

Most of the exceptions come from the type of paint job you are undertaking. We talked more about the various stages of paint jobs in the previous chapter, but they have a bearing on what we're discussing here. For instance, when to remove and replace window glass doesn't matter if you don't intend to take any glass out.

But, in general, the process should go like this:

1. Mechanical work comes first. If you're going to rebuild the engine, transmission, brake system, suspension, or any similar components, do it now. Most builders suggest, and I agree, that after you rebuild such components, you should reinstall, adjust, align, and hook-up all the mechanical components, and drive the vehicle enough to make sure that everything works properly before you proceed further. This brings up two big questions. First, it's easiest to paint and detail each of these mechanical components when it's out of the chassis and being rebuilt. But if you do, and then reinstall everything to get it running and test drive it, you have to mask and seal all of the mechanical and engine components during the messy bodywork and paint stages. Some prefer to remove, rebuild, and detail the mechanical components, but not to reinstall them until the painting and rub out are complete. Still others do the mechanical work, reinstall and test the components, but wait to do all engine/chassis detailing after the body painting is done. We're already dealing with exceptions, and the choice is really up to you. (And, obviously, many cars being painted are new enough that mechanical components don't need rebuilding; and such cars do not need reupholstering or other steps of the "building" process.) Second is the "body-off" debate. We discuss this much more later. I'm personally against it in most cases for post-'30s cars. But if you're going to take the body off the frame, either because it's simple to do (i.e., a pre-'40s car), or because it's so rusty you need to dip it in a chemical strip bath, now is the time to do it. Without debating the issue, if you decided to remove the body from the chassis, paint it separately, and reinstall it when it's all done, then you can rebuild, paint, and detail all the chassis/mechanical components separately and put them in a corner, covered, and clean for the rest of the process.

2. Strip the body as much as possible. Again, this depends largely on the "stage" of paint job you are undertaking. But don't be lazy or cut corners. Unbolt or peel off everything possible from the exterior of the car: lights, handles, chrome trim, bumpers (even new painted types), wipers, license plates…you get the idea. If you're going all the way, this is the time to strip out all upholstery and glass, too. Basically, this depends on your levels of energy and commitment, buffered by some common sense. The more you take the car apart (for sanding, prep, paint coverage, and rub out) the better-quality paint job you produce. But how good a paint job does this project deserve?

3. We're assuming (hoping) that for the vast majority of you, your car needs no more than minor bodywork. But this is the time to do it. If your car needs any major work, and it's beyond your abilities, take it to a good bodyshop now. They'll appreciate having the body stripped (especially of interior and glass) because they would probably have to do that, anyway. If the body is so bad that it needs to be removed and paint/rust stripped, now is obviously the time to do it. However, if large patch panels or other major portions of metal (such as floors) need to be welded into the body, this is best done when the body is properly installed and shimmed on the chassis (even if temporarily), so that such pieces align correctly as they are welded in place. This step would also include swapping crunched bolt-on body parts (front fenders, doors, hood, trunk) for straighter ones. But let's hope that all your paint project needs is minor bodywork, which we cover in Chapter 3. When it's done, spray those areas with primer, preferably a high-fill variety.

4. Next comes sanding or the other type of stripping—paint stripping. Again, for the vast majority of you, it will be the former. But for most of you, this step is basic, even boring, grunt work. Yes, there's a little skill and finesse involved, and we cover that in Chapter 6. But the deal in this step is to get all surfaces to be painted (in door-jambs, under the hood and trunk, firewall, fender panels—wherever you're going to repaint) not only sanded smooth, but scuffed sufficiently so that the new paint adheres properly.

5. No matter what "stage" of paint job you're doing, this is the time to align all body panels. Newer cars shouldn't need adjustment or realignment, but you might be surprised how many car or truck bodies are improperly fit at the factory (especially older ones, which very likely have settled and shifted over years of driving/chassis flex/other abuse). Maybe you don't really care. For those that do, it might mean double work. Assemble all body panels and then adjust, shim, bend, tweak, grind, or whatever it takes to get all the fit and gaps right, then mark them and take them all back apart for painting. Many people paint all the parts first, then try to make them fit; it's certainly possible, but can lead to chips, frustration, or even redoing certain areas.

6. Now is the time to mask off everything you want to protect from paint or overspray. After a thorough cleaning of all surfaces to be painted with a good degreaser, I'd follow with a coat of sealer/etching primer in any cases (1) where you've got bare metal, or (2) you've got one or more layers of paint on the car (maybe including primed bodywork) of possibly dubious origins. In either case, I'd follow this with a good, full coat of a modern catalyzed primer, followed by a second, complete round of dry sanding (assuming there's masking in place). If you're repainting a relatively new car, or one you're convinced has a "stable substrate," you can simply mask it after a good sanding, and you're ready to repaint.

7. Paint

8. If you're going to color-sand and rub out, do both now.

9. Then remove all masking/paper/etc. If you're not rubbing it out, make sure the paint is sufficiently dry before peeling back any tape. If you do color-sand (wet, of course) and rub the paint, be sure to remove all masking before it dries out and sticks in place (don't leave it overnight).

10. If you've removed glass, now is the time to reinstall it, along with new felt strips, channels, rubber, and so on. However, check with your upholsterer, because many rear windows, windshields, and other components you might not think of (dome light, wiring, antenna, stereo speakers, air conditioning) need to be installed in conjunction with the headliner or other upholstery panels. Also, on many cars exterior chrome trim and things like door handles must be reinstalled before upholstery is in place. And this would be the time to install all new weatherstripping and any body seals, assuming you removed them for paint.

11. Finally, last comes new upholstery, if that's part of the rebuild. Assuming you removed all the old upholstery back in Step 2, most upholsterers request that you paint as much of the inside of the car as possible (especially around doors, kick panels, dash area, and so on). Certain cars, such as early VW bugs, have lots of body-color-painted areas inside. Others might need pieces such as window frames, dashboards, seat kick-panels, arm-rest bottoms, ash-tray covers—you name it—painted. They can either match the outside of the car or be painted another color, but they should be painted before (or at least as) the new upholstery is installed. Work closely with your upholsterer, and pray that he doesn't scratch up your new paint job too much.

As we said at the beginning of this list, there are plenty of exceptions. Most of the cars being painted by readers of this book won't have interiors or glass removed. Of examples shown in this book, at least two should either have been upholstered after paint, or had more of the existing interior removed. These are guidelines, not rules.

BODYWORK 101

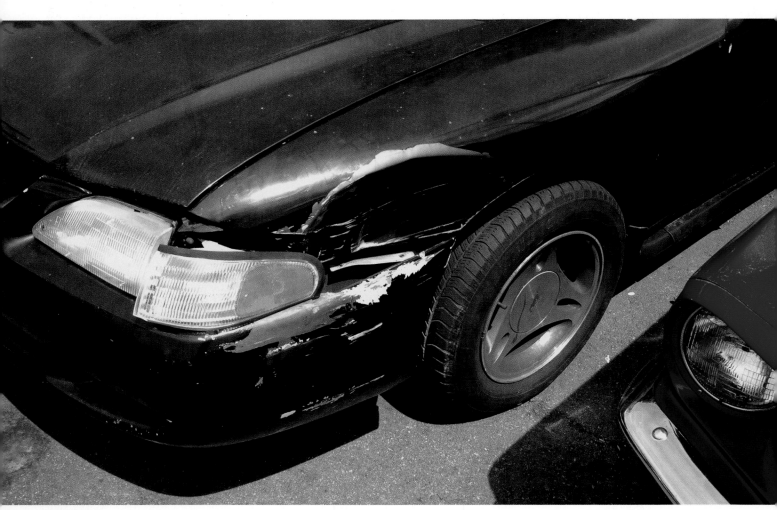

This Mustang fender doesn't look seriously dented, but the way it's crumpled around the headlight and bumper flange, plus the fact that it's an easily removable part, means it would be simpler and smarter to swap this for a good used replacement, rather than try to straighten it.

Believe it or not, there was a time when using lead as a filler when doing automotive bodywork was considered "quick and cheap." The proper method, then, was called "metalworking," and it consisted of hammer-and-dollying the metal straight as much as possible; shrinking or stretching other areas of metal as needed, possibly using heat from a torch; and finally filing very small ripples or imperfections from the surface with a Vixen body file. Only a precious few expert "metalmen" can do this today on sheet-metal bodies, whether steel or aluminum. They can also cut out bad sections of the body, hand-form new ones to fit perfectly, weld them in place, and finish the area so you can hardly see, or feel, where the work was done. We don't expect you to do this, or to even know—let alone afford—someone who can.

Someone who was at *Hot Rod* magazine in the early '50s told me a funny story at the other extreme. At that time

There are many books on bodywork and metal finishing, but here we focus only on very basic body straightening, done primarily with hand tools. Your first necessity is a bodyman's hammer and dolly. Start with the hammer with a flat, round head on one side and a pick on the other, plus a dolly with one flat and one curved side, such as the second from right. Add more as you go. Do not use other types of hammers on sheetmetal.

Don't even think about sanding plastic filler level and smooth without using a hard rubber block or the longer board made for this purpose. They now make even longer blocks than these that curve to fit metal surfaces. Always use as long a block as possible to level filler quickly and evenly.

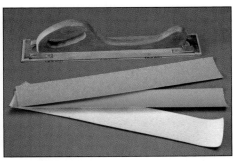

Buy strips of 36, 80, and 180 grit paper made to fit the "longboard" or "filler board." Cut them to fit shorter blocks. Most bodywork sanding is done with 36 grit. Use 80 grit on high-fill primers and spot putty. The 180 and finer-grit papers are covered under prepping and block sanding in Chapter 6.

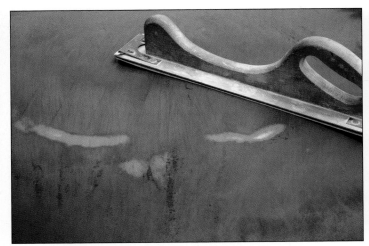

Surprisingly, not all dents are readily apparent to the eye. A trained open-palm hand helps locate minor creases and ripples. But one sure way to locate them is to sand the area with a block or board with 80-grit paper. They show up quickly through existing paint, such as these crescent creases common to roof areas.

The pick end of a body hammer is often misused, but it's good for erasing such creases. Use it to tap along the exposed raised edge, using little more than the weight of the hammer to do the work. Feel the area with the palm of your other hand as you go. When you're good at this, no filler is needed.

the magazine had a Ford panel truck with its logo painted on its sides, flames on the front, and Von Dutch pinstriping. Someone, somehow, flipped it over and damaged one side. So they took it to a well-known custom shop to have it straightened and repaired. The funny part is that the customizer had some sort of "gun" that could melt and spray lead onto a body. Instead of properly straightening the truck, the shop hammered the panels close to shape and sprayed the imperfections full of lead, grinding and filing to contour afterward. The repaired truck looked all right but was noticeably heavier. This was a genuine "lead sled," a term for a vehicle repaired with copious amounts of lead instead of proper metalwork.

The short cuts that made *Hot Rod*'s lead sled can still be taken today, but with plastic filler instead of toxic metal. There is nothing wrong with good-quality filler applied properly and sparingly. In fact, there are a few reasons why filler *is better* than lead. First, it's much lighter and considerably cheaper and easier to apply—without special tools, talents, or products. Second, applying lead requires heating the sheetmetal with a torch, which warps it. And, third, the leading process involves acids and other chemicals (in the lead, tinning, etc.) that can come back to lift, bubble, or craze the final paint, sometimes years later, if not thoroughly washed and cleaned away. Believe it or not, I have seen more paint jobs (especially on classic or custom cars) marred by bad lead work than by bad filler.

On the other hand, plastic or resin-based fillers were just coming on the market when I first started trying, and thereby learning, to do bodywork. I did experience some cracking, but that was because (1) the fillers weren't perfected yet, (2) I didn't properly clean and prepare the surfaces, and (3) without experience and a proper hammer and dolly, I had to apply too much filler over not-straight-enough

metal. But it didn't take that long for fillers to improve, along with my bodywork skills. All of my vehicles have minor amounts of plastic filler, some—I'm afraid I must admit—I applied 20 to 40 years ago. These vehicles see plenty of use, most have been repainted more than once, but not one has ever shown any evidence of plastic body filler cracking, lifting, bubbling, checking, or anything else. Nothing. Ever.

Get the Metal Straight

Before you ever lift the lid on a can of filler, you need to get the metal as straight as you can.

Let's start with the obvious: dents you can see. If any of these come in the category of rips, crumples, or crashes, they're probably outside the scope of this book. If your car has been whacked so badly the frame is crooked and the doors no longer close properly, you need professional help with big professional tools (like a frame-puller). You are, of course, welcome to tackle any bodywork you want, with whatever tools you have, and you'll undoubtedly learn something. But that's not what we're teaching here.

If the vehicle has sustained some major damage (or rust) that you're not

Some metalmen cringe at the thought of using a grinder on sheetmetal, but in a relatively small area like this, it's the most efficient way to clean the metal. Use a 36-grit disc, do not use much pressure, and don't make big sparks or turn the metal blue.

In this case, the creases were visible as you sighted down the rear fender, but I sanded them with a 36-grit board so you could see them.

going to fix with a hammer, dolly, and a little filler, you can take it to a reputable body shop to have the work done. Depending on what they agree to, how much you trust them, and how much you want to spend (or try to save), you might have three options: (1) have them do the big work like frame straightening, panel-patching or replacing, and then "roughing out" any remaining metalwork so that you can fill and block-sand it at home; (2) have them include filler work, which they can do quickly with their professional shop and air tools; or (3) have them also prime and spot-putty the area so that it's "ready to block and

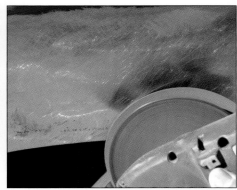

This body had some surface rust under the chrome strips, and the grinder quickly cleans this off. Make sure it's all gone before you put any filler or paint over it.

The grinder roughs up the surface so the filler bonds better. Be sure to clean more than the dented area, so you won't have any filler over paint.

paint." Unless you know a shop well, they probably won't do (1) or (2), and if they do (3), you've got to trust them because you won't be able to see what they did or how much filler they used. As we've advised, don't invest in major bodywork unless the car is worth it.

If the wrinkle or crunch damage is isolated to a body part that is unboltable, such as a front fender or door, you can replace it with a decent one from a wrecking yard, or other source. Should it need stripping or a little ding repair, fine. You can do that.

Between major damage for someone else to repair and metal you can swap out lies moderate damage to a panel not easily replaced. We're talking about metal that isn't cracked or split, folded over on itself, badly stretched, and does not have holes in it (from rust, or otherwise). To start on this type of repair, I'd suggest getting a body hammer with a round, flat head on one side and a dull-pointed "pick" on the other, and a universal dolly with at least one flat side and one curved side. Both last a lifetime, and together they can do a whole lot of metalwork. A couple of other shapes or sizes of dollies would help, but most any flat or curved, easily held piece of heavy metal will do. You should find plenty of other "metal persuaders" in your garage, as well. But, as a general rule, don't use a ball-peen hammer for bodywork and don't pound

on sheetmetal with anything like a screwdriver blade or center punch. In fact, do not use the "pick" end of the body hammer for anything other than light tapping.

Before talking about straightening metal, let's consider what doesn't need straightening. A lot of door-dings, nicks, and deep scratches can actually be filled with today's good, catalyzed, high-fill primers. There's some controversy on this point. Certain bodymen dislike adding and block-sanding heavy layers of primer; they prefer to work on bare metal with thin coats of filler. This is a tough call. The advantage of modern primers and catalyzed spot putties is that they can be applied over existing paint. If you don't need to strip the car to bare metal, this is the most expedient way to fill these minor dings, scrapes and scratches— those less than 1/8-inch deep. If you grind or strip the paint to bare metal to fill such small dings with filler, first (on newer cars) you'll be removing the factory-applied base coats and, second, creating a rough, jagged edge around the repair that has to be feather-edged, primed, and maybe even spot-puttied to make it level and smooth with the existing paint, anyway. If you're stripping the car to bare metal, by all means use plastic filler on these very shallow dings, especially if you can see them. Conversely, the rule is to never apply filler over existing paint or primer. PPG claims that filler should be applied over its high-adhesion DP-series sealers, claiming it sticks better than to the bare metal. I'm too old school to try it. See what your paint dealer or professional recommends.

Let's talk about metal that needs straightening—that means anything that's 1/8-inch or more out of shape. Start gently. Especially on newer cars, it's amazing how much you can straighten sheetmetal with your bare hands. Massage it; bump it. On larger dents, see if it pops back out just by pushing on it from the back side. You

might be surprised. If it leaves a crescent crease around the edge, try tapping this out with the flat or pick end of your hammer—tap, tap, tap lightly along it, back and forth. Someone caved-in the rear quarter of my son's '50 Ford in a parking lot, just behind the door. After removing interior panels, I was able to push it back out from inside with my feet, pressing on it repeatedly until it was all gone. It didn't even crack the paint. Another time, something fell on the fender of my VW bug, making a crease about an inch deep and four inches long. I massaged this out with the round end of a large plastic screwdriver handle. You can do a lot of bodywork with your hands, and what's at hand in your garage.

Hammer-and-dolly work is a talent most can acquire with practice. Two things: most dents in sheetmetal cause some stretching of the metal; hammering sheetmetal directly on a dolly stretches it further, as it "squeezes" the metal between the hammer and dolly. When sheetmetal gets stretched too far from its original shape, it begins to "oil can"—that is, to pop in or out as you press on it. You don't want this. Fixing it can only be done by shrinking the metal, with heat, in some manner that is beyond the scope of this book. (Sheetmetal expands, like most substances, when it is heated, but then shrinks to smaller than its original size when it cools. Don't ask me why. But that's why welding or any other severe heating of sheetmetal warps it.)

So when you're hammer-and-dollying to work out dents, do not start aggressively. Further, it is better to hammer off-dolly rather than on-dolly. That is, to lower a high spot in the metal, place the dolly under a low spot next to it, and push up with the dolly as you tap or hammer down the high spot. With practice you can use this method to lower high spots, raise low spots, or do both at the same time, all the while hammering on the outer surface with the dolly on the inside. Of course there are places where you can't get your hand or the dolly inside. You might have to remove some body panels, and definitely interior panels, to work them properly. You can gently use the hammer to tap down some high spots without using a dolly behind it, and a dolly can be very effective, by itself, to bump or knock low spots up, or out (even big ones, to start with).

But the main thing is, when you're straightening sheetmetal with a hammer and dolly (or anything else), try not to stretch it any more than it already is. That's why you should never beat sheetmetal aggressively with just a hammer (and especially not a peen or a pick) to try to straighten or undent it. You just make it worse, and possibly ruin it. The more you work metal, the harder and more brittle it gets, until it cracks.

Also, since you're going to be filling the surface after you have straightened it as much as possible, you want all the irregularities to be low spots, with no high spots. That is, you want all the sheetmetal to be at, or slightly below, its original surface level so that you can fill-in just these low spots with

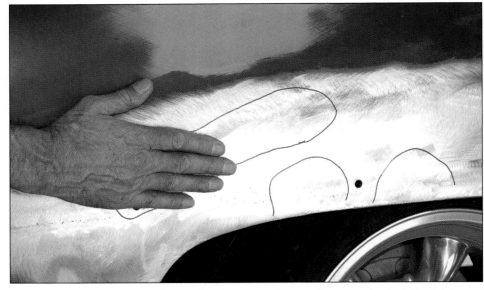

Run your open hand, as shown, back and forth over the area to feel the high and low spots in the metal. It takes practice to develop this "feel," but it is essential to bodywork. I have marked one high area (near hand) and two low spots.

the least overall amount of material possible.

One last word here. We've been talking about dents in the metal that you can *see*, even when the body is stripped to bare metal. These are obvious, and you must fix them. A good, experienced bodyman, however, doesn't look for metal imperfections with his eyes, he *feels* for them with his hand. To acquire this bodyman's touch does take some practice. You use the outstretched hand, palm down, and lightly run it back and forth, with a minimum of pressure. Move your hand fairly quickly, just sort of skimming the surface, in a linear motion

Fortunately I can get a flat dolly behind the high area. To gently tap it down, I hold the dolly firmly next to the crease, and hammer directly on the high spot. This is called "hammer-off-dolly." Hammering directly on the dolly, especially with force, stretches the metal (by hammering it thinner), which leads to "oil canning," where the metal pops in and out. Expert metalmen can hammer, shrink, and stretch the surface perfectly straight. We're not experts (few are). We want to get it as level as possible, with no high spots and only minor low spots.

(straight back-and-forth). As you learn the feel, any high or low spots in what should be flat sheetmetal are immediately detected, even when you can't readily see them. Further, you can tell where the metal is high and where it is low. If you're having a hard time developing this feel, try using a clean, dry, unfolded shop rag between your hand and the surface. Experienced bodymen feel the surface before they start hammer-and-dollying it, at intervals during the process to check progress, and then again at intervals as they are sanding it down with filler or primer, until it feels straight and smooth enough to pass the "touch test." You want to learn how to do this now, during the bodywork and sanding stage, because once you spray the paint, color-sand it, and rub it out nice and glossy, that mirror finish will definitely visually show any dips, bumps, dings, or ripples your eye couldn't see before, but your hand should have felt.

Fill It

Now do you think you're ready to open that can of plastic filler? How big a can did you get? You might as well buy a gallon, since it's more economical, and it lasts for years until you mix it with the hardener to use it. But you better not put that whole gallon on one car. If you do, the majority of it better end up on the floor as shaving particles and sanding dust. In fact, if you're a first-timer, don't

When the area is as straight as you can get it, it's time to mix filler. I use a piece of heavy-gauge sheetmetal to mix it on, and a screwdriver blade as a stirrer. Especially for beginners, start with small amounts of filler so it doesn't harden before you're done spreading it. You can always add more.

Some important things: Squish the hardener in its tube several times to mix it before opening. You have to add the right amount of hardener; adding more than enough won't make the filler harden faster, it weakens it because the extra won't ever "dry." Likewise, be sure to mix the filler and hardener completely (until it's all one color), because any that doesn't mix also stays soft.

You want different sizes of spreaders to apply the mixed filler to larger or smaller areas. The big one is rubber, and bends to conform to body contours. The smallest one is for spot putty. If you can't find a size you need, cut one to the shape you want (as the two black ones in the middle have been).

feel bad if you go through a gallon of this stuff pretty quickly. Put it on, sand it off; put more on, and sand it off a few times before you start to learn how much to apply, and how much to sand off. The typical beginner puts too much on, which is okay, but then sands too much off, which means you have to apply a second coat and sand again. Two or three tries is normal for starters.

Here's another tip: They sell plastic filler-mixing boards, but you either have to clean them with acetone or throw them away. I use a piece of metal because I can wipe it fairly clean with a spreader after each use, and then hit it with my grinder to quickly clean it when too much hardened filler builds up. I've been using this same piece—part of a '56 Chevy fender—for many years.

Preparing the surface: Only apply filler to clean, bare metal (or fiberglass). "Bare" is self-explanatory, but I must emphasize "clean." This not only means no paint, dirt, scale, rust, or other obvious crud, but it also means no oils of any kind. You've got oil of all kinds in your garage. If you use any air tools (more next chapter) up to this stage, you should oil them, and they spit some of this oil out as they work. And you have oils in your hands. Your sweat has oil in it. So, before you get ready to spread any filler, I suggest you wipe down the work area with lacquer thinner or acetone, and wipe it dry with a clean cloth.

Second, we have another controversy. Many metalmen shudder at the thought of putting a grinder to sheetmetal. Any grinder with a 24- to 36-grit disc can remove metal in a hurry. This goes against the laws and religion of "metalwork," as opposed to "bodywork." I can see their point. Their mantra is to save sheetmetal, not grind it away. On the other hand, they didn't get the name "body grinder" for no reason. They've been a staple in bodyshops and even custom shops for decades. (Of course, they've been grossly misused there for decades, as well.) Used carefully and sparingly, a large body grinder with a 7- or 8-inch 24- to 36-grit sanding disc (or the smaller, right-angle, air-driven die grinder type with a 1-1/2- to 2-inch disc) can be a helpful body tool. If you're not stripping paint by other means, it is the quickest and most effective way to remove paint from an area that needs bodywork. It is also the best way to remove old filler. And it obviously cleans the surface to shiny metal that you're going to spread filler over. Just don't overdo it. Clean the metal, don't gouge or grind it. As soon as you see sparks start to fly, you're removing metal. If the metal on the body starts to turn blue in spots, you're not only removing metal, but heating it enough to warp it. Don't do that.

Here are some tips. I use a slow-speed body grinder (2,400 rpm, as opposed to the normal 5,000 to 6,000 rpm) for two reasons: first, it's not nearly as aggressive when used as a grinder; but, second, I can also use it for a buffer when I'm rubbing out paint (which I do much more often). Also, I use 36- to 50-grit discs on sheetmetal (actually I use these grits on the small die grinder on sheetmetal, these days, much more often than on the big body grinder). Never use a body grinder, or a rotary grinder/sander of any type, to try to smooth and shape filler. That's usually disastrous, and we explain why later.

On the other hand, it says right on the body filler can, in the directions, first thing, "Grind/sand surface with 24 to 80 grit sandpaper down to bare metal." Admitted, it doesn't say to use a body grinder for this, and I would emphasize "down *to* bare metal," not into it, or through it. Many other books, manuals, and bodymen say to "rough up" the metal surface to be filled with 24- to 36-grit paper (or disc) to give a better bonding surface between metal and filler. I would agree with this. Just stop at "roughing up."

So you've got the area that needs bodywork cleaned to bare metal. You've hammer-and-dollied it as close to straight as you can, keeping any dips or wiggles below the original surface as much as possible. And you've roughed up the surface with a coarse disc or paper. And it's clean of any oils or grease. You're ready to mix and spread filler.

First you need something to mix it on. They sell large plastic "palettes" for this, which are fine and easy to hold, but require cleaning with acetone after each use. You don't want a piece of cardboard or anything that might have wax or other impurities in it. I prefer a piece of sheetmetal. Mine happens to be cut out of a '56 Chevy fender, and I've used it for many years. I scrape it with the squeegee after each use, but it still builds up. So every so often I hold it on the floor with

In this case using a medium-size pliable plastic spreader, I apply the mixed filler quickly, but smoothly and evenly, to the dented area. One tip: when "spreading" filler, don't just wipe it onto the surface, actually press it onto the metal to make sure it adheres.

my foot and grind it back down with my grinder. If you reuse a mixing surface, it's important to keep it free of any small chunks or hard particles that might get in the freshly mixed filler. For a stirrer, I've always used a big, old screwdriver blade. Squeegees or spreaders are made in pliable plastic or rubber, in various sizes (get two or three), and they must be wiped clean after each use with a paper towel, possibly with acetone. If the lip of the spreader isn't clean, it leaves lines or grooves in the filler as you spread it.

Mixing filler properly is extremely important. Unfortunately, there's no good way to measure amounts. Again, you learn by experience. Basically, it's a dab of catalyst (hardener) to a glob of filler. Be sure to knead the hardener in the tube to make it uniform before you open it (if liquid comes out before paste, you didn't squish it enough). The hardener is a darker color than the filler—usually red—and once you have added it, you must quickly, but very thoroughly, mix the two with your stirrer until it's all one uniform color (i.e.,

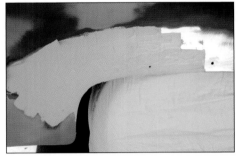

Just as in mixing the filler, it takes some experience to learn how much to apply at one time. A bit too much is better than too little, because you're going to sand off as much as possible. But you can always add more; it's no big deal.

pink). This is very important. Any filler that doesn't get mixed with catalyst never hardens. You don't want soft spots, bubbles, or cavities in your body filler.

The chemical reaction of filler and hardener is highly dependent on room temperature. On a warm or hot day, don't try mixing a big glob. It will probably harden halfway through the job.

What doesn't get evenly spread on the body in time goes in the trash. Mix a smaller amount and start over in a smaller area. In cold climates, on the other hand, the filler can take forever to harden. Bodyshops in such locales usually have banks of heat lamps they can direct on the mixed and spread filler to make it "set up" quicker, so they can start sanding it. Here's the important part: *Adding more or less hardener to the filler does not make it set up faster or slower.* Too little hardener, and the filler never fully hardens. This is rare. The more common problem is adding extra catalyst to try to make it harden sooner. The filler can only bond with a set amount of hardener; any extra catalyst remains soft, just like filler that didn't get fully mixed. Some of you are going to learn this the hard way.

Modern plastic filler is very good if mixed and applied properly. If it's not mixed properly, for either of the above reasons, hopefully you will find out during the sanding process. If not, it can ruin an otherwise good paint job, either right away, or much later. If you use it wrong, don't blame the filler.

Finally, one of the most overused and misused terms pertaining to body and paint work today is a "skim coat" of filler. This has somehow come to mean a relatively thin layer of filler over an entire body panel, if not over the entire body of the vehicle. No, no, no! Just as bad as putting too much filler in one place (too thick), is putting too much filler every place—even if it is thin. In general, you want the minimum amount of total material build-up on top of the sheetmetal of your car, including filler, primers, color, clear—everything. That's a basic rule of painting that gets broken way too often. I know production shops do it; and now lots of custom shops do it to get show-winning body fit and finish as quickly and practically as they can. They look great on the show circuit for a year or so. Or they might get driven a few times a year. But we assume you're fixing

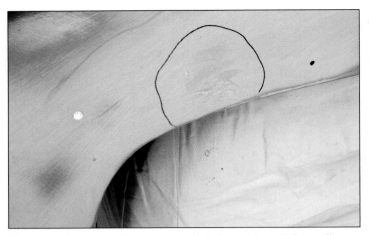

If you've done your hammer-and-dolly work well (i.e., all metal at or below the intended final surface), sand until a few bare spots in the metal just begin to show, as at lower left. (If one or more obviously high spots appear quickly, get out the hammer and dolly again and work them down.) In this case, one low spot (circled) appeared.

After the first board sanding with 36-grit, whether you had to hammer down some high spots or found a low spot or two—or both, apply another thin coat of filler either to those areas or over the whole area, and begin the process again.

The idea is to sand the majority of the filler back off—meaning you have to get the metal pretty straight to begin with. All filler here is less than 1/8-inch thick. Note that no filler covers paint.

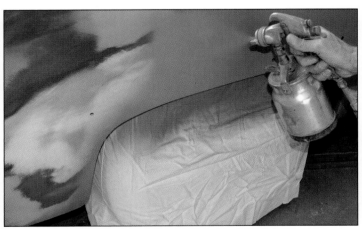

You could resand the area with 80-grit and featheredge the paint, but with today's high-fill primers, it's more efficient to spray a couple layers of that first, and then start block-sanding with 80-grit.

up and painting a car you're going to use and keep for a while. Don't build it out of filler. Don't do what you might see in some magazines or on some TV shows. You've got more than a week to finish this project. Spread a thin, even layer of filler over any areas you have body-worked, covering all the sheetmetal in areas that were dented and that you hammer-and-dollied, plus 2 to 3 inches

extra around it. That's all. Avoid filler at the edges of doors, hoods, and other body panels, as well as in doorjambs. It can get knocked or chipped out of such areas. Poor door or body panel gaps or fitment need to be fixed by realignment, shims, or methods that involve welding—not plastic filler. Spread filler only where it's needed, and then sand most of that off.

Sand It

Sanding is addressed partly here, and more later. When it comes to paint and bodywork, the home hobbyist's best friend is the "filler board" or "long board." We're assuming you are working primarily with hand tools; however, even if you had a shelf full of air sanders of every kind, hand-sanding in long strokes

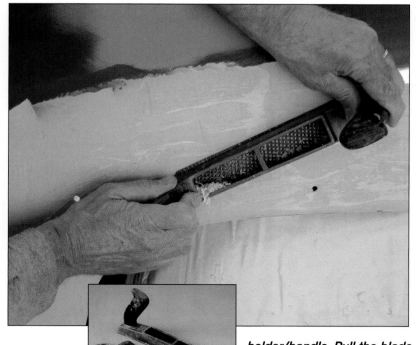

If you've ever seen an article on bodywork, you've undoubtedly read that you should first shave the filler with a "cheesegrater" blade. There's more to it than that. These perforated, sharpened, flat or rounded metal blades were first known by the Stanley trade name "Surform," and were invented to work, in appropriate holders, like a wood plane. They also work great for shaping or sculpting semi-soft substances such as foam blanks for surfboards. But we don't want so much filler on your car that it needs sculpting or shaping. The purpose of the cheesegrater in the filler process is twofold—(1) to quickly "knock down" (shave off) any rough edges, overlaps, etc. to smooth the surface, and (2), more importantly, to remove a sticky film that develops on the surface of the filler as it hardens. It's easiest to "cheesegrate" the filler just before it fully hardens (when it's like hard rubber). The flat blades curve to a rounded surface (when not used in a holder); either flat or rounded blades can be used with or without a holder/handle. Pull the blade, without much down-pressure, in long sweeps, to shave the high spots off the filler. And even if the filler has hardened, you should "cheesegrate" it; otherwise your sandpaper immediately clogs with sticky, small blobs of filler.

with the filler board is the fastest and surest way to get a flat, level surface on your vehicle's body. This holds true whether you're sanding with 36-grit on filler, 80-grit to level high-fill primer and spot putty, or 180-grit over a final coat of primer on the whole body. Never sand filler without some kind of backing block, and the longer the block you can use, the faster the surface gets flat or straight. Body shops use air-powered DA (dual action) sanders on filler almost exclusively. They're fast and easy to handle for everyday production work, but it takes practice to level filler evenly with one. I finally got one, but I hardly ever use it. Especially for a beginner, it can make your filler uneven in a hurry, especially in large areas. The filler board is only a little slower, but it's much better at leveling the surface.

But before you start sanding fresh filler at all, you should always knock down the surface with a Surform blade,

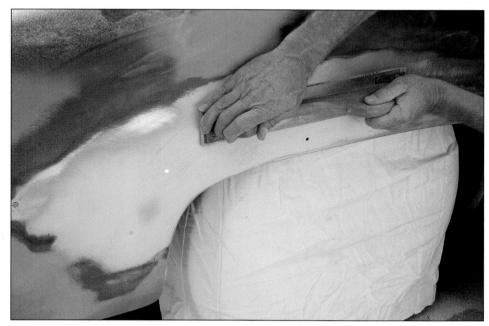

After you've shaved the sticky surface off the bondo and leveled it a bit, it's time to go to work with the "longboard" and some 36-grit paper. Again, let the tool do the work; sand in long sweeps and at angles so the edge doesn't cut a straight line. Feel the surface with your hand as you go, but you can usually see high spots (they sand first) and low spots (they don't sand) as you go.

The repaired area looks ready for paint here, but it's not. The 36-grit leaves deep sanding scratches and the ground paint edges are still not smooth. That comes from block sanding with 80- and 180-grit. But the fender is now straight, with no creases, bumps, or dips.

Not all areas that need bodywork are flat. In the rear corner of the right front fender, where I have "frenched" the aerial, there is a convex crown with a concave area between it and the fender inner edge. Here I am using a rounded cheesegrater, without a holder, in the convex area.

commonly known as a "cheese grater." These come in flat or rounded shapes, in various lengths, and you can use them by themselves, or in various types of holders. I recommend the longer ones, one flat and one round. The round one works on flat surfaces (drag it at an angle), and is easier to hold by itself. The flat one bends to concave or convex surfaces, but I also like to use it in a holder with handles, like a wood plane. Use the grater blade after the filler has started to harden, but before it's fully set-up (when it's a little harder than rubbery). Don't be too aggressive with it. Primarily, you want to shave off the "ridges" and uneven surface of the filler and, depending on how much you put on, get it down close to the surface you want, quickly—but not too far. The other major purpose for always using the blade before sanding is that the filler, as it hardens, forms some sort of film on the surface—I don't know what it is and you can't see it; it feels a little sticky to the touch. But it clogs your 36-grit sandpaper the minute you start to sand it, and you can't clean it out. Sandpaper's too expensive to waste. But if you shave the surface of the filler with a cheese grater blade first, even if it has hardened, it prevents it from clogging the paper.

The photos in this book show various sanding boards, blocks, and tubes. But use the longest practical one, with 36-grit paper, to start working the filler flat. On most surfaces, but particularly on convex-curved ones, I like to sand at 45 degrees, both ways, with the board pointing

Next I use a strip of 36-grit paper held around a round rubber "block" made for such areas. A straight piece of radiator hose would work as well, and pieces of smaller hose work in tighter-curved areas.

On the crowned part I use a medium-size flat block, but sand at 45-degree angles to the crown. Whenever sanding filler, be careful not to cut grooves or troughs in it.

The last step for professional bodymen is to add daubs of "spot putty" over the primer to fill any bubble holes, deep scratches, or other minor indents in the surface, leaving it to the painter to block smooth (sometimes to the painter's consternation). Since you're (probably) the bodyman and painter, do the filler work properly and use spot putty very sparingly. I have also, surprisingly, seen painters using lacquer putty recently. It's quick and easy, but it's nothing more than lacquer primer in paste form. I strongly recommend you use a good, catalyzed spot putty. It only takes a couple of seconds to mix (as shown), and hardens like filler, permanently.

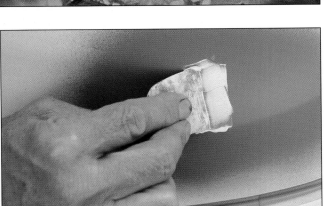

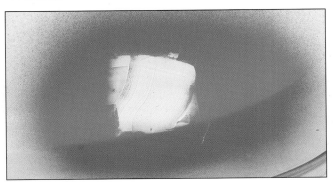

Catalyzed spot putties are usually lighter and easier to sand, but the main difference is that filler is made to go on bare metal, and putty over primer (neither should be used vice-versa). Besides pinholes and sand-scratches in filler, putty is good for filling typical door-dings and shopping-cart gouges. After scuffing the paint and squirting the area with primer, I am adding putty with a small squeegee to a small, round door ding.

toward the front of the car (or at 90 degrees, whatever the surface calls for). But you don't want to sand ruts or grooves into the filler by sanding too long in the same place, in the same direction. Let the long board level the surface.

Keep sanding until you just start to uncover patches or spots of bare metal. Run your hand over the surface, as we described, to feel if these are high spots. If they appeared quickly, in small spots, they probably are. If so, get out your body hammer once again and, depending on their size, tap them down just a bit with the flat or pick end. You probably don't need a dolly for this. Then mix and spread another "skim coat" of filler over this same area, and sand it with the board and 36-grit once again. Hopefully it will level out (your bare hand should tell you this) before, or just as, you uncover bare metal again.

You don't have to get it perfect now. But if you get it reasonably level in two tries, you're doing a good job. You could follow with 80-grit on the board, but most would stop here, and spray an ample coat of high-fill primer over the worked area, before going to 80-grit sanding. If you ground paint away to do the bodywork, feather edge it with 80- or 180-grit paper on a block or with a pad before shooting the primer. We'll talk more about sanding after this stage in Chapter 6.

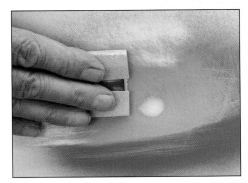

To sand the putty smooth, I wrapped a piece of 80-grit paper around a flat, hard rubber squeegee as a sanding block. Once it's smooth, re-prime the area before painting.

EQUIPMENT FOR HOME PAINTING

All sorts of home shop compressors, including ones with rotary pumps and vertical tanks, are available from a variety of sources, but an old standard for many years is the 2-hp, 2-piston Sears unit with a 20-gallon tank. It puts out 10 cfm at 40 psi, or 8.5 cfm at 90 psi, which is fine for old-style spray guns and most air tools, but not for HVLP guns. After years of winding and unwinding a 50-ft. hose, I recently got the spring-loaded reel and highly recommend it.

You can improve your car's finish in a couple ways without a compressor and spray gun. One way is to buff and polish the paint to make it look new again; the other is to disassemble and partially prep the car yourself before taking it to a one-day-type paint shop. We've covered the first already, and the other is shown in Chapter 7. But even in these two cases, it's nice to have home spray equipment so you can at least spray some professional-quality (i.e., not spray can) primer during the sand-and-prep stage, or spot-in a few bad places on an old paint job that can then be otherwise rubbed out and saved without a full respray.

There are a couple other ways to paint a car without buying your own compressor and other spray equipment, but I don't recommend them. In fact, they might not even be available in most places anymore. The first is to rent a compressor (and possibly other equipment) to use at home. But a quick check of equipment rental yards recently produced slim results. They either had low-capacity gasoline-powered portable compressors (or the small electric ones, with no air tank, more compatible with air brushes), or "airless" units designed for house painting. In the past, I have rented spray equipment from my local automotive paint store—obviously of the type needed for car painting—but a round of calls to such paint supply houses recently produced no positive results. I think the main problem is the recent change in paint equipment technology, primarily due to HVLP (high-volume, low-pressure) systems and government demands that such systems be used by professional shops with no provisions for the occasional, at-home painter. Perhaps you could do better in your area.

Another approach, at least in the past, was a rental spray booth. I have used these a few times. The good part was that you got to paint your car in a clean, filtered, well-lit professional-type

To run most HVLP guns, you need a larger, industrial-type compressor, such as this 5-hp unit with a 50-gallon tank, which puts out 14 cfm at 125 psi. Unfortunately they cost about $1,000 new, and buying a used unit is risky. The vertical tank is a definite space-saver.

booth that had a nice, big compressor, filters, hose, etc. All you had to bring was your gun, paint materials, and a prepped car to paint. The bad part was getting the car there and back, stripped—especially after it was painted. You couldn't leave the car in the booth overnight. But it's probably a moot point, because I couldn't find any spray booths for rent, and if you can't find one in car-crazy Southern California, perhaps they are a thing of the past. Can't hurt checking your area, though.

Get a Compressor

If you were only going to paint one or two cars in your life, you could consider trying to rent or borrow a compressor. In the long run, however, the amount you save going that route hardly justifies not buying your own. Compared to other shop tools, and especially compared to the cost of a professional paint job, a good home air compressor is downright cheap. In fact, you can get one for about (or less than) the cost of an entry-level one-day paint job, and way less than something like a home welder, band saw, or the like. A recent check of Sears (the old stand-by for home-shop tools) and other home builder big-box stores yielded a decent selection of good compressors in the $300 to $500 range and even big, shop-quality ones for less than $1,000.

Normally, I would say get the best compressor you can afford, because as soon as you have one, you find all sorts of uses for it, and you probably want to add some air tools to your garage closet. But since we're concerned with the low-buck approach here, my first advice is to get your own compressor, period. My second admonition is to get one that operates a spray gun adequately and continually throughout a paint job. This immediately brings up the question of what type of spray gun to get, including HVLP (high-volume, low-pressure). We will get to this shortly.

Several 110-volt compressor models are available, with horsepower ratings manufacturers are playing with to make them more appealing. What was a 2-hp compressor is suddenly a 6-hp compressor—until it's running. Obviously a HP rating "when running" or "under load" is the only one that counts. I'd recommend at least 1-1/2 and preferably 2 hp (while working), and a 25 to 30 gallon air tank. Even more important is the compressor's air rating in cubic-feet per minute. The designation is SCFM, for standard cubic feet per minute. This is often

Large or small, I highly recommend a 220-volt compressor to avoid blowing circuits in the middle of a paint job. Plug shapes and sizes vary; make them match. When rewiring the garage, you'll find that an in-line off/on switch is helpful. A bright red "on" light is even more so, since the compressor shuts itself off at a set pressure, but starts back up in the middle of the night (after leaking down) if you forget to turn this switch off.

Since compressing air causes any moisture in it to condense, you need a water trap in the line for painting. This one, mounted at the compressor outlet, is doing some good (you can see water in it, which needs draining), but it really should be 20-ft. downstream to work effectively, which can be difficult to do in your garage.

given at air-pressure levels of 40 pounds per square inch (PSI) and at 90 psi. A regular siphon-feed spray gun requires 6 to 8 scfm at 40 psi, while many air tools, such as sanders, can require 6 to 8 scfm at 90 psi. If all you're going to do is paint, the lower rating is fine, but it's always better to have more capacity than less.

My personal choice, and therefore my recommendation to you, is to acquire a 220-volt compressor. The last thing you want to do in the middle of a paint job is blow a fuse (i.e., trip a circuit breaker)—which very likely not only shuts off the compressor, but turns off all the lights as well. Most houses are wired with 220 volts from the power pole; running it to your garage is not a big deal. If you're at all serious about working in your garage—on cars or whatever—I strongly recommend wiring it with a 220-volt circuit. Other shop equipment, specifically MIG welders, are available in 110 and 220 volt types, too, and 220-volt is better. I speak from experience.

The smart choice in the long run is to get the best practical compressor that you can afford. "Practical" means don't go to the machinery auction and buy some huge industrial unit that takes a crane to lift and is very likely worn out. It also means don't go to the "Offshore Tool Shack" or the "Backdoor Freight

Dock Emporium" and buy something cheap just because it *looks* like something good. If you're saving $1,000 to $2,000 (or much more) on just one paint job, why not spend a little more money on your compressor? It lasts a lot longer than one paint job. And get one now that runs air tools because eventually you'll want some.

A couple of other considerations: every home garage needs more room, so a good choice is a compressor with a vertical tank (if you're in earthquake country, bolt it to the floor). Also, most home compressors have wheels, but I'd suggest finding a permanent location for it, and attaching a hose long enough to reach wherever you need it. You need at least 25 feet to get around a car to paint it—50 feet is much better—with at least 3/8-inch internal diameter. Be advised that air hose creates a pressure drop (sort of like resistance in electrical wire). The longer and smaller (i.d.) the hose, the greater the pressure drop is between the compressor and the end of the hose—it can be as much as 10 psi per 25 feet of length with 3/8-inch hose. That's another reason to get a better compressor.

Since compressing air separates water from it (turns humidity into water drops), you need a good water trap at the compressor outlet (actually 25 feet from

the outlet is best), and another one (possibly disposable) at the end of the hose, near the gun. The compressor tank also has a water outlet on it; drain it regularly.

Obviously you don't want water in the air that you're using to spray paint. You don't want anything else in it, either. All compressors have an air intake port somewhere, and it should come with a replaceable filter of some sort. Buy extra filters, keep them handy, and change them regularly. Most people have the compressor somewhere in the garage, where you're going to be

Most industrial applications locate the compressor outside the spray booth, with hard pipe running to a water trap (with adjustable pressure regulator, in this case) inside the booth, to attach the hose to. If you can do this at home, it would be optimum.

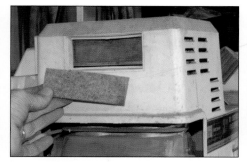

Just as you don't want water in your air, you don't want dirt or dust. Your compressor intake should have an air filter of some sort, such as this "felt pad" type. Keep replacements on hand and change them regularly, especially if the compressor is located near where you paint (because it sucks in overspray, which clogs the filter).

painting. That means the compressor is inhaling air filled with paint overspray. Check the filter on your compressor after a paint job, and you'll be surprised. In most garages, there's not much you can do about it. Just locate the compressor where it can breathe the cleanest air possible. Pro shops put the compressor outside and plumb air into the spray area with hard piping, fitted with quick-connect outlets at various locations around the room. You could do this at home.

Speaking of quick-connect couplers, by all means use them, even if all you have is one spray gun (believe me, you'll have more air stuff later). They make everything, from cleaning that gun, to attaching your tire filler, much easier. Just be advised that different brands use different shapes and sizes; get them all (male and female) at the same place.

In the last chapter we showed the use of an electric rotary disc grinder (top), but only alluded to air-powered sanders such as the jitterbug type or oscillating type (such as the "DA"— dual action—at lower right).

I got this water trap that hangs on your belt or pocket years ago, and drain it periodically as I paint or use air tools. Even in dry California, it's amazing how much water it collects (which you don't want mixing in your paint). An alternative is a small, disposable trap that mounts to the gun's air inlet.

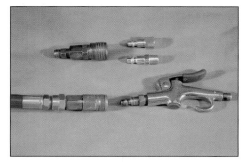

If you have a compressor, it's nuts not to attach a quick-connect coupler to the end of the hose, and matching receptacles for your guns, tools, and accessories. One of the first accessories you should get, especially for painting, is a blow-gun.

When you have a compressor, your collection of air tools grows. These small die grinders, with straight or right-angle chucks, do a variety of jobs with interchangeable tools or mandrels. Squirt a couple drops of oil directly into the inlet of all your air tools every time you use them. Never use an in-line oiler in the hose if you plan to paint.

We won't cover air tools in this book because, for the home car painter, they really are a luxury. If you do get some, however, add a few drops of air tool oil to the inlet, before you attach the air line, every time you use one. Never install an air tool oil mister at the compressor if you ever intend to spray paint with the same hose.

Spray Guns

The spray gun and supporting equipment primarily serve the purpose of depositing the liquid paint on the vehicle surface in a practical—hopefully somewhat artistic—manner so that it bonds and hardens (i.e., "dries") properly. If you have any kind of decent, properly maintained, and properly adjusted spray gun, and you know how to use it, you can lay on a smooth, even, glossy coat of paint that won't need further rubbing out (assuming it's a gloss coat). Even if your painting skills and equipment are not top notch, you can probably still get a layer of paint on the car that you can sand smooth and rub out to look pretty darn good (assuming

Like most of my stuff, my small arsenal of spray guns is old, but well-kept. In fact, the JGA DeVilbiss was well used when someone gave it to me 30+ years ago, and it still works fine. The small touch-up gun is great for what its name implies, as well as countless small jobs, from doorjambs to model cars or bicycles. These are all siphon-feed, non-HVLP guns.

Even if you have a regulator on the compressor, it's nearly mandatory to have an air adjuster at the gun, since different paints require different pressures, and even the length of your hose changes air pressure. Note each gun has an adjuster attached. Although I usually adjust pressure by "feel," some painters like a dial gauge at the gun.

Keeping your guns clean is paramount to proper spraying as well as long life. Especially important is keeping the inside of the nozzle area free of any dried paint.

you're using modern two-part paint and you mixed the chemicals properly).

All this is to say that there's no magic to a spray gun. The most expensive or most sophisticated one won't spray paint any better than any other good, clean, properly adjusted one. A good spray job comes from a rather prosaic combination of a clean, consistent, properly regulated air supply; good-quality paint products, properly mixed; a clean, well-lit, ventilated environment in a specified temperature range; of course the always-mentioned proper surface preperation; and, finally, a deft, practiced hand with a good-quality, clean, and properly adjusted spray gun.

I got my first spray gun, a standard DeVilbiss Model JGA 502, nearly 40 years ago. It was lying on someone's garage floor, and the owner gave it to me. Lord knows how old it was then. But it was my only spray gun for 25 years. I used it for everything from lacquers to urethanes, candies and pearls, high-build primers and high-solid clears. I keep it

clean, I change the packings once in a while, put a little white grease on the needle shaft, and have maybe changed the nozzle head once, and it works just as well now as ever. I still use it today, mostly for primers. Kept clean (without using sharp objects) and maintained, a good spray gun never wears out.

But we have a quandary here. Just as all paint products are in a major state of

change, as we discuss in the next chapter, so is automotive paint spraying equipment. The industry is shifting from "siphon-feed" guns to "gravity feed" types. The age-old siphon-feed guns mount the paint pot under the spray handle/nozzle, and the paint is sucked out of the cup by the pressure-drop of the air passing through the nozzle, a process very similar to the venturi effect that draws fuel into the air stream in a carburetor. On better guns, the paint cup quick-disconnects from the gun for easy filling on the workbench. The only disadvantages to this type of gun involve the paint cup. Sometimes the seal at the top can leak if the top is not tightened properly or if the gasket is worn out. Also, the air vent hole in the top can get plugged with paint or leak if you tip the gun (with a full pot of paint) at too much of an angle while painting something like a horizontal surface. In the old days, many painters would tie a shop rag around the top of the cup to guard against any drips. Later guns have a small, coiled tube connected to this vent hole to prevent such drips.

On the gravity-feed gun (which we used to think of as "European-style" because they were common there for years) the paint cup mounts on top of the nozzle/handle, and the paint feeds by gravity into the gun. To fill the cup, you remove a vented screw cap on top. The cup screws into the top of the gun, and the two remain attached while you fill the gun. This design requires a special rack to hold the gun while you fill it, and does not allow you to set the gun down on a workbench when it has paint in it. Obviously, you would have to modify your hand motions to accommodate the new size and shape when changing from one type of gun to the other.

The major advantages of the gravity-feed gun are that it is much less prone to dripping or leaking (one drip can spoil a coat of paint); it does not start spitting when paint nears the bottom of the cup;

and you are able to spray all the mixed paint in the cup, without that little extra left in the bottom you otherwise have to throw out if it is catalyzed. A few painters I questioned asserted that the gravity-feed gun was better at "breaking up" or mixing modern metallics and pearls for a more even coat, but others said this was psychological. Most of the gravity-feed guns available today are HVLP models.

HVLP Systems

HVLP stands for high volume, low pressure. The vast majority of painters tend to adjust air pressure at the gun by "feel" rather than checking a gauge. I think the old rule of thumb was 50 psi at the gun for spraying regular enamels, and 30 psi for lacquers. I don't think I've heard a rule for two-part paints, but they're in that range, depending on whether they're base coats or clear coats. The new HVLP guns, however, are designed to spray at pressures in the 3 to 5 psi range. Nearly all the professional painters I asked admitted they shoot at higher pressures than that—but only about 10 psi.

The HVLP spray gun was invented by a man named Ross Mattson in the 1980s to spray candy colors on production-line motorcycle parts more evenly. Its advantage over older, higher-pressure systems, is that it produces much less overspray—and therefore much less waste and pollution. It was strictly a practical improvement on the age-old paint spray gun. Mattson manufactured and sold his guns, and in the beginning they were the only ones that worked really well. The only problem was that they were quite expensive. But then the air quality government guys got wind of this and said, "Hey, that's good for the environment...less overspray means less pollutants in the air." And, in controlled areas, they immediately mandated HVLP spray equipment for all production (i.e., professional in any way) shops. I just visited and called all the automo-

This is a more modern HVLP gun, nearly all of which are the gravity-feed (cup on top) type. Although they may be in different locations, most also have adjusting knobs for fluid (paint) flow, airflow, and fan-pattern width. This one also has an adjustable air pressure regulator, with a dial gauge, between the inlet and the hose.

tive paint supply stores (which is where you go to buy a good spray gun) in my area, and they all told me that they are only allowed to sell HVLP guns. Worse, I was told that I really needed to buy three of these guns (at about $350 each), with slightly different-sized nozzles and tips for spraying undercoats, color base coats, and high-solid clears. "That's what all the professionals do," they said.

So here's the quandary: HVLP spray guns really are better. They spray more evenly and they cut down significantly on overspray. HVLP cuts your paint use (and cost) as much as 50%. That's good. Very good. The problem is the "high volume" part of HVLP.

The big advantage of HVLP guns is that they greatly reduce overspray, and therefore use (and waste) far less paint. The disadvantage of any gravity-feed gun, however, is that you can't set it down, or fill it, without a special holding rack, such as this homemade one. The upper ring is for holding a strainer.

Most "pro" paint shops and mail-order houses sell only HVLP guns, which can be expensive (and require a big compressor). However, we found most "big store" home centers, as well as our local Tool Shack, carried both inexpensive HVLP guns (left) as well as non-HVLP guns (right; this one labeled as an "LVLP"—Low Volume Low Pressure—gun).

Most compressors can build high pressures for short periods of time, but to sustain a large volume of airflow at any pressure—even 5 to 10 psi—requires a big compressor with large pistons and, more important, a big tank (like 50-plus gallons). We're talking about an industrial-size compressor. You need one of these compressors to run a good HVLP gun. As one professional painter said, "With the new urethane paints, you can't stop and wait for the compressor to catch up, like you could with lacquers." Under any circumstances, you want the pressure you set at your gun to remain constant (whether it's 30 psi with a regular gun or 5 to 10 psi with an HVLP) all the time you're painting, which means the pressure in the compressor tank has to be more than that—at all times. Obviously, if the pressure drops or varies in any way while you're painting, the spray pattern and paint flow from the gun varies (or even stops). You don't want this.

I would certainly recommend a good HVLP gun if you had the budget, the room, and the wiring circuitry in your garage for an industrial-size compressor—but I have to assume you don't.

At the other end of the scale, several types of "home HVLP systems" are offered by mail-order houses and some big-buy tool stores. These can be in the form of a pseudo-HVLP gun that works with a home-shop compressor, but more often include some sort of "turbine" air-blower rather than a compressor with a tank. The types I have tried in the past do not work well. They might have better ones by the time you read this. But cheap is cheap. If possible, try something before you buy it.

Presently, the best solution for the home garage painter is to use the older-style (non-HVLP) gun, whether in a siphon-feed or gravity-feed configuration, with a good quality, home-type compressor. Such guns might not be available at your automotive paint store (which caters to the professional market, not you), but they are plentiful at home-builder stores and through mail-order sources. Again, you have three main choices. The same pro painter I quoted above says he buys the cheap "off-shore" HVLP knock-off guns for $69.95, and uses the same one for all types of paints with no problem (including candies,

pearls, and clear coats). When it gets worn or malfunctions, instead of rebuilding it, he just buys another. That's one option, but it means you have to be able to tell a good "knock-off" from a junk one. The second and probably preferable option is to buy a name-brand, good-quality non-HVLP spray gun. The third option is to buy a good-quality, used, name-brand spray gun—whether at a swap meet, through the "recycler" ads, or on the Internet. If it hasn't been abused, it should be fine. And rebuild parts should be available for quite some time.

Final Equipment Notes

Lots of painters like to keep an old, or cheap, gun for painting primers, in addition to a better "top-coat gun." There's no real need to do this unless you're lazy about cleaning your primer gun, or you just like to buy equipment. I can't imagine you'd be painting primer and color coats at the same time, and you can't leave today's catalyzed paints sitting in a gun for any length of time. I would suggest, instead, that you first invest in a smaller "touch-up" gun. You can adjust the spray pattern and material feed on your full-size gun to spray in small areas, but the smaller gun is better for getting into areas such as doorjambs, and for painting smaller parts such as dashboards, window frames, chassis components, whatever. You can keep it adjusted for small areas, and if you're only using a small amount of paint, the smaller cup wastes less and cleans up more easily. They come in siphon or gravity-feed styles.

Plus, get a charcoal respirator face-mask—and use it. In fact, as with air filters for your compressor, keep some extra "refill" mask inserts on hand. I don't think you need the whole "space suit" that some professional painters are made to (and probably should) wear.

A note on the environmental impact of automotive painting: I'm very pro-envi-

Another "accessory" that should be in any painter's cabinet is a good breathing mask with replaceable charcoal filters (and extra filters, as shown). Unlike old lacquer, which only made you high from breathing too many fumes, recent paints contain isocyanates and other bad stuff that can kill you if you breathe (or even absorb) too much. If you paint daily, you want the full-on "space suit" with fresh air pumped into it to breathe. Most hobby painters do less than one car a year, but you should still use a good filter mask every time you spray. Fortunately, they're making paints safer now.

This plastic shower curtain, hung on nails, covers a bicycle.

ronmental protection. I recycle, I never pour used oil down any drains, and I spend a lot of time outside among trees. But the typical hobbyist, like me, who paints cars in his garage at home cannot be compared to any sort of production paint or body shop, where several cars are painted daily. How many cars are you going to paint, realistically? One, two, maybe three in your lifetime? Even if you averaged one a year, how many would that be, total? Not nearly enough to be in any way environmentally measurable. Now multiply or divide that by the number of automotive hobbyists in your city or state who actually paint their own cars. The point is, you don't need the full-on EPA-approved shop, equipment, cloth-

ing, and so on to protect the environment from the type of painting you do (in my opinion). But I still wouldn't paint any large amounts (i.e., a whole car) of any type of paint—and especially not catalyzed ones—in my garage without a good, filtered, respirator face mask.

Preparing the Garage

Let's hope you have a garage, it has a paved floor, it's big enough to paint a car in, and it isn't full of junk. If it is full

If you have a garage to paint in, hopefully it's a clean, well-lit place, with enough room to move all around the vehicle. For painting, you need lights overhead, as well as on the sides, to really see what you're doing. This garage has about the minimum.

Note the door is propped open slightly on a regular house fan. It is turned to blow air out of the garage (exhaust). This is mandatory. Likewise, there should be some vents elsewhere (preferably at the other end) to let outside air in. You don't want any fans blowing toward your paint job, because they blow dirt (or bugs) into it. Don't paint at night if you can help it. Morning, when the air outside is still, is best.

of junk, clean it out. Even if it's not full of junk, clean it. Use an air nozzle on your compressor hose to blow all dirt, dust, cobwebs, etc., out of all nooks and crannies of your garage, especially anywhere above where you will be painting. Do this well before you're ready to paint. If possible, finish the garage cleaning process by hosing out the floor with water. Both the blowing out and hosing out are highly recommended if you've done all your filler and primer block sanding in the garage. Some old-school painters like to wet down the floor and keep it wet while painting, to keep any dust down. But I don't like having water anywhere near where I'm painting—not on the floor, not in the air hose, not absorbed in the primer, and I'd prefer not to paint on a humid day if I can help it.

Just as getting dust in your paint is a problem, so is getting paint overspray (especially with today's urethane paints) on everything in the garage. To help control both, tape up plastic sheeting, such as Visqueen, wherever necessary.

You also need ventilation. Never paint in a closed garage. Most garages have built-in vents around the lower walls and at the peaks of the roof. This is good, but you also need a fan to move air (and overspray) while you're painting. A typical portable house fan, in a 3 x 3 foot frame, is excellent for this. You want it to blow air out (exhaust), not in. You could put it in

Even with a good exhaust fan, overspray from urethane paints can be very messy in your garage. The best way to keep it off stuff is to hang clear plastic sheeting—available at your auto paint or hardware store—on the walls and over anything else you want to keep clean. Use plastic shipping tape, or thumbtacks, for easy installation and removal. The boxes on the shelf also have plastic on top.

Form-fit car covers, such as these with elastic around the bottom, are excellent for keeping overspray (and other stuff) off vehicles that might be in the garage while you're priming, spot painting, or doing bodywork. If you're painting a whole car, move any others out of, and well away from, the garage.

a window (if you have one), but the simplest is to prop the garage door on it. Start the fan before you start painting, and keep it going for a good while after you're done to exhaust vapors as the paint dries. You can get more elaborate than this, as we show later, using air conditioner filters for inlet air, or even building a mini-booth of plastic sheeting in your garage (or outside—some of these have been available commercially). But making your garage relatively dust-free and rigging an adequate exhaust fan are the first requisites.

Another "must-have" for home painting is proper lighting. You can't paint properly if you can't see what you're doing. Overhead lights won't cut it. You could rig up temporary lights to shine on the sides, front, and back of the car as you paint, but fluorescent light fixtures are not expensive, and are easy to attach to your garage walls, positioned to light all sides of the vehicle. Professional spray booths often have lights in the floor as well as the walls, and the entire inside is painted white for further reflectivity. You try painting a car black, or some other dark color, in a poorly lit garage, and you will see why.

We've already discussed wiring to some extent. I recommend a separate 220-volt circuit for the compressor, if possible. Also make sure you have electrical capacity (enough circuits and breakers) for plenty of lights and at least one fan. As I said before, you don't want the lights going out in the middle of a paint job.

Another thing that doesn't get discussed often enough in paint books and articles is temperature control. Even old-style paints are very temperature-sensitive in terms of drying, and newer paints won't chemically harden (or "crosslink") if not kept above a certain temperature for a certain period of time (read the information sheet, or talk to your paint supplier about this). The question is: how do you control the temperature in your garage? Few garages have any sort of air conditioning (but being too hot usually isn't the problem...for the paint). One option is to wait to paint when the weather is optimal, but that is often impractical, especially in seasonal areas. Many of you auto hobbyists in colder climates do have good garage heaters, either of per-

Cabinets with doors are good for keeping out overspray, as well as hanging posters. Just make sure the doors close tightly.

manent or portable varieties. But this brings up two questions. First, how do you maintain heat in the garage and good ventilation at the same time? I'm not sure, but ventilation is very necessary. Second, most garage heaters are gas-fed, and most paints are highly flammable (especially when atomized in a closed garage). I have been told not to paint in a garage that even has a gas water heater in it, because the pilot light could ignite the whole thing when it's full of lacquer overspray. I must say I've never heard of this actually happening—

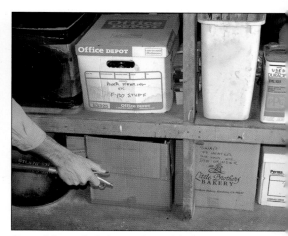

One big difference between a spray booth and your garage is that the booth doesn't have shelves, cabinets, and junk in it—that's the idea. But the painter still needs a place to mix paints, fill his gun, clean it, and store paints, reducers, cleaners, strainers, stirring sticks, and so on—not to mention a trash can, paper towels, rags, and other clean-up items. So professional booths usually have a small "mixing table" in one corner, with a small storage shelf to hold such things.

You do lots of things other than paint in your garage, and you undoubtedly have a bench to work on. When it's time to paint, clear and clean a section of the bench to use for mixing paint, filling your guns, and so on. It's probably a good idea to spread out a few layers of absorbent newspaper, and tape it down. And if you paint very often, it also helps to have paint supplies—especially cleaning thinners, rags, strainers, sticks, tape, and so on, stored on shelves or in cupboards nearby.

Speaking of doing other things in your garage (including bodywork and sanding on the car you're going to paint), most create dust and dirt. Before painting, at least sweep the floor thoroughly and knock down any cobwebs from the rafters, etc. Many painters like to spray water on the floor when they're painting to catch dust and lint, but that doesn't work very well in a garage (and I'm personally averse to having water—which evaporates into the air—anywhere near my paint). So I use the air-gun with high-pressure to blow any dust, dirt, bugs, cobwebs and so on from the rafters, walls, shelves, along the baseboards, and the whole floor, with the exhaust fan going, working from the back of the garage toward the front. Do this an hour or two before you paint to let things settle.

If your garage looks like this, I'm afraid you might be better off painting in the driveway. Even if you cleaned all the junk out of it, (1) it's barely one-car size without enough room to walk around a car to paint it, and (2) it's so old and decrepit it will rain dust and dirt on your paint job (especially when a flock of pigeons lands on the roof in the middle of a job).

On the other hand, painting is not some sort of religious rite that must be performed in an immaculate temple. At least this guy has a two-car garage, lights, fans, and he has hung plastic sheeting over some stuff. And he's wearing a good facemask. This is not where I'd want to spray a car, but color sanding and rubbing out will erase most imperfections in the spray job.

Then again, you can go from one extreme to another. Literally painting a car in your driveway is certainly possible (I've done it), but I'd have to consider it a last resort. A portable awning, preferably in the back yard, would be better than this.

As you can see, the finished product looks as good as any high-dollar pro paint job done in a fancy spray booth.

and I have heard of a lot of people who paint cars in garages, during winter, with gas heaters going. I'm from California, however, and the amount of heating required is minimal compared to what a person would have to do in a frigid northern state. Talk to your paint supplier about your proposed painting space, how you plan to heat and ventilate it, and the associated risks.

Legality and Neighbors

In most "controlled areas," stores are highly restricted on what types of paints and products they can sell (including spray guns, and so on), but there are no restrictions on what you can use in your home garage. So, in most areas, if you buy paint such as acrylic lacquer in an area where it's still legal to sell, and bring it home and spray it in your garage, even if you're in a "restricted area," it's okay.

If you live in a rural area, you should have no problems. But if you want to paint a car in your garage in an urban or (probably worse) suburban area, you have several considerations. Even though I live in a densely populated city near Los Angeles, the way my garage is built (large) and situated (at the back of a deep lot), most of my neighbors neither see, hear, nor smell what I'm doing in there. My one close neighbor (his garage is three feet from mine) builds special effects things for the movie studios, and I often help weld or paint something for him, or loan him a tool when he needs it. No problem. And as long as I recycle my used oil, thinner, or other paint products through their special program, the city seems to have no other restrictions on painting in garages.

At my previous house, however, on a typical residential street in a different city, a next-door neighbor called both the police and the fire department while I was spraying my wife's VW bug with urethane paint. The neighbor didn't like the smell. I suppose I can't blame her. But the officials made me stop painting,

Two things here: rather than hang plastic or get overspray on stuff, you might use the driveway to spray the numerous smaller parts that need painting or priming during any paint job. Secondly, whether in the driveway or garage, you need something to hang or prop such parts on while painting them. A trash can works well for medium-size parts like a door, hood, or gas tank, but notice plastic over it to keep dust from flying out. I also keep two wooden orange crates for parts spraying, with a stash of cardboard boxes if I need more. Cut and bent coat hangers work well for hanging parts from the ceiling or rafters.

Customizer/sculptor Lee Pratt lives in a large, open "artist's loft." To keep overspray from drifting out or dust and dirt from floating in, he built this temporary, self-contained spray booth from 2 x 4s and plastic sheeting.

good idea to get to know your immediate neighbors, and at least feel them out to see if they might have any objections to what you might be doing in your garage. Regardless of any specific laws in your community, a complaining neighbor is a problem. You have two possible choices here. One is to make friends with your neighbors; let them know what you are (or "might be") doing, tell them to call or come to you first if they have any complaints about noise, dust, fumes, whatever; and maybe even offer to fix a dent or two in their cars, touch up some scratches—it can help (if you can do a good job). On the other hand, to be blunt, a neighbor won't complain if they don't know what you're doing. This is just a statement, not a recommendation.

But use some common sense. This book is about painting your own car in your home garage. Many, if not most, home garages are in neighborhoods. So you have to consider your neighbors. We're not talking about any kind of professional activity; it's strictly a hobby, or you could even consider it maintenance/upkeep. I've never heard of anyone getting in trouble for painting their own house—or even having professionals do it. Who would, or could, complain about that? But the same neighbor who has any army of lawn-mowing, weed-whacking,

informed me that it was illegal to paint a car in a home garage in that city (a table, bike, or boat was fine), and further that it was illegal to have more than one gallon of flammable material, of any kind, in my garage. I had painted at least three other cars in the same garage with no

problems. But this time I was stuck. I sold the house and moved.

Of course other solutions are available. The first is to find out what the laws are in your particular area. This is more a consideration than a solution. Second— and this can be touchy—it's probably a

It has a sealed ceiling and four walls, a small door for access (which has plastic over it during painting), and electric lights inside plus plenty of natural light through the clear plastic from nearby windows. Since he doesn't paint regularly, he builds the booth to fit the car he's doing—in this case a fiberglass Porsche Speedster for his wife.

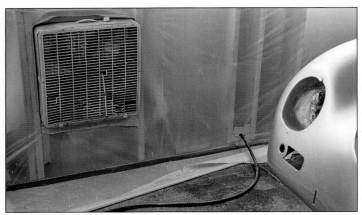

A regular house fan is built in to exhaust overspray, with ducting to carry it out of the building. Also note the air hose from the compressor, which is just outside the "booth."

To let clean air in, Lee installed a couple of air conditioner filters in the back wall, where he also hung a paper/tape dispenser. Also note that the hood and deck are hung from the ceiling beams with wires for easy painting on both sides.

After the Porsche was done, Lee took that booth down and built a bigger one to spray this '58 Impala in gorgeous black lacquer with a purple candy, lace-painted top. This car wasn't done by a professional in a fancy booth using the latest paints and equipment, but by someone spraying lacquer in a hand-built, sheet-plastic, makeshift "booth" at home. Sure he's had some practice and knows what he's doing—but you can do the same, even if you don't have a garage to work in. Have you been practicing?

leaf-blowing "gardeners" invade her yard for an hour or two every week will be the first to complain that your compressor makes too much noise. So don't be out in your garage sanding, grinding, or body-hammering late at night. I especially don't recommend painting in your garage at night for several reasons, only the first being neighbor consideration. Bright lights at night attract bugs. Do your masking and prep the night before, then spray paint in the morning, just about the time the neighbors leave for work, when the air is still and the rest of the day is hopefully warm and dry for the paint to cure. Make sense? Other considerations would include not placing your exhaust fan where it blows fumes into your neighbor's yard.

Finally, if your home garage really isn't suited to painting a car (or you don't have a garage), you might be able to rent a space to do it, which would still be much less expensive than a professional paint job in most cases. Public storage-type garages used to allow this when they first became popular, but most no longer do. Finding an industrial space in an urban area can be difficult or expensive in some cases, easy in others. In one case, I found someone who already had his own shop space for doing bodywork and paint, and I sub-rented space from him to do a couple paint jobs of my own. In another case, members of my car club rented a shop, and I was able to use that. There are plenty of options. In fact, there might even be some rental spray booths operating in certain parts of the country. Or, there's always the possibility of talking a local pro painter into renting you his booth for a day, when he's not using it.

TODAY'S PAINT PRODUCTS

I swore I wouldn't bore you with a bunch of paint cans, but it's inevitable in this chapter. This grouping represents just the color and clear, with attendant reducers and catalysts, for the paint on one car. It doesn't include any primers, sealers, cleaners, or other "prep" products. These happen to be all PPG (formerly Ditzler) brand, purchased at the same place at the same time. The color, mixed at the paint store, is a Lincoln Mark VIII dark green metallic with pearl for my '52 Chevy, which was dark green metallic originally. This is a 2-stage system, with base coat (DBU) and clear coat (2021). While most normal-size vehicles won't require more than a gallon of mixed color, or clear, I ordered 1-1/2 gallons of color (to have plenty for dash, window frames, under hood, etc.) in two gallon cans, so I can mix the two back and forth to make sure all the color is the same before painting. The two quarts (DAR) are the same color mixed in a single-stage, which dries very glossy, for use in areas (firewall, under trunk, etc.) where I don't need the extra work of 2-stage or rub out. The only problem with buying all these products now is that the bodywork/prep on the car has taken longer than expected, and the reducer/catalyst (DRR— "RR" stands for "reactive reducer") "goes bad" after time. Hopefully it is okay stored in a cool place, unopened.

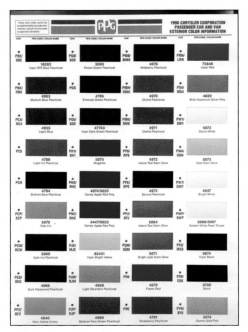

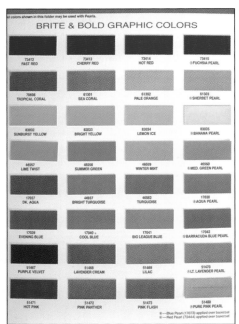

How do you choose a new paint color for your car? Thousands are available. The auto paint store should have a large rack (or stack) of "color paint chip" books with small samples of all the colors used on domestic and foreign cars and trucks, going back several years. You can choose one of these colors, have the shop mix up a small amount (say, a pint) from the formula, and go home and spray it on something to see how you like it. Another alternative is to look at cars and trucks on the highway; if you see a color you like, note the brand and approximate age of the vehicle, and then look for that color in the books. Plus there are usually pages of "custom colors," with formulas, and "fleet colors" (a whole page of different shades of red, or yellow, for example). Or, a good paint shop can mix (or match) virtually any color you want, though you won't have a "formula" for ordering it again, later.

You might think it's impossible to write a book about how to paint cars without talking about paint, but that is essentially what I intend to do. If it weren't such a cliché (and if it weren't largely untrue), I would say that the paint itself is one of the least important parts of this whole process. Yes, the surface preparation—from the bare metal to the final, sanded undercoats—is the most important element of a good quality and long-lasting automotive paint job. Secondly, given moderate skill with the spray gun (and given excellent surface preparation), the final color-sand and rub out are what make any paint job look professional and ultimately award-winning. Good paint, compatibility of products and, especially today, proper mixing of the elements of each product, are all very important to a good paint job. But talking about paint is about as exciting as watching paint dry. And looking at pictures of paint cans in a book is worse than boring, even in color.

But those aren't the real reasons why we're not going to discuss specific paint products here. We describe paint as solid particles suspended in a liquid "carrier" so that those particles can be transported, by pressurized air, and deposited on a surface, where they adhere once the liquids all evaporate away. That's the way paint had been for decades (centuries if you substitute a brush for the spray gun), but no longer. The main reason we're not going to talk about paint in this "How to Paint" book is that we're not using paint to paint cars any more. We're using chemicals. The process might not seem or look much different. We mix assorted liquids in set proportions and spray them with a "gun," using pressurized air, onto the surface of a car in the age-old manner. Then they "dry" either hard and shiny, or smooth and dull so that we can buff them out to a lustrous shine. It all seems pretty much the same as before, but it's not.

Now, when you mix those liquids together, one of which is the color you want to put on your car, you are no longer mixing a solids-bearing liquid paint with a highly evaporative thinner to make it sprayable and so that it dries relatively quickly. Now the colored particles are suspended in a liquid that is a reactive

It's obviously better to buy your paint when you're ready to use it. This is the pearl base coat and clear we used for the "scuff and squirt" job you see in Chapter 8. Again, all products are the same brand, and represent just the pearl and clear, with catalyst/reducer (the white base coat already being on the car). The bad news is that this amount of paint cost nearly $500; the good news is that we only used half of it for the job. Further, if you spray it yourself, $500 is a whole lot less than a $2,000 to $3,000 (or much more) pearl-and-clear custom paint job.

The simplest and easiest color to repaint any car is its original color. Even for decades-old cars, the original color(s) should be listed as a "color code" on an I.D. tag somewhere on the body, such as this one in a doorjamb.

chemical compound. The other liquid you mix with it—even though it may contain evaporatives or thinners—primarily contains a catalyst, which is a chemical agent that instigates a molecular change over a relatively short period of time once the two chemicals are mixed. Today's paints don't just dry, they also chemically *bond*, which in current auto painting parlance is called "cross-linking."

Chemistry, even though I took plenty of it, was never my favorite subject in school. So I won't go into textbook details. But if you remember any of your high school courses, you know that in any chemical equation only so many atoms or molecules of one substance will combine with so many of another to produce a set number of molecules of the new substance. Two hydrogen atoms will combine with one oxygen atom to produce one molecule of water. No less, no more. And if you want a whole bunch of water, you must combine a lot of hydrogen and oxygen in a ratio of 2-to-1, exactly. Reactions involving catalysts are a bit different, but the emphasis here is on exact mixing ratios. To work properly,

to chemically bond as designed, today's paints must be mixed in the exact proportions specified by the manufacturer.

You may also remember that heat (temperature) has a bearing on all chemical processes. Heat is energy, and most chemical reactions require some energy to occur. In an article I did for *Rod & Custom* magazine in 1991 called "New Age Painting," I quoted a PPG paint expert as saying, "With all catalyzed urethanes (clear or color), room temperature must be maintained above 50 degrees F for 24 hours for the paint to fully crosslink (harden). If not, it never fully crosslinks, and can break down with age. This is critical." This is something I have not heard mentioned much, before or since. Good, modern paint booths are heated, and most professional painters leave a freshly painted car in the heated booth overnight to "dry" (or chemically harden). But this is pretty hard to do, even in warm climates, if you're painting in your garage.

The worst problem is that, in most cases these days, none of this information is on the paint can. Even the type of catalyst to use, and the mixing proportions (which used to be printed in plain diagrams on the label), are often left off. Instead, you need to get a special "information leaflet" for the given type of paint, at the specific time you're going to use it, which is filled with more precautions and legalese jargon than actual instructions on how to mix and use the product. You need help.

Then, when and if you do figure out how to use the paint product properly, the next time you go back to get some more, you are told bluntly, "Sorry, that product is no longer legal. We can't sell it to you. You have to use such-and-such instead." Which means, of course, that you have to *learn* how to use the new product. Not only that, but whatever mixing agents you had for the old product (if they had a shelf-life of more than a few days anyway) are now obsolete, and must be replaced with new, different

ones. This is not only annoying, it also gets expensive quickly.

Make Friends With Your Paint Dealer

This is another major reason why we are not going to talk about specific types, brands, or product names (or numbers) of paints in this book. As I have said more than once, we are in a tumultuous, rapidly changing period in terms of automotive painting (among many things). Painters in many parts of the U.S. can still buy acrylic paints and reducers. Where I live lacquer is illegal, and I've had to change nearly all types of paint I use three times in three years. At the same time, custom water-base paints are just coming on the market, available for home-painters, but they are not perfected (at the moment they take multiple coats to cover and still must be top-coated with a urethane-type clear). I used to dread the day when I would have to paint my car with "water colors." But the more I

Not too long ago automotive paint cans had mixing and spraying directions printed on the label—even easily read diagrams. Not any more. Now you have to get a "tech sheet" to go with the specific paint, and they are hard to store, easy to lose, and even harder to decipher. It's much easier to write mixing proportions right on the can, with a marker, when you get it.

When mixing old paints, you could add more or less thinner to your liking. But today's "paint chemicals" require exact catalyst and reducer proportions. Paint stores sell plastic mixing cups (middle) printed with specific ratios for several types of paint, but these are "use once and throw away" items. In the past, I always used large or small coffee cans with equally spaced rings for simple mixing (and lacquer cleans easily). Today, I find paper cups of various sizes an expedient, and expendable, mixing device. Or, you can simply measure and mark a mixing stick (2 to 1 ratio shown) and hold it upright in a container as you pour in ingredients to the mark. Mixing sticks and strainers should be free at the paint store; keep plenty on hand.

think about it now, I hope they perfect it quickly. If manufacturers get it figured out, hopefully the paint (once it's on the car) will be as durable, shiny, and vibrant as anything we have now, but you could (hopefully) mix it with water, clean up with water, and not have any toxic chemicals or vapors to deal with. We'll see.

But I can't tell you what exactly is coming in the future. And there's no point in talking about specific products available today, because they'll very likely change by the time you read this. So….

We will talk about general types of paints and products that are used in the painting process (such as primers, sealers, color coats, clear coats, etc.). But to

find out what specific brands, names, and numbers of those types of paints you can get, legally, in your area, at a given time, you need a knowledgeable advisor. Hopefully that is your local automotive paint dealer, with whom you should start to cultivate a friendly relationship. This is someone you're going to have to trust.

The reason you need a separate mixing container is so you can thoroughly mix the components with the stirring stick, but more importantly so that you can strain this mixture as you pour it into the spray gun pot. Never mix paint in the gun without straining.

Fortunately, most paint products mix in ratio multiples of one. For instance, this high-fill primer should be mixed two parts paint to one part catalyst (no reducer). After thoroughly stirring the paint with the stick, I'm using the paper cup method (do not use plastic or Styrofoam; they can melt) to pour out two cups of paint...

...To which I add one cup of catalyst in a mixing container—in this case a clean coffee can (I keep several for this purpose, and usually throw them away after use).

I suppose these days you should be able to get some sort of product information from the major paint manufacturers over the Internet, but it wouldn't be the first place I'd try. The deal is that motor vehicles are in every part of this vast land of ours—no matter where you live—and they have an amazing propensity for bumping into each other or into stationary objects. Most car and truck dealers have a collision repair shop (dealers make much more money off of repairing your car than they do selling it to you); separate, independent, collision repair shops are in every town, big or small; and a few shops around the country still specialize in automotive painting, custom or otherwise.

All of these places have to buy their paint and related supplies from an automotive paint store, whether it's a business of its own or a corner of the local auto parts dealer. This is not a boutique business. Where there are cars and trucks, there are places to repair and repaint them, and there are stores to sell them the products needed to do so. Anyone can buy paint and supplies (and usually equipment) at these paint stores. You don't have to be a professional or anything like that. The automotive paint stores know what products they can get from the manufacturers (what's currently legal; what supersedes what; and so on), and they should be able to provide you with the proper catalyst/reducer, tell you the exact proportions for mixing, and what undercoats/topcoats are compatible. They need to know this, and stay on top of it, because their primary customers—the repair and paint shops—have to use these paint materials on a regular basis, and can't afford screwups and redos. They know what works and what doesn't, from using them daily. If a new product doesn't work well, or if a certain combination isn't compatible, they (the painters) let the paint store know right away, and demand something better.

Pro paint shops prefer the printed mixing cups because they use lots of types of paint, daily. Romulo, who sprays our Camry in Chapter 8, shows a simple trick of outlining the proper mixing proportions on the cup with a couple pieces of tape. Also note how he pours from the gallon can to avoid splashing, and that he wears cheap, disposable rubber gloves to avoid stained, cracked "painter's hands."

As always—as stated in every article or book about automotive painting—the rule of thumb is to use the same brand of products for one whole paint job. The manufacturer should know, and state, what works with what. But today, more than ever, there can be exceptions to that rule, as manufacturers keep bringing new products to market, many to meet tightening government regulations.

So my advice to you is to try to find and get to know a friendly, knowledgeable, and helpful automotive paint salesman. The easy part is that automotive paint stores are common. The hard part is that you, the hobbyist/home car painter, are not their primary customer, by any means. So don't pester them with questions or waste their time. You might have to pay retail rather than "shop rate" for your stuff. But tell them what you're doing, and ask what specific combination of products they recommend for the job, and what their regular customers (the professional painters) seem to prefer. Reading this book should give you a pretty good idea of what you, and they, are talking about.

One more thing, and this can get really iffy depending on which "stage" of paint job you plan, how fast you work, and how well you stick to your plans. In an ideal world, you should get all the paint products you need for one paint job at the same time. In fact, you should probably get a little more than you think you need. I'm talking about stuff that comes in cans: primer, sealer, mixed-color paint, clear, and proportional amounts of all necessary compatible catalysts/hardeners/reducers. I say this for a few reasons. First, no matter how carefully paint colors are mixed (by formula), they can vary slightly from can to can. So it's always best to get all your color mixed at the same time, by the same person, and to get a little extra to save for potential touch-up later. If you need more than one gallon of mixed-color paint, it's even advisable to get an extra empty can, and pour the cans of paint back and forth to thoroughly mix all the color. I'd also recommend getting an extra, smaller, empty can, say a quart, to store your leftover paint for touch-up, with minimal air in the can.

Second, get the proper catalyst/reducer, in the corresponding amount, at the same time you buy the paint. If you come back later for more, it might very well be "no longer available," having been superseded by something incompatible with the paint you have. Further, keep these cans of paints and (especially) catalyst/reducer closed until you're ready to use them. Most have a long shelf life, but some "go bad" within weeks—if not

Looking at what's in the can is much more fun than looking at the outside. This is white pearl, which gave the paint its name. In the old days you made it by mixing powder in clear lacquer. Today you can get it pre-mixed in a variety of translucent hues (besides white). A 3-stage paint, this dull-drying "base coat" must be sprayed over a similar, but solid, base color, then top coated with glossy clear, which can be rubbed out or left as is.

A large, glass kitchen mixing cup seems an obvious and convenient device for measuring paint, especially since it has a variety of ratio combinations printed on it. It is shown here with a 2:1 ratio of high-fill primer and catalyst, before stirring. The only problem—especially with today's sticky paints—is cleaning it after each use.

days—of being exposed to air (and there's really no way to test them).

Third, these days certain primers/base coats and, more particularly, certain clears are only compatible with certain types of paints. This is where the time element comes in. If it's going to take you a couple years, or more, to prep and paint this car and you buy all your products now, will they still be good when you're finally ready to use them? (If you keep them tightly sealed, and in a cool place, they probably will—but check with your paint dealer when purchasing.) Probably the worst situation is to buy a mixed-color paint now, and find out after you have applied it some time later that no compatible clear is available to put over it. In a slightly different situation, I had to throw away (properly dispose of) two gallons of very expensive urethane clear because no correct catalyst was available any longer, anywhere in the country. While the natural impulse is to buy your paint color first, a better plan would be to buy your sealer and sanding primer now, because the body-

work/sanding process takes the longest in any paint job, and because most all catalyzed primers can be covered with any types of paint. Then, when the car all straight, primed, blocked, sanded, and really ready for paint, have your color mixed and get a compatible clear at the same time (if you're using a clear coat), along with the necessary additives. Once you've done what masking is needed, it should then only take a couple days to spray the color and the clear.

Types of Paints and Related Products

Obviously we're going to speak generically here. And since this chapter is titled "Today's Paint Products," we won't discuss lacquers or enamels in any detail other than in the accompanying sidebar. Lacquers were great for custom paint jobs, but they are virtually unavailable today. Enamels are used for house paint and spray cans—though I think all house paint will be water-based soon. In short, today's catalyzed (i.e., "two-part") paints are far superior in numerous ways to old lacquers and enamels. Given that, we start with a couple of non-paint products that come in bottles or cans.

Wax and Grease Remover. Known in the old days by the popular brand "Pre-Kleeno," this is a clear liquid cleaner that removes wax, grease, oils, and (today) any dreaded silicone residue that might be on the vehicle surface. Its application is simple, but specific: apply it with a *clean* (preferably white) cloth or towel in a rubbing motion to a relatively small area (one or two square yards), and then immediately wipe it off with another clean, dry towel before the liquid evaporates. If you're repainting (or touching-up) a vehicle that still has paint on it, this is a very important first step, especially if it might have any traces of wax (many of which contains silicones today) on the surface. Even more obvious is to wash the car with detergent and water to begin with. Then use wax and

No paint job—unless it's been stripped to bare metal and treated with an etching agent and/or sealer—should be started without a thorough cleaning with a "wax and grease remover" or better yet, a "Silicone Remover," as shown. Silicone wax is a painter's nemesis; don't use it. But any wax, oil, road tar, etc., should be cleaned off the surface before you do anything else (sanding just embeds it). Then, just before color coats, clean it again (being sure to wipe it off before it dries, as directed), because hand oils, or even sweat drops, can lead to fisheyes in the paint.

Another too-little-known product that should be in every garage is 3M Adhesive Cleaner. Made specifically to clean off excess 3M Weatherstrip Adhesive glue (it's about the only thing that will), it is also excellent for cleaning adhesive residue from masking tape left on too long (as shown here), or anything else. Once you use it, you'll wonder how you ever did without it.

grease remover on all painted surfaces or surfaces to be painted, including in door jambs and so on, after you have stripped the car of trim, but before you start sanding (sanding imbeds oils or silicone in the paint). Then, after all the sanding or priming, just before you're ready to shoot your final coat of sealer or first coat of paint, degrease the whole car again. You never know what might have gotten on the car that would cause the paint to fisheye: your sweat, oil from your hands during sanding, whatever.

Metal Conditioner. If you have stripped your car to bare metal, your first step should be a metal conditioner, such as "Metalprep." This is a mildly acidic wash (usually reduced with water) that is applied to the bare metal with something like steel wool or 3M abrasive pads to remove any minor surface rust that has formed from prior washing and, more importantly, to "etch" the metal surface to make it bond with your first coat of primer or primer/sealer. Wear rubber gloves and eye protection when applying it; follow directions carefully; and be sure

to wash/neutralize it thoroughly and dry the surface before it can rust some more.

Self-etching Primer. This is one you should ask your paint dealer about. I'm not sure what types are available or applicable by the time you read this. Basically, they do the same thing as metal conditioner (other than removing rust): they chemically etch the surface when applied, so this non-sandable first primer coat really bites into and adheres to the metal.

Sealers. These were common in the days of non-catalyzed lacquers and enamels. They are applied over existing (and sometimes unknown) layers of paint before repainting. Their primary function was to act as a "hold back" shield to keep thinners in the new paint from seeping into, and possibly crazing or lifting, the old paint. At the same time it keeps old paint colors (especially reds) from "bleeding back through" the new layers of paint, causing discoloration. There were a variety of such sealers, some to be applied as a first layer over sanded existing substrate, some to be sprayed as a final layer (over sanded primer, etc.) just before the color-coat, and some used more for adhesion than for color-bleed.

High-adhesion Primer-Sealers. I said I wasn't going to name names or numbers, but here's the exception. When PPG introduced its DP-series of catalyzed primer-sealers more than 15 years ago, they simply called them "Epoxy Primer." When I wrote about and tested it in '91, I

called it their "new wonder-grip...primer. This stuff adheres so well, they recommend you put filler *over* it, 'cause it sticks to metal better than the filler." I still haven't tried that, but that's what they say, and the product is still on the market (if it's gone when you read this, ask what its replacement might be). It's excellent, very easy to use, and basically replaces both products listed above. In fact, without getting into chemistry, I'd call it a "double etching" primer: applied over steel, aluminum, or fiberglass, it not only "grips" the surface material, but it also grips the paint (or filler) applied on top of it. And, since it's catalyzed, it acts as an even better blocking shield than old sealers over existing old paint, or over your own bodywork and primers. So, it is excellent to use both as a first adhesion coat over bare metal, as well as a final sealer/adhesion coat when the surface is sanded and ready for color coats. Don't sand the DP.

I mention it by name because it's pretty much in a class by itself. It also serves as a good example of a couple of general considerations. First is to follow directions explicitly. Mix the DP with its catalyst, DP 401, one-to-one. The catalyst also acts as reducer (don't add anything else). Once mixed, let this concoction sit for a 1/2-hour "induction" period before spraying. Got that? After spraying, let it dry at least one hour before topcoating with other paint (2 to 3 hours before plastic

PPG's DP-series primer-sealer, mentioned in the text, easily mixes at a 1:1 ratio with its 401 catalyst. It comes in several colors, but DP40 is green, so I used it on my green Chevy's roof to cover some bare metal spots and seal the old, original paint.

filler). And—pay attention—you must add topcoats over the DP within seven days, otherwise it dries (or "links") so hard it won't grip the paint on top of it. If you do let it go more than a week, however, you can spray another coat of DP and start again (following all the same directions, of course). I'm making a big deal of this because none of these directions are printed on the label. You've got to ask for the "poop sheet" that goes with the paint, and you've got to dig through the cautions and other legal mumbo jumbo to find the real application directions—but they are very important!

Second, like old lacquer primer, DP comes in several colors. The original, DP 40, is grey-green, DP 90 is black (which makes a great hot rod "suede primer" coat), DP 48 is white, and so on. Did you ever stop to wonder why primers came in different shades and colors? Judging from primer spots on cars from years past, apparently not. Two reasons: If you're doing spot body or paint work on a car that's already painted, you should cover the repair with a shade/color of primer that most closely matches the color on the car. Don't use white or light gray primer in spots on a black or dark-colored vehicle. All paints, especially lighter colors, are transparent to some small extent. If your prepared surface has light and dark sections, these either cause lighter and darker areas in your finished paint job, or you have to spray several extra coats of color to fully, and homogenously, cover the substrate.

The primer doesn't have to be the same color as the existing paint, just a similar shade; for instance, use light gray over yellow, tan, or silver. On the other hand, if you are going to change the color of the car significantly (or are starting from bare metal), prime the whole thing (and/or use a final DP seal coat) in a color/shade that most closely matches your final color. This makes spraying an even color-coat easier, and requires less paint. Plus, an added bonus is that when you get

inevitable rock chips later, they won't show up horribly like they would if you sprayed a dark color over a light primer.

High-Build Primer. In the old days of lacquer and enamel painting, we used lots of primer. It was usually lacquer primer, and it was technically primer-surfacer, or "sandable primer." This is what you used, in multiple coats, block sanding after each coat, to get the body smooth, all scratches filled, and so on. Today we don't really have any "universal primer" like that anymore (and don't use lacquer primer under catalyzed paint—it wrinkles). Instead, we have non-sandable primer-sealers like DP 40, and "high-build," "high-solids," or "fast-fill" catalyzed primer-surfacers to make the job of block sanding much quicker and easier. Because they are catalyzed, (1) they "dry" very quickly for ready sanding, and (2) they also act as an excellent sealer to block against any gremlins creeping up through old layers of paint. High-solids is probably the most accurate name for this stuff, because it literally has a *lot* of solid material in it—a gallon of it is really heavy.

During the sand-and-prep stage, you spray on one or more heavy coats of this material, let it set, and then (ideally) block-sand most of it back off. It doesn't clog paper; it doesn't shrink or swell; it holds back underlying color; it doesn't absorb water. It's really good stuff.

The first universally popular product of this type was PPG's yellowish K 200. Unfortunately, it (and its successor, gray K 36), have been "outlawed," so ask your paint dealer what is currently good and available. I have also heard that a few similar products are available that are essentially "sprayable filler." This didn't sound good to me, and I haven't tried it, but I have been getting very good reports on it from professional painters. Again, ask your trusted paint dealer's advice.

Two-Part Paints. Known by various names (such as "two-pack" in England),

these are any of the modern catalyzed paints, be they urethanes, epoxies, acrylics or other types, that chemically harden (or "cross-link") rather than just air-dry. Some can be a little harder to spray, more "touchy" about fisheyes or separation, and more critical as to mixing proportions, but they are far superior to older non-catalyzed paints in most respects, as outlined in the accompanying sidebar. One drawback to these paints (besides pervasive overspray) is that they are considerably more toxic than older types, especially those containing isocyanates. You *must* wear a good charcoal-filter breathing mask when applying them, and effective exhaust ventilation of the spraying area is mandatory. If you paint with it regularly without protection (a full ventilated body suit is recommended), it can definitely kill you. Then again, many two-part paints were available in non-isocyanate versions several years ago, which seem to work just as well. It's something to ask your paint dealer.

Two-Step Paints. These are also known as two-stage (or three-stage, or more) paint, or often just "base coat-clear coat." Whereas old lacquers were often clear-coated (with clear lacquer), the two-step generally refers to a "system" of two-part (i.e., catalyzed) paints that consists of a color base coat that sprays easily and evenly, and dries very quickly to a dull, satin-like finish, very much like the old lacquers, followed by a clear gloss-coat. Since the clear coat dries very glossy, it can be left as-is, but it is most often color-sanded and rubbed out for a glass-like finish. Whereas base coats are available in any color, including non-metallics (red, black, white, etc.), the system was designed primarily for modern metallic, or metallic-with-pearl, colors. All of these colors are available in two-part, one-step formulations (that is, catalyzed paint that dries glossy, so it doesn't *have* to be rubbed out—though it *could* be—plus it could be clear-coated, too). But don't get confused.

In the old days, hot rodders drove their cars in primer as they worked on them, but lacquer primer is porous, allowing water to seep through and rust the metal underneath. While the old-time primer or "suede" look is popular again, today's 2-part, catalyzed primers are much better at sealing the metal from moisture. Black DP50 works well for this, but my son, Bill, used a common product called "Trim Black" (used on hoods of '60s/'70s muscle cars) on his custom '50 Ford, which has withstood a couple seasons of outdoor San Francisco weather well.

The point of the two-step system is that the usually metallic base color can be sprayed in thin, even coats without problems of streaking, running, or mottling (because it doesn't have to be "flowed out" in a heavy, wet coat). It dries very quickly, so if you do screw up you can just scuff or sand it down and re-shoot it immediately. And the thicker, glossy clear coat not only adds depth to the color, but protects the metallic particles from being "disturbed" during the color-sand/rub out process.

A three-step paint job would include a solid-color base coat, followed by a transparent-color pearl or candy coat, followed by a clear coat. These are for advanced painters, and are only briefly illustrated in this book. True base coats, which dry satin-dull, cannot be rubbed out. Gloss-finish catalyzed metallics, pearls, or candies can be rubbed out, but it's not recommended without a clear coat. On the other hand, I do not understand why painters would apply straight non-metallic colors such as red, yellow, orange, white, or especially black as a base coat-clear coat two-step process.

These colors can be ordered and sprayed in high-gloss one-step catalyzed paints, which can be color-sanded and rubbed out for an even smoother, glassier finish. Adding a clear coat (in my opinion) just means buying more paint, adding another step, and—if you're painting in your garage—incurring the risk of a bug or dirt getting in the clear coat, which is much harder to fix than just sanding, spotting-in, and rubbing out the affected area in a one-step, non-metallic paint.

Reducers. In the old days we called these thinners. They allowed you to thin the paint to the consistency you liked best for spraying. More importantly, lacquer and enamel thinners came in different "speeds" (fast, medium, slow) to allow you to speed up or slow down the paint drying time, given the temperature where you were painting.

Many two-part paints don't account for temperature; some offer a "fast" or a "slow" catalyst; others (such as high-fill primers) allow you to add reducer to the catalyzed paint, both to thin it and adjust drying time, thus making it, technically, "three-part" paint. Further, other new paints (such as

color base coats) might use what is called "reactive reducer." This does three jobs: it thins the paint; it adjusts drying time (in PPG's current case, the last two numbers indicate its temperature range—DRR 1185 is for use in 85-degree weather); and it also contains the catalyst agent. This makes things simple for shops that spray a lot of paint daily. They can change reducer to match the weather. But the big problem for hobby painters is that the shelf life of this reducer is quite short, once it's opened. And even if you keep the can closed, the weather might change significantly between the time you buy it and are ready to use it. Further, if you buy your mixed base coat color now, and wait to buy the reactive reducer for it when you're ready to paint, there's a strong possibility it might be superseded by a new product, and you are stuck with mixed paint for which there is no available, fresh reducer/catalyst. Solution? Buy your paint and matching reducer when you're really ready to paint—and you know which way the wind's blowing.

The above catalog is neither comprehensive nor exhaustive. We've listed generic types of paints that might come in acrylics, urethanes, or other chemical formulations. We've ignored old lacquers and enamels. We've also ignored strange breeds such as "alkyds" or the all-inclusive, but mysterious, "synthetics." We haven't explored water-based automotive paints because they don't seem perfected yet for amateur use. We have little idea what the future holds for them, and any other new types of paints we may not have even imagined yet. We repeat: try to find a knowledgeable and helpful paint store person who can keep you abreast of new automotive paint products, and tell you which ones he or she recommends given feedback from professional customers. Further, when trying a new product, buy a small quantity and test it on something other than your favorite car, first, to see how it works and whether you like it (or, perhaps more important, to learn to use it properly).

Old Paints Vs. New Paints

Old Enamel

- Must be sprayed in a booth
- Takes overnight to dry
- Requires expert spray technique to avoid runs/sags/mottling (of metallics)/ vs. orange peel
- Takes about 3 to 6 months to dry sufficiently to sand and repaint to fix mistakes
- Can (usually) be applied in one coat
- Dries glossy
- Cannot be rubbed out
- Can be sprayed over most other old paints/substrates
- Thick paint film; good coverage
- "Fills" minor sandscratches/imperfections
- Minimal shrinkage
- Remains relatively soft
- Cannot be spot-painted (because you cannot rub out overspray "edges")
- Not scratch/chip resistant, especially when new
- Ages well; does not crack, check, etc. unless abused or neglected
- Thinning ratio not critical, but overthinning can lead to runs/sags, underthinning to orange peel
- Thinner "speed" not as critical as lacquer
- Leftover paint can be poured back in can; unused paint stores relatively well
- Overspray is not a major problem

Old Lacquer

- Can be sprayed most anywhere
- Dries very quickly
- Can be sanded and resprayed right away
- Easy to spray; doesn't run/sag easily; orange peel is not a problem
- Dries dull; requires rub out (but rubs very easily)
- Can be clear-coated (with clear lacquer); clear is highly recommended over metallics, necessary over candies or pearls
- Thin paint film; usually requires multiple coats for good coverage
- Shows sand-scratches/surface imperfections; excellent surface prep and fine sanding required
- Multiple primer coats usually required
- Cannot be applied over enamel or most other old paints (will wrinkle)
- Shrinks after about 6 months (including lacquer primer), showing sand-scratches
and other surface imperfections; often requires re-rubout.
- Brittle, relatively fragile; chips easily
- Very easily spotted-in or touched-up
- Does not age well, especially if exposed to elements. Often cracks/checks with age, even kept covered (especially if applied in multiple coats and kept in hot/cold climates)
- Thinning proportions not critical
- Thinner speed is important to match ambient temperature; too "fast" thinner leads to dry spray/overspray buildup on paint surface
- Unused paint stores indefinitely if sealed; can pour leftover paint (even thinned) back in can
- Overspray is no problem; falls to floor as "dust" that can be swept up or blown away

New Catalyzed Acrylics/Urethanes (One Stage)

- Should be sprayed in booth; can be sprayed in garage (with ventilation)
- Dries in about 20 minutes to allow sand and respray
- Mixing proportions must be exact
- Once mixed with catalyst, must be sprayed right away; gun must be thoroughly cleaned immediately after use
- Leftover mixed paint must be disposed of
- Can be sprayed over most substrates, with or without catalyzed primer (only)
- Relatively thick paint film; "fills" sand scratches, etc.
- Can usually cover in one coat
- Does not shrink
- Dries very glossy; does not need rub out if sprayed well
- Difficult to spray; runs easily; "fisheyes" easily if surface not thoroughly clean and dust-free
- Can be color-sanded and rubbed out
- Usually not clear-coated, but can be
- Can be spot-painted or touched up
- Very tough paint; does not rock-chip easily; scratches can often be rubbed out
- Ages very well; can be rubbed and buffed if faded
- Overspray is a major problem when not sprayed in a vacuum booth; different types of paints (epoxies, urethanes) are worse than others

New Catalyzed Paints (Two-Stage–Base coat-Clear coat)

- Base coat sprays like lacquer; can be sprayed anywhere
- Base coat dries very quickly; can be sanded and resprayed
- Base coat cannot be sanded without recoating before clear coat
- Most base coat drying time controlled by "reactive reducer"; must be matched to ambient temperature, but not as critical as lacquer
- Shelf-life of "reactive reducer" is short; cannot be checked without spray-testing
- Once mixed, paints must be sprayed, gun cleaned, left over disposed of, etc.
- Un-mixed left over paint products do not keep well
- Mixing ratios for most paint products critical
- Clear coat should be sprayed in a booth; can be sprayed in a clean, bug-free, indoor, ventilated space
- Clear coat requires expert spray technique; runs/fisheyes easily, but also orange-peels easily
- Runs/sags can often be color-sanded out of clear
- Dirt, bugs, other problems require respraying base coat (can be spotted-in), and re-clearing.
- If sprayed well, clear dries smooth and very glossy; but is usually color-sanded and rubbed out for best finish
- Clear coat is tough, ages well; but peels if left to elements
- Can be repaired/spotted-in/touched up; but requires several steps, increasing coverage area of each step (primer, base coat, clear coat)
- Base coat overspray is minimal, like lacquer; clear coat overspray is not readily visible, but leaves rough residue on surfaces

PREP, SAND, AND MASK

The first "prep" step of any good paint job is to remove as many parts from the car as feasible that aren't supposed to be painted. This not only makes the ensuing bodywork, sanding, masking, and painting steps much easier, it also allows you to paint all surfaces that were painted originally. Here I am just beginning the process on my '52 Chevy. The taillights and license come off, as does the door (and other) upholstery panels. Also detach parts such as the front and rear gravel pans and interior window frames, which are easily prepped and painted separately. In this case, I repainted the dashboard in the car, and left the rear window (and trim) in place.

Preparation ("prep work," or just "prep") is certainly very important to a good, long-lasting paint job, but not necessarily in the same ways it used to be.

In the old days stripping the car to bare metal wasn't nearly as prevalent, and we didn't have high-fill, catalyzed primers. So carefully hand-sanding the entire surface of the existing paint was absolutely necessary to ensure a smooth, unblemished finish for the final paint layer. You had to painstakingly hand-sand out every rock chip, scratch, or crack, featheredging it until you could no longer feel any imperfection in the surface. A few coats of lacquer primer, in between sanding, helped. But the heavily solvent-based lacquer primer often seeped into exposed undercoat layers, especially in feather-edged areas, causing them to wrinkle or lift. Or, lacquer primers or putties would absorb solvents from paint layers, causing them to swell, or shrink, or both.

So painting a car in the fairly recent old days meant starting by laboriously hand wet-sanding the entire body (after any necessary bodywork, of course) with 180 to 220 grit paper, feathering out chips and scratches as mentioned, and then going back over the whole thing with 360 to 400 grit wet-sanding. The latter process might be repeated two or three times, with layers of lacquer primer in between. Painting with lacquers could produce glorious results, but the preparation process was laborious and could be very frustrating.

Preparation these days means something different and more inclusive. Today's products are better, easier to use, faster, and certainly longer lasting.

Instead of starting the prep process with sanding the old paint, let's rethink the whole procedure. Obviously, if you're going to strip the car to bare metal (or fiberglass), that negates sanding the old paint entirely. Similarly, which of the following prep steps you follow depends more or less or the "stage" of

paint job you're doing on your vehicle. But the basics of prep include: (1) Straightening the body. This includes major and minor metalwork, use of fillers, and board-sanding surfaces smooth with 36 and 80 grit paper. (2) Cleaning and adhesion. We've covered products and methods for cleaning the surface, but before you sand anything, the surface must be clean of any dirt, oil, grease, or other contaminants such as silicones. And it must be re-cleaned more than once before you shoot final paint. Equally important, you must use paint products (undercoats or topcoats) that ensure maximum adhesion to whatever surface you're dealing with, above or below it. A major, though often overlooked, part of the prep process is making sure the final paint does not bubble or lift anytime after it is applied. (3) Priming and sanding. If you're repainting a relatively new car with decent paint, then maybe all you need to do is

clean and fully sand the existing surface, possibly spray an adhesion coat, then shoot your color. But most cars that need a paint job need more than that. The details are discussed later in the book, but this is where high-fill primer (usually) comes in, and *lots* of sanding—block sanding, careful sanding, complete sanding in all nooks and corners. It's still somewhat laborious, but usually not frustrating.

Let's briefly delineate the basic steps of paint preparation in the order in which they should be done.

Disassembly. Start by detaching, or peeling off, anything that gets in the way of painting the basic surface of the car—that is, all that was originally painted by the factory (or more, if you want). This might even include removing some pieces (such as large, plastic bumpers or body "cladding" on newer cars) that should be painted separately and reinstalled on or over the repainted body.

Even on older cars, the way to remove certain clipped-on trim strips can be a mystery. First, check inside the body for any studs with nuts, and remove them. Then it's usually a matter of prying the trim piece off the clips any way you can without bending or kinking the strips, the clips, or the car body. Use patience and creativity.

Once you get trim strips off, it's best to remove all the clips (again, carefully and creatively). Put them, and any other fasteners or small parts groups, in zip-lock plastic bags or small cardboard boxes marked with a felt-tip pen and store them in the same place as other items from this project. Do this. Believe me, you'll be thankful later.

"Dechroming" newer cars is fun—most of the badges and emblems are held on with adhesive and simply peel off, as shown (again, check for any studs/nuts inside; if the adhesive is stubborn, a heat gun helps). If you want to replace them after painting, however, get new ones, with fresh adhesive, at the dealer (though we saw a guy at one shop replacing individual used letters with clear weatherstrip glue).

If you have a car made during those unlucky years when they put black rubber "gaskets" around door handles and other body parts, as shown, they must be removed for proper painting. There's no feasible way to mask them. You've got to disassemble the inside of the door, remove the handle and rubber, paint the handle separately, then reassemble everything (with new rubber) after the body is painted (and rubbed out, if you're going that far).

Disassembly is almost done. The headlight and door handles will come off. Maybe the windwings. Probably the front fender. I shouldn't have done upholstery first, and the windshield wasn't supposed to come out, but those are other stories. Wheels and tires can be easily covered with old beach towels or, better, cheap covers with elastic bands available at your paint store.

This step depends on which class of paint job you're doing and your own levels of energy, patience, and perfection. When taking parts off, it's a good idea to bag and label them and their fasteners, because it may be a while before you're ready to reinstall them.

Bodywork. We won't discuss this here because we covered it in Chapter 3, but it is definitely one of the steps of paint prep, and it should be done now, after disassembly (and paint stripping, if that's included). If you have bodywork done by someone else, they usually cover the area with a coat of high-fill primer (unfortunately, many times so you can't see what exactly they've done). The running jibe between bodymen and painters is that the bodyman gets the surface "close enough," shoots it with sanding primer, and leaves it to the painter to block-sand smooth. Painters, of course, yell that the bodyman didn't get it close enough. If you're doing both bodywork and paint, you want to get it "really close" during the bodywork stage. Then, depending on other factors, you can shoot a coat of primer over the body-worked areas as you do them, or wait and

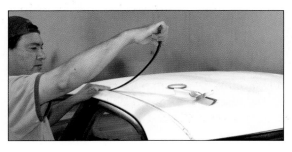

Trim on newer cars is minimal, but its removal can be mysterious, too. The black rubber strips in the roof (what are they for, anyway?) are usually held by clips at each end and pop and peel out easily after a little wiggling.

Where does the body-work process end and sanding begin? That's an ongoing debate between bodymen and painters, but if you're doing it all yourself, it's a moot point. We showed bodywork on this fender in Chapter 3, ending with board sanding with 36-grit paper followed by a coat of high-fill primer. Most bodymen would then deliver the car to the painter, as shown, with catalyzed spot putty used sparingly to fill deep scratches or filler pits.

prime the whole car at once, before block sanding.

Cleaning/Degreasing. This step might start with soap and water or a pressure washer. We've discussed degreasing agents. They come with directions, and should be used before any new layer of material is sprayed on the car if you've worked, touched, or sweated on it in between. If you strip the car to bare metal, you can skip this step for now.

Sanding. If the paint on your project vehicle is significantly cracked, checked, peeling, bubbling, or flaking, you are much better off stripping it down to bare metal (by whatever method you choose). If the current paint on the car is not adhering properly, whatever paint you put on top of it will not adhere properly either.

Stripping paint "by whatever method you choose" includes those we have discussed—it does not include *sanding* all the paint off the car. If you try hand-sanding your car to bare metal you're nuts or a masochist (probably both), and the same goes for (usually drill-motor-powered) strappers, flappers, rotary wire brushes, or whatever else is being hawked on late-night TV. There are good types, such as 3M abrasive wheels, that work well in small spots, especially for metal cleaning, but not for a whole car body. Most importantly, *do not try to sand all the paint off your car with a rotary sander of any type.* Most true

metalmen cringe at the thought of a body grinder touching sheetmetal. Others, including plastic filler manufacturers, actually recommend using a coarse-disc grinder (i.e., 24 to 36 grit) to both clean and rough-up a body-worked area for best filler adhesion. I'll go with that, to a minor degree. But don't take a body grinder to the whole outside of your car—or even major portions of it—just to strip paint off. Just as bad (and I've seen this way too many times) is using any sort of rotary sanding discs, whether in your electric drill or its own machine, to sand down a car. These are for sanding the flaking paint on the wood trim of your house. On a car they only gouge the surface and grind ruts in the metal. At this stage of the paint job we assume any major bodywork has

been done, and sanded as level and smooth as possible with at least 36-grit paper on sanding boards or blocks. We want to make the entire surface smoother, not gash and gouge it.

You don't need air tools for the occasional at-home automotive paint job, at least not for sanding. But if you're a tool collector, a couple types are acceptable. They are of the orbital (i.e, vibratory, rather than rotary) type, and they incorporate a semi-hard, flat backing to act as a block to help level the surface. Jitter-bugs come in various sizes, from hand-block up to Bondo-board. They are most effective when used with coarser papers to level out layers of plastic filler, but can be used with 180-grit dry paper to sand and level paint surfaces, too. Although a dual-action (D.A.) sander uses a round pad, it vibrates rather than spins. A favorite of production bodymen, it takes more practice to get surfaces smooth. But for the home-painter it's good for feathering-out rock chips, deep scratches, and other surface imperfections in small areas. It's not designed to sand large surfaces smooth.

Completely hand-sanding a car for paint, properly, only takes a good day or two, at most. When painting one car, at home on your own time, that's not much. So take the time to do it thoroughly. Here are a few tips to make the job go well:

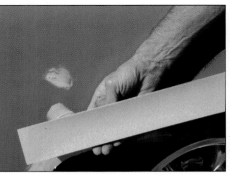 

You can start the block-sanding process with 180-grit paper (wet or dry). But if some filler work has been done, spot putty added, or just a layer or two of high-fill primer needs leveling, I prefer to start with 80-grit paper (dry) on a long-board to work down large areas quickly, followed by 180 grit (with, perhaps, another coat of primer in between).

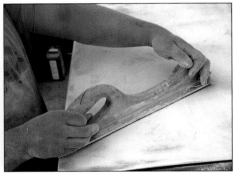

If you're lucky, as in this case, you are able to sand all the guide coat off (meaning the high spots and all the low spots) evenly. If you uncover bare metal, however, or low spots remain, it's time for more primer and more sanding—or even a little more bodywork.

The key to any great paint job is careful and thorough block sanding of the whole body, which is usually repetitive (prime, block sand, prime, block sand). The longer the sanding board or block the better, especially on large panels. Sanding without one is useless for getting panels straight. High-fill primers are a big help in this process, especially if you start with a "guide coat" on top. This is simply a dusting of a contrasting color of paint—spray can black is cheap and handy—wafted over the primer coat.

In this example on a flat deck lid with a good coat of high-fill primer, a quick sanding with 80-grit on a long board quickly shows bare high spots, dark low spots, and sand scratches.

• Use quality sandpaper made for automotive paint work (3M, Makita, Norton are some common brands; there are others). I suggest you get it at your automotive paint supply store. It may seem expensive at first, but it pays for itself in the long run by lasting longer and not clogging as easily as general-purpose sandpaper. For hand-sanding, tear a full sheet of paper in half, then fold it in thirds. If you do enough sanding, buying sandpaper by the pack or box saves bucks, and saves trips to the store (especially late at night and on weekends when they're closed, but you're working on your hobby project).

• Use a semi-hard rubber pad inside the folded paper as often as possible to even the sanding pressure and give a blocking effect. Use your fingertips, and the corners of the paper, to get into corners and concave ridges, which are very important to sand. But—as you have undoubtedly heard many times—don't sand with your fingertips in open areas. It leaves uneven ridges. Use the palm of your hand, or turn your hand at an angle. Also, especially with a block, do not sand parallel to an edge or a ridge. Sand at an angle. Otherwise the outer edge of the block/paper cuts a ridge in the surface.

• Speaking of fingertips—this one hint is worth the price of this book. The reason painters fold their paper in thirds is so it won't wrinkle or ball up, is easier to hold onto, and can be turned regularly for a fresh surface (plus, it makes a good size to fit your hand). But as one side is sanding the car, the other side is sanding your hand. After a day of this, believe me, your hand is going to be bloody and it *hurts!* Especially your fingertips. I've seen painters wrap their fingers in tape to guard against this. But the hot tip is to wear a pair of rubber dishwashing gloves. You want the kind you

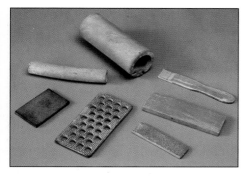

We emphasize using the longest sanding blocks practical on most body panels to get all the dips and waves out. But many body areas, especially on older cars, aren't big and flat. Sanding in corners, curves, and up to beltlines or raised bodylines is very important—but so is using an appropriate-size block behind the sandpaper rather than your fingers. Pieces of hose, hard rubber squeegees, paint sticks, small blocks of wood, or other flat or curved shapes can be used, either with paper wrapped around them, or glued on (several kinds of sandpaper come with adhesive backing).

For instance, this fender, which has been repaired and primed, has a convex surface on top—being sanded with 80-grit wrapped around a slightly pliable hard rubber squeegee—and a concave area next to the edge, calling for a short piece of heater hose as a "block."

 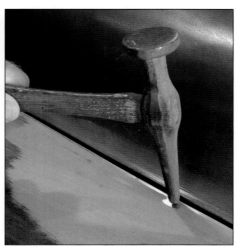

Low spots can be filled with more primer or a little spot putty. But if your sanding uncovers a high area, such as this obvious spot of bare metal, you probably have to hammer it down. If you did your initial hammer-and-dolly work adequately, you shouldn't have to get aggressive at this stage. A little careful and gentle tapping with a pick hammer leveled this so it only needed one more priming and sanding.

can pick up a dime with; they come in large, and they stretch to fit your big hands. They're especially helpful when wet sanding. In fact, get two or three pairs, because you'll wear holes in them—instead of your fingers. You'll thank me for this one!

Wet or Dry?

It's your preference. Only "wet-or-dry" paper, which is typically black, works wet. You can use it dry—some do—but I don't. The primary advantage to wet sanding is that the paper lasts longer and tends not to clog as much. It is messy, though, both on the car and on the floor; you have to wash the residue off, and you have to wait till the washed surface dries to see how you've done and whether it needs more sanding. On the other hand, dry sanding produces lots of dust, which some people hate more.

Personally, I wet-sand existing paint, starting with 220 to 240 grit and going finer. (Color sanding, which we get to, is always done wet.) Anything that requires 180-grit sanding, especially with a board or block, I prefer to do dry. And because of years of using lacquer primers, which can absorb and hold water, even when they look dry, I refuse to wet-sand primers of any kind. With modern catalyzed primers it's really okay, and a lot of painters prefer to wet-sand everything. But I like the gray Fre-Cut paper for dry sanding; I think dust blows off a lot easier than cleaning up after wet sanding; and I'd much prefer to block- or board-sand with dry paper. After any kind of wet sanding, especially on primer, be sure that you have completely washed off all residue, and allowed the surface to *thoroughly* dry, before spraying any paint product on top of it.

You probably think you're sanding the surface to make it smooth. That's only partially true, and not nearly as true as it once was. You're sanding for two reasons: (1) to level the surface, and (2) to

Some painters like to wet-sand everything. I prefer dry sanding, especially on primer. Special tan or gray paper (such as 3M Fre-Cut) is made for this. Do not use cheap sandpaper (or masking tape); it's not worth it in the long run. If you use a lot, buying it in packs saves quite a bit (I get 180 and 320 grit). Whether sanding with your hand or a rubber pad, start by creasing and tearing a sheet in half, then fold that in thirds. This fits your hand (or pad), keeps the paper flat, and allows you to keep turning to a fresh side.

scuff it up to promote adhesion of the next layer of paint. In the days of lacquers, which were thin and contained solvents that bit into the layer beneath it, it was common to do multiple layers of paint, sanding with 400- to 600-grit paper in between, to get a glass-smooth finish. Today's catalyzed paints (especially with a clear coat) are thicker, and they "cross-link," which means their molecules chemically bond with each other—but not necessarily with the layer below. So fine-grit sanding is not only a waste of time and effort (because the paint—or high-fill primer—fills in scratches and other imperfections), but can actually *decrease* adhesion of the next layer of paint. Most of today's painters say that sanding to 240-, 320-, or 360-grit, at most, is plenty. If you're sanding down an existing paint job, it's much more important

to make the entire surface uniformly dull and abraded than it is to make it silky smooth. This is especially true in areas such as doorjambs (if you're painting them), around windows, in body creases and indentations, and so on.

Prime and Block. *(Read Masking below, too, before you prime.)* In the above scenario, we're assuming the car has decent (undamaged, non-peeling) paint on it, and requires little or no body-

While it's always preferable to use a pad, if you're just sanding down existing paint for repainting, you can hand-sand, as shown, starting with 240 or 320 grit paper. Note masking tape protecting stainless trim around the window.

This area needed more than simple hand-sanding, so we switched to 180-grit on a sanding block. However, never block-sand directly along a body edge or line as shown; the outer edge of the block will cut a groove parallel to the body line that will show distinctly after you paint the car.

work. But most cars that *need* painting don't fit that description. For these, we welcome catalyzed high-fill primers and catalyzed spot-putties. Yes, they can be abused. But, boy, do they make paint-prep easier than it used to be.

We don't need to say it again—if the old paint isn't adhering to the body, strip it. Once it's stripped, do any necessary bodywork, board-sanding filler at least to 36 to 40-grit, if not 80-grit. Since you're

The trouble with dry-sanding painted surfaces (as opposed to primer) is that it usually quickly clogs the paper, as shown, and makes grooves in the surface. You can clean the paper by slapping it between your hands (do this regularly when dry-sanding anything).

For sanding paint, especially a whole car, I strongly recommend wet sanding, for which you need dark-colored Wet-or-Dry paper. It works dry, but it's the only kind that works wet. Tear it in half, then fold it in thirds for use. This configuration is the only way to grip the paper and keep it flat while sanding—but it means that one side of the folded paper is sanding your hand while the other side is sanding the car. And soaking your hand in water only makes your skin softer. So here's the hot tip worth well more than the price of this book: Get two or three pairs of large-size rubber dish-washing gloves to wear while wet-sanding your car. It's not to keep your hands soft and clean—it's to keep them from bleeding!

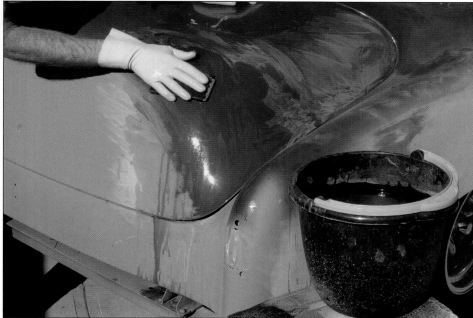

Some people like to wet-sand with a dribbling hose. I think dipping the paper in a bucket of water (keep it nearby) is simpler and keeps your feet drier. If the paint on your car isn't cracked or flakey, a thorough sanding with 360-grit will probably do (some like to go finer, but I think the new paint needs a good "grip"). Otherwise, start with 240, or even 180, and finish with 360.

painting the whole car, not just doing spot bodywork, we then suggest you spray the whole body with a coat of sealer/etching-type primer, followed by a coat of high-fill catalyzed primer. If the body is really straight enough that it doesn't need block sanding, fine; shoot it with the sealer and shoot your color coat. But I haven't seen many bodies needing paint that are that straight. Most have some door-dings, scrapes, or other little wobblies that don't require filler, but can be block-sanded out of a high-fill primer coat, or filled with catalyzed spot putty over the primer (the putty is not made to go on bare metal), and then

block-sanded level. You could just spray the high-fill primer where you see it's needed, but most painters find it faster and simpler in the long run to prime the whole car at once. The problem is that you usually can't see (or even feel, with a well-trained hand) all the little imperfections that show up in the final, glossy paint coat.

The same usually applies to a vehicle you don't need to strip. If it's been around the block a few times, you've probably already done some bodywork to it, and it very likely has its share of rock chips, door dings, scrapes, and so on. First, wet or dry sand the existing paint in the manner, and for the reasons, outlined above. However, you don't need to fully feather edge every rock chip or scrape until it's smooth. Just knock down the rough edges and make sure the paint isn't flaking around the chip (check it with your fingernail—or something similar if you're wearing rubber gloves). If the paint has any cracks or splits in it,

these you have to "chase"—keep sanding them, even to bare metal, until you're confident the paint remaining around them is adhering properly.

Then you have two choices. You can spot-paint high-fill primer over any body-worked areas, and all the chips, scrapes, dings, and minor dents that didn't require filler, but might need some spot putty. Or you can spray the whole body with a sealer, followed by a generous coat of high-fill primer. This would usually be followed by a guide coat and block sanding of the whole body.

It all depends, once again, on how much work you want to do and how good a paint job you want.

The two things that separate a regular paint job from a first-class, show-quality one are full, careful block sanding of the entire body and equally careful color sanding and rubbing-out of the final gloss coat. Both add considerable time and work (though very little cost) to your paint job. It's your time and your effort.

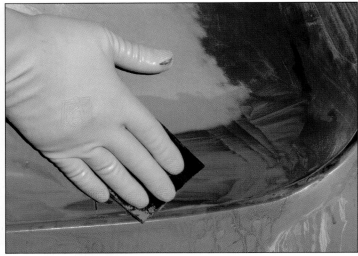

Even wet sanding with finer paper, you should use a rubber backing pad. If you're hand-sanding, however, do not use your fingertips, especially in a parallel motion, because it makes grooves as seen in the first photo. Instead, turn your hand at an angle to the direction of sanding, as demonstrated in the second picture.

Block sanding has levels, or stages, just as paint jobs have levels. Since the majority of paint jobs don't involve bare-metal stripping, the most common scenario is: do necessary bodywork; sand the rest of the car (as described); spot-in the bodyworked areas as well as any chipped, scratched, or dinged areas with high-fill primer; use catalyzed spot putty, sparingly, to further fill chips, scratches, dings, and very minor ripples or dents; block-sand these areas smooth with 80-grit paper (using a long-board on larger areas); and then respray these areas—and probably the rest of the car—with another coat of high-fill primer, followed by another round of block-sanding.

How many times you're willing to do this, over what percentage of the vehicle's body, and with what grits of sandpaper, determine what level of block sanding you achieve. It's up to you.

Personally, after priming, puttying, and board-sanding bodyworked areas to 80-grit (dry), I prefer to prime the whole car (with high-fill, catalyzed primer) and block-sand the whole thing with 80-grit on a long-board wherever possible, using smaller blocks as necessary in smaller areas. By dry sanding with relatively coarse paper, I've never found the need

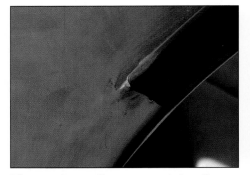
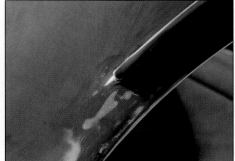

Thorough sanding means into all corners and crevices. The first photo shows lack of sanding around the drip rail, while the second shows not only complete sanding, but also a process called "featheredging" to remove chips or cracks and blend the area around them to level the surface. This area now needs a sealer or etching primer since bare metal has been exposed.

for a guide coat. You know high spots when you uncover bare metal. Low spots are visible because they remain unsanded (sort of shiny). Depending on the magnitude of these high and low spots, they might require a little more tapping with a body hammer at this point (I prefer not to use putty in large low spots, only in small nicks or dings. Never add filler over primer; if an area needs further filling—and this is often discovered during the blocking stage—strip or grind it to bare metal first). Then spray more primer and continue block/board sanding until all high and low areas are gone. I then follow with a full-body sanding with 180-grit, dry, by hand, using a rubber pad, until all visible 80-grit sand scratches disappear (adding more primer, as needed, if I hit bare metal in spots). Then I do it again with 320 to 360-grit paper, dry, with or without a pad.

Those who prefer to wet sand while blocking benefit from a guide coat, because you can't see low areas otherwise. The guide coat can be a light fogging of any different color paint, usually from a black spray can over a light primer. The type of paint doesn't matter,

The sanded surface (only the trunk has been done here) should have a uniform, satiny look. If it has any shiny spots, it needs more sanding; if you can see pits, scratches, or cracks, it probably needs more sanding, then more primer, then more sanding. It's your time and labor; how good a paint job do you want?

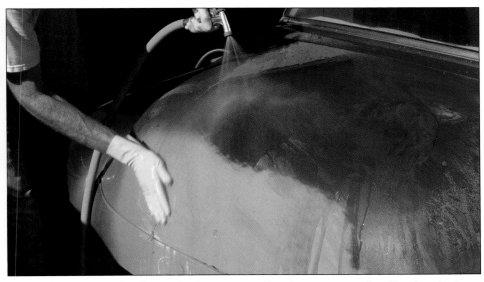

While dry sanding is plenty dusty, wet sanding is even messier. Be sure to tape from the inside any holes that you don't want water going through. And when you're done, thoroughly rinse all residue off the surface and out of any seams or cracks.

because it all gets sanded off, if you do your blocking properly.

I should mention here that there is some controversy between painters and bodymen today over whether the majority of block sanding should be done with filler over bare metal, or with high-fill primer. I think it's a moot point (in fact, there are a few brands of high-fill primer now that are essentially spray-on filler). Too much of either is bad, and not an acceptable substitute for proper metal-work and body straightening. But that takes more talent and experience. My personal opinion is that 80 to 90 percent of whatever type of body filler you put on the car should end up as dust on the floor.

Masking. I hate masking. It's worse than wrapping Christmas presents. I'd prefer to remove parts than mask them, any day. And that is the preferred method for car painting, anyway. But some masking is usually necessary (especially for home hobby-type paint jobs, as opposed to body-off-frame restorations), and some rules and several tips apply.

We could have covered masking before priming/blocking, because you have to mask before you can start spray-ing anything, including primer. On the other hand, you need to remove and re-mask everything after block sanding, anyway, as you will see. Once again, some basics:

• The quality of masking tape varies greatly in terms of sticking, unsticking, bending around corners, and so on. *Do not use cheap tape.* I use only 3M brand, and the tan type (not blue or red, or what-ever). You probably need to get it at the automotive paint store. It's not cheap, but cheap tape isn't worth the price. Any amount you could possibly save with cheap tape is overshadowed by the annoy-ance and wasted time you suffer trying to apply and remove it properly.

•Likewise, use only automotive masking paper; it's usually light green and comes in large rolls of various widths, again, at the auto paint place. Newspaper is free, but it's cumbersome to unfold and fold, it is porous, it sheds lint, it holds dust, and the newsprint can rub off. Newspaper is not masking paper.

• They make caddies that hold a cou-ple sizes of paper rolls, plus tape, that apply the tape to the edge of the paper, allowing you to tear off paper the length you want, taped and ready to go. They work great (when they work properly). But I've never gotten one, mainly because it takes up too much garage space for the lit-tle time I'd actually use it. However, the real tip is to attach the tape to the edge of the paper *before* you try to tape the paper to the car. Masking is tedious, but this makes it many times easier.

• Never leave tape on the car after it gets wet. Don't mask a car and leave it outside over night. Once it gets wet and dries on the car, it might as well be glued on. It won't peel off. And if it's taped over paint, it can peel the paint off. If you're going to wet-sand existing paint on the car, do it before you do any masking (assuming the windows are still in place). Wash the car off, and thoroughly dry it, before masking. If you're wet-sanding primer coats, you must remove masking tape and paper before it dries on the car.

• Whether you wet-sand or dry-sand the car, always remove and replace all masking paper before shooting final coats. Otherwise sanding residue that collects in the folds of the paper (and tape) invariably blows out into your fresh

After you've spent untold hours sanding and prepping the body until it's ready for smooth and glossy paint, you've still got the usually considerable task of masking it before you can start spraying stuff. Use good tape and real masking paper, which comes in rolls of various widths at your automotive paint store (newspaper is porous, linty, and can smudge ink on the surface). A masking dispenser, which applies the tape to the paper edge and then tears both off cleanly, makes the job much easier, but it is a luxury most home painters can't justify, or don't have room for.

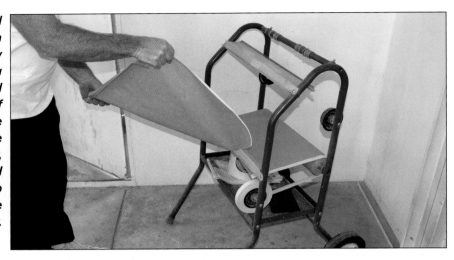

paint as you're spraying, no matter how hard you try to clean it out beforehand.

Other considerations regarding masking pertain to the level of paint job/car build you're doing. Obviously, if you're doing the bare body off the frame, you don't have to mask anything. At the other extreme, if you're doing the "scuff and squirt," with the doors, hood, etc., closed, take off as much exterior trim as you can, and then mask all windows and everything else on the outside of the car you don't want painted. In between are several variations, ranging from pulling all the interior and glass out, to masking (sealing) off these areas completely (if you leave the interior in). Bottom line, masking is pretty intuitive. If you don't

want paint on it, take it off or mask it off.

A couple of further things: In the old days, painters masked off the interior and shot the doorjambs first (and under the hood and trunk, if they were going to do them), in fast-drying lacquer, then closed them a few minutes later and shot the whole outside of the car in enamel (both mixed to the same color). These days, with relatively fast-drying catalyzed paints, most painters mask off the interior, windows (and engine, maybe), if they're still in place, and paint the car, doorjambs, under the hood, etc., all at the same time, as we show in the example in Chapter 9. This is really the most practical way to do it these days, involving the least amount of masking and tape

seams. Plus, if you're painting in your own garage, there's no rush to get the car out of the "booth." You can leave it sitting overnight to fully dry with the doors and hood slightly open.

But what if you want the chassis and engine painted and detailed on your hobby car? Painting the body and frame separately (body-off-frame) is obviously the most effective and most arduous. Next comes removing the engine, painting and detailing it separately, painting the engine compartment while it's out (possibly while painting the rest of the car), and then reinstalling the engine. But it's not really that hard to get even show-quality chassis detailing without taking everything apart.

 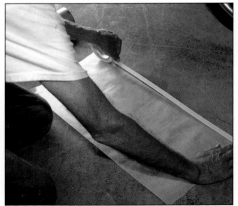 

The alternative is to clean a spot on the floor or your bench, roll out a piece of paper, tear it off the roll with a quick snap, stick a piece of 3/4-inch tape to the paper and surface at one corner, stretch it carefully along the edge of the paper, then tear the tape off and press it firmly to the paper (only). You can do it quickly when you get the hang of it. But the main point is to attach the tape to the paper first, then use the taped paper to do the masking.

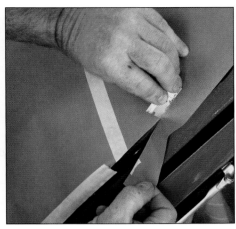

You can mask around corners with the taped paper to a certain extent, but you still have to tape some edges. You can fold them under to fit, or trim them with a razor blade, as shown.

In this case the painter removed the chrome molding around the window, so it was easy to fit the taped paper along the top edge, then add tape to the sides and bottom.

In some areas with tight corners, rubber moldings, and so on (such as this door window and vent), it's easier to run a piece of tape around it first, making sure it fits right next to the painted surface all around, then add the taped paper to this to cover the window.

Good masking requires care and patience. If you're going to get sloppy, however, do it as shown. It's much easier to clean a little paint off chrome or rubber afterwards, than it is to have to sand, remask, and repaint a body part that tape strayed onto.

You have two choices: paint the chassis/engine first, and mask it all off while you paint the car; or, do all your messy bodywork, sanding, priming, and painting on the body first, then detail the undercarriage second. Doing it the first way is easier to mask. I'd do the messy sanding/bodywork/priming first. Then detail the chassis. Then, once the car is in position for painting, mask it from the rocker panels down to the floor, all around the car (this requires some creativity in the wheelwell areas). You can do this with masking paper, but it's probably easier with plastic sheeting, such as Visqueen, taping it to the floor and all around the

car. In similar fashion, you can "wrap up" the engine, as well as other under-hood components that shouldn't be body-color (radiator, horns, wiring, etc.).

The biggest problem with today's paints, in this regard, however, is pervasive overspray that seems to get onto and into places you'd never dream. That's one reason why some painters like to mask a car down to the floor, all around the perimeter, even if the undercarriage isn't already detailed (I had one instance where I found overspray *inside* my dashboard gauges!).

For this and other reasons, I prefer to paint the car first, then go back and detail

the chassis, using mostly (if not exclusively) spray cans, which have far less overspray problem (besides being simple and cheap to use). You can tape masking paper along the rocker sills, either taping it to the garage floor, or just letting it hang down close to it. But a simple trick I discovered is to apply a coat of wax (car polish) to the entire outside of the car (windows, chrome, paint—whatever's there). Then do all your chassis detail painting. When you're finished, just buff all the wax off the car, and any overspray

For newer cars, which usually have black, square-edged, plastic trim around windows, headlights, etc., 3M has developed this trick new tape (#06349 Trim Masking Tape). It has a stiff, non-stick backing that fits easily down into the crack between the trim and the painted surface, then folds over and attaches to the window, light, or other non-painted surface with an adhesive strip.

Here's a trick Romulo showed us to tape around black rubber at window edges on newer cars, but it works anywhere you need to mask a rubber gasket or molding next to paint, or a chrome piece that's not coming off. Mask with regular paper and tape around the window, but leave about 1/8-inch of the rubber, next to the paint, untaped. Then cover this edge exactly with 3M's blue, thinner, plastic "Fineline" tape, which has a much crisper edge.

The trick is to quickly but carefully pull this blue tape back off just after you've finished your clear coat, before it hardens, so the clear can "settle" right up to the trim. This photo also shows how you should remove any masking tape next to a painted edge, even after the paint is dry: pull it back at a sharp angle, and away from the paint, to minimize the possibility of pulling up any fresh paint (from the body) as you remove the masking.

Although we show several "stages" of paint jobs in the following chapters (including more examples of masking), most typical at-home paint projects look like this when they're sanded, masked, and finally ready to spray. However, note that the trim, lights, handles, etc., are off, body openings are masked from the inside, chassis parts (i.e, exhaust pipes) are covered, as are wheels/tires, and the doors are ajar because interior openings are masked and the doorjambs will be painted along with the rest of the car.

comes off with it—plus your car is waxed and ready to go to the show!

Finally, when masking, always err on the side of what you're masking off, not what you're painting. It's much easier to clean or scrape paint off a window or chrome molding or piece of rubber than it is to repaint or touch-up a spot on the body that didn't get painted because it had tape over it.

In general, as far as everything in this chapter is concerned, the primary job is to thoroughly sand, prep, and paint every square millimeter of the body that's supposed to have paint on it. Once that's accomplished, it's relatively easy to clean up, detail, or even paint other areas—to the extent that you want them detailed.

ONE-DAY WONDER

Steve Dalton's neighbor had this slightly scruffy '91 Camaro and it quit running. A fuel-injected car, he figured it would cost too much to fix, so he was going to sell it to the local Pick-A-Part wrecking yard for $200. Steve offered him $200 for it, ascertained it was a bad fuel pump in the tank, replaced it, and had the car running fine in a few days. It had alloy wheels, a decent interior, and other amenities, but the body had some scrapes and dings (and prior work) and the paint was sad. So Steve started doing some bodywork on it and planned to take it to a one-day type shop for a repaint in the original color.

GM had some primer coat problems around this time, and the paint on the roof and trunk had peeled. Steve had already stripped these areas and primed them, along with some other areas he'd bodyworked, when I contacted him about following the paint job for this book.

Besides removing emblems and doing spot-priming, Steve wet-sanded areas that needed special attention, but decided to leave most sanding to the paint shop.

Steve did any bodywork that needed metal straightening or plastic body filler, since he trusted his own work and it would be a considerable extra expense at the paint shop.

The shop we chose is actually called 1-Day Paint & Body, a small chain located in the Southwest. Steve drove the car there then removed the taillights, license-plate bracket, and side-view mirrors.

You've got a car or truck that needs painting. But you can't afford—or don't want to pay—the two, three, or five thousand dollars it realistically costs to have a local body and paint shop do the work.

Or maybe the vehicle in question really isn't worth a two to five thousand dollar paint job, but you'd like a nice paint job on it anyway.

That is, *if* you could find a body and paint shop that even *does* a regular, full paint job. I don't know about where you live, but in most metropolitan areas these days, such shops make their money on collision repair, paid for by insurance companies. They pull frames straight, replace fenders, glass, and so on with new pieces, then spot-paint what's needed to match the finish on relatively new cars. Most such shops won't even work on anything resembling an "old" vehicle, let alone do a full paint job—especially one requiring a color change—which would require some hours of hand-work like sanding, masking, and so on.

And given that situation, if you can find a shop that is willing to paint your car, for whatever price, how good are they? Car painting is probably not their primary business. For whatever reasons—government regulations, cost of materials, cost of labor,

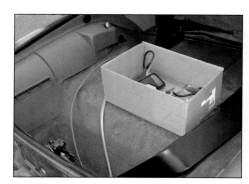

Some shops don't like to paint loose parts, but 1-Day said it was no problem. So Steve put the mirrors, side molding strips, and a new front air dam in the trunk for painting separately.

When we visited, 1-Day offered four levels of paint jobs, ranging from about $300 to $1,400 (extra for a color-change or doorjambs), but a big selling point for us was that they all used DuPont Chromabase urethane (catalyzed) paint. Steve chose the highest-level job because (1) it was the only base-coat/clear-coat option, (2) they could match the color to the original on the car, and (3) it included a color sand and rub out, which Steve hadn't planned on, but would gladly accept for the price. It took a while to find the color code for this car; Steve is pointing to it on a label found in a storage compartment in the trunk area.

You could do even more sanding and parts-removal if you wanted, but this is how Steve's car entered the shop.

Check the just-painted cars out front to judge a shop's quality. These looked good. However, those at a competing (well-known) shop across the street showed grinder marks, surprisingly bad orange-peel, and a "Help Wanted" sign on the door—not good indicators.

or more likely the marked improvement in factory paint jobs that last much longer than they used to—there just aren't many "auto painting" businesses anymore. There are a few high-dollar custom-paint specialists (where you'll pay several thousand dollars—often into five figures). And then there are the low-buck one-day in-and-out paint places, such as Earl Scheib or Maaco, that have franchises all across the country (where you can get in-and-out for as little as a few hundred bucks).

Since you get what you pay for in this world, a few hundred bucks doesn't promise a great paint job. The way we would turn a bottom-dollar finish into a decent one in the old days was to do a lot of the work ourselves, pay more, and make special requests on how the shop handled the job. Our first task, of course, was to take everything possible off the car that you didn't want them to get paint on (otherwise they would). Second was to hand-sand all the paint, being

sure to feather-edge any chips or scratches as much as possible, without sanding to bare metal. Third, the real trick was to pay twice the going rate (which was still plenty cheap) just to get them to spray on twice the allotted amount of paint. To tightly control costs, The Earl only allowed something like two quarts of paint per car, which barely covered a sedan, let alone a wagon. For the extra money you could get two coats of paint, including the rocker moldings, around wheelwells, and so on. Fourth—and this was important—was to ask them to paint the car with the doors shut. This way they couldn't get any paint on the interior, which would invariably happen otherwise. Plus, the extra paint that would have been used in doorjambs could go on the outside of the car. Finally, we'd ask them not to paint the wheels, because no cool car had body-color wheels (especially not Earl Scheib body color), and they'd always get paint on the tires, too. Then, when we got the car home, after letting the paint dry for a week or so (so it wouldn't pull off with masking tape), we'd sand and mask the doorjambs and paint them with spray cans in black, a color to match the dash/interior, or a shade as close to the outside as possible. And we'd paint the wheels white, black, or red and add whatever hubcaps were coolest at the time. Then after waiting the prescribed six months or so, we would wax the car. The remaining task was to keep it clean and take care of it. Even an old-days Earl Scheib paint job responded very well to care and upkeep. The more you waxed it (especially as the enamel paint finally hardened somewhat), the better it looked. If you did it right and kept the car up, even other car nuts probably couldn't tell it came from Uncle Earl's. Especially if you had it painted black.

The Don't-Do-it-Yourself Paint Job

Like so many things in our modern world, the quality of one-day "in-and-out" paint jobs has improved significantly. Of course, as you might suspect, so has the price. But at most such auto-painting places, you now get choices. As I mentioned, the old "spray it, bake it, and drive it away" job now costs about $250 to $500 depending on the place, but that's still dirt cheap. But now most such shops offer a range of paint stage options, starting with name-brand two-part (catalyzed) paint and a wide range of color choices. Additional levels include masking and painting doorjambs, under hood, and so on; base coat/clear coat in even more colors; and even (at at least one chain we checked) a complete color-sanded and rubbed out modern paint finish for about $1,500. As of this writing, that's about half what a similar paint job would cost elsewhere (at the cheapest, if you could find a shop to do it).

So don't ridicule the "drive-thru" auto paint shops these days. Let's take a look at a few reasons why one might be a better option than painting your car in your own garage. And then let's see what you can do at home—and with your choices at such a shop—to optimize the paint job you can get for a very good price.

Let's say you don't have an air compressor, or a spray gun, and all the other equipment necessary to paint a car. If you're starting from zero, it adds up to quite a bit of stuff. It would cost quite a bit more than one or two one-day paint jobs.

First stop was the sanding booth in back, where Romulo started on it with 220 dry paper on a jitterbug.

Although Steve had filled most of them, Romulo found a few more spots that required spot putty. Then he continued working the car with an orbital palm-sander, first with 220, then with 320 paper.

Unlike many such shops, this one did a significant amount of hand sanding, especially in critical areas such as around handles, locks, and door/hood/trunk edges.

Even if you have some or all of the equipment, maybe you keep a pretty tidy garage, and you don't like the idea of filling it with catalyzed paint fumes and overspray: or the prospect of hanging up all that plastic sheeting and sealing everything off looks like more work than you want to do just to paint this one old

We were also surprised that Romulo finished by spot-priming areas, especially where he had spot-puttied. Plus, he used lacquer primer (as had Steve), which is usually a no-no under today's catalyzed paints. But he explained that 1-Day starts the painting process with a catalyzed sealer to stabilize what's on the surface and (hopefully) whatever gremlins might be underneath. Smart move.

And, perhaps most importantly, their painters know how to spray paint. They do it all day long, every day. The gun-wielders in such places have usually worked their way up, and have plenty of experience. The management knows they can't have painters that cause runs, drips, or ugly orange-peel, because at their prices and with their schedule, they can't afford to have "re-dos." Besides, learning to lay on a good, even, smooth coat of paint isn't that difficult. It just takes practice and experience. These guys have plenty.

Finally, even given the advantages listed above, the one big drawback to old-day $19.95 paint chains was that they used their own, usually low-quality, non-brand paint. No matter how well it was sprayed on, it had an evil tendency to peel back off (especially given their

minimal—if any—surface sanding or prep). Well, the quality of paint in general has improved significantly since then, in most cases (though we will see what happens when and if water-based paints are phased in). But the better news is that most of these places, for a moderate increase in price, offer two-part (catalyzed) paints in name brands (i.e., Dupont, PPG, etc.), a much larger choice of contemporary colors, and even two-stage (base coat/clear coat) options.

We don't know which chains, franchises, or local one-off auto paint shops of this type exist in your area, but they are plentiful. To check one out, pay a visit, find out what level of options they offer (including brand and type of paint used), and what the warranty is. But much more importantly, look at some of the finished cars in the lot, waiting to be picked up by

car. At the other end of this spectrum, maybe you don't even have a garage to paint your car in, or the one you have isn't really big enough to do the job.

Regardless of whether you have the equipment or the space, perhaps you've never spray-painted anything in your life, or the few attempts you've made have been less than satisfactory. You'd really prefer to have someone who knows how to handle a spray gun shoot the color on your project car.

Fine. Given those parameters, let's look at what the one-day paint emporium can offer you.

For starters, they all have professional, well-ventilated and filtered, usually temperature-controlled spray booths to spray the paint in. You don't have to prepare the space, plus your car is painted where there is no dust, no dirt, and no bugs, m'lady.

Not only do they have good, up-to-date spray booths, but they have industrial-size compressors, industrial-quality water-traps and air filters, the latest HVLP spray equipment, and so on. They have to. The government mandates it and checks on them regularly.

Next stop was the masking station where Alisa— "Fastest Masker in the West"—looked like she was ready for anything with her well-equipped taping cart.

Most one-day type paint shops are used to masking everything on a vehicle, so Alisa made quick work of all the windows...

...and didn't hesitate with small parts like door handles, locks, and headlights.

Steve removed the door panels (mainly to get the side mirrors off). Since this was to be a "doors closed" paint job, we figured that'd be it. But, again surprisingly, Alisa masked off both the doorjambs and the inside of the doors, all around.

customers. That tells you much more about their quality than any front-office salesman.

What You Can Do

You don't need a book to tell you how to take your car to a shop to get it painted. We wouldn't have included this chapter if there weren't some ways in which you could participate—add your own effort—to make a one-day paint job turn out better than average, and to make it an acceptable substitute for either painting the car yourself or taking it to the high-dollar shop (which, we should mention, takes a *whole lot* longer than one day to prep and paint your car).

If you've been reading this book front-to-back, you've probably already surmised that the two primary things you can do at home to improve a one-day type paint job are to: (1) take as much stuff off the exterior of the car you don't want painted as possible; and (2) thoroughly hand sand the existing paint on the car.

In the first category, how much you disassemble the car depends on a few factors, including its age, and assuming you want to drive the car to the paint shop and back. Older cars have readily detachable non-painted components such as chrome bumpers and grille, headlights, taillights, mirrors, door handles, hood ornaments, and so on. These are all relatively easy to unbolt and remove. If you're driving the car to the shop, you need at least taillights and brake lights, and you may want things like turn signals, door handles, and mirrors. One trick is to loosen these components and pull them slightly away from the body (about 1/8 to 1/4 inch) so paint can get behind them; but don't let them hang down, covering metal that should be painted.

Newer cars with body-color bumpers, handles, mirrors, and so on are problematic. Most one-day paint shops don't want

Further, she masked the inside of the tailgate, from the weatherstrip in (leaving the painted edge to get repainted), and similarly sealed the trunk area with tape and clear plastic.

This is how the car looked before it went in the spray booth. You can see it's well-sanded and there wasn't a lot to mask (the whole masking job took about 15 minutes). They wouldn't let us in the booth to take pictures, but you can see it in the background. It's actually a spray booth attached to a separate drying/heating booth. The painter mixed the base coat from toners in the shop to the formula for the color code of the car.

to deal with any loose parts; they want to roll the car into the booth and paint it as a whole, with all parts at least semi-attached. Ask your chosen shop how much disassembly they do or don't allow.

Likewise, we assume that a vehicle being painted this way will not be getting all new interior, glass, and so on. So, obviously, leave all windows in place. On some cars, chrome or stainless trim around windows is easy to remove and greatly simplifies masking. On others it cannot be removed without removing the glass, gasket, and all. Do not try to take off trim that you're not sure how to put back on. Masking it is much simpler, and in this case better.

On the other hand, don't rule out a full-on glass-out/interior-out paint job at a one-day paint shop. It would require a way of trailering or towing the vehicle to and from the shop. And, obviously, you'd have to make arrangements with the shop to do this (though it's actually much easier for them, since little or no masking would be needed). You'd have to leave the doors, hood, and trunk attached. But all the other stripping is hand work you can do at home. So if you don't have the equipment, space, or experience to paint it yourself, but you do have the time and energy to completely disassemble and reassemble the car, this is one viable option, especially if you pay for the better or best paint they offer. I know of one vintage dragster that was painted during restoration by Maaco, and is now on display in a museum.

As far as sanding is concerned, that's covered in the preceding chapter. A full hand sanding of the car is the one thing none of the in-and-out paint shops do, because it's way too time-consuming for them. But it doesn't really take that long, and you can easily do it at home. It doesn't take any tools or dedicated space. Just some time and sweat.

The other thing you can do at home, as outlined here in Chapter 3, is basic bodywork. Again, you can do

The actual painting process—sealer, base coat, clear coat, drying time—doesn't take all that long. The car came out looking smooth and glossy, and looked even better when all the masking was removed.

The shop told us up front that, despite their name, the top-of-the-line job, including rub out, was going to take longer than one day. That was fine. When we arrived early next morning, 1-Day's "roving rub-out expert" had beaten us there and already color sanded the whole car with 1500-2000-grit paper. After having taped window edges for protection, he was just starting to buff the roof with a variable-speed electric buffer with a foam-cutting pad, using liquid compound. You can see in these photos how the color sanding dulls the glossy clear coat to a velvety finish, but then the compound-buffing quickly brings it back to an even smoother and glossier luster.

We'll talk much more about the color sand and rub out process in Chapter 11, and it is pretty unusual for a one-day type paint shop to offer this option. But, as we say in the text, if they know they have to sand and rub it, they'll be sure to put enough paint on. Here the "buff guy" adds a minimal amount of compound from a plastic squirt bottle, then quickly brings up a gloss with the power buffer on the hood. The whole sand-and-rub took about half a day.

While many such shops won't do them, 1-Day was fine with painting a few parts separately, including the side mirrors and front dam, seen here coming out of the spray booth.

Back at the shop to pick up his painted and buffed $200 ride, customer Steve was quite satisfied. After reinstalling the taillights, license, and mirrors, he drove it home.

much of this with hand tools. And it can save you quite a bit of money. A big caveat is that no paint shop wants to guarantee a paint job over somebody else's bodywork—you have to deal with the individual paint shop on that. But, if the vehicle in question needs bodywork, I think that leaves you two choices. Maybe two and a half. The half is to straighten any bent sheetmetal as best you can, using hammer-and-dolly or whatever tools you have available. But leave it in bare metal or pre-existing paint—don't use any filler or primer. Depending on your skill and the predilections of the paint shop, this might save you some money on bodywork costs—but not necessarily. The first full option is to let the paint place do whatever bodywork/priming they (or you) deem necessary, and pay their price. The second is to do the bodywork yourself and forego any guarantee on the paint. This is well worth considering if (1) your bodywork is good, and (2) you're going for a lower-priced paint job, anyway. In fact, even if you're getting their best spray job, the point is that the chances of the paint going bad are slim (especially if you do good prep on your part, and keep up the paint job afterwards), and the cost of having them do the bodywork could often be more than having the car repainted, if it does go bad. See how that logic works?

Tips and Tricks

The old "pay more for extra paint" trick might still apply, though you probably wouldn't want to pay double the price just for an extra coat of paint. But ask them how much they'd charge.

Some places include a color sand and rub-out with their highest-priced paint job. Depending on the extra cost, this could be well worth the money, because then they know they have to put enough paint (or clear) on the car so as not to rub through it—and if they do, they have to fix it.

Otherwise, the hot tip is to get the catalyzed paint (or base coat/clear coat), because then you can rub it out yourself as we show in Chapter 11. Most one-day type paint places won't do a rub out because it's so labor-intensive—or charge accordingly if they do. But the problem here is the same as trying to rub-out a factory paint job—you don't know how much paint they put on the car, but you know they didn't intend it to be rubbed out. You might be able to buff it out (carefully), or you might go through. If you can get them to add an extra coat of paint or clear for a decent price, then

you can color sand and rub it out at your cost (free) with much less fear of rubbing through. On the other hand, if you're happy with a glossy finish like a new car (not rubbed out), that's all you need. Wax it and enjoy it.

Most of these paint places are onto the "doors closed" trick. Their lowest-priced paint job is usually a doors-closed deal. That doesn't mean you get any extra paint on the outside, but at least it insures you don't get paint on

For the rubber and plastic side moldings, repainted by the shop, Steve used double-sided, highly adhesive "trim tape," available at dealers or most parts stores, to reattach them, asking a friend to help align them and get them straight.

the interior, and you can paint or otherwise detail the doorjambs and other such areas yourself.

If you are paying them to paint the doorjambs, they'll probably do a good job of masking off the interior opening. But it's very difficult to mask the doors' rubber weatherstrip seals. Unfortunately (especially for newer cars) they can be expensive to replace. But if you care about such things as detailed doorjambs, you should really remove the rubber seals, clean the area with adhesive remover and sand it, and then install new seals after the painting is done. It also wouldn't cost you anything but your time to remove the upholstered door panels and the window frames (if any).

Speaking of masking, you might think you can do a more meticulous job than the entry-level laborers doing it at the paint shop. You might be right, and it could benefit you to run a single layer of 3/4-inch tape around such things as window frames or openings. This allows you to drive the car, and the maskers can add taped paper over your tape. On the other hand, these guys mask cars all day, every day. They might not like the way you tape something, or even be offended by it. Remember in the last chapter I mentioned that it's always better when masking to err in favor of getting a little paint on the trim, rather than not getting paint on the body where it belongs. This is taught to most of the maskers at these

paint shops, and part of their job is to go around the car when it's done, cleaning paint off any chrome trim, rubber, or other parts that shouldn't have gotten paint on them. You can do the same at home. Using lacquer thinner (*very carefully*) on a rag or razor blades, you can clean areas that might have gotten some stray paint on them. This is generally easier than trying to pre-mask the car yourself. If, by chance, the paint shop did miss a spot—because of mis-masking or bad spraying—they should fix it, immediately, under their warranty. It's not that hard to do.

Such detailing goes for the rest of the car, too. One telltale sign of a recent quickie paint job is body-color overspray on the gas tank, exhaust pipe, or other undercarriage parts visible from road level. After you get the car home from the one-day paint store, another day spent with a wire brush, maybe some coarse sandpaper, some masking paper and tape, and a few spray cans of semi-gloss black or some other neutral color (i.e., dark gray), can finish off the undercarriage, engine compartment, trunk, and so on.

But speaking of spray cans, *do not* use any on the exterior of the vehicle before you have it painted, especially by a one-day shop. If you're doing the one-day paint job because you don't have your own paint equipment, you might feel strong urges to touch up spots, as you're sanding, with spray can primer.

To be honest, we didn't think the paint shop was going to mask the doorjambs, and you can see some hints of primer overspray in there (from Steve's prior bodywork). But this is much preferable to having painted upholstery. Steve will now mask and detail the jambs with his own small compressor and spray gun.

Don't do it. You never know what's in spray cans these days, and whatever it might be, new two-part paints usually don't like it. I found through bad experience that the same is true for old-style lacquer primers—even good-quality lacquer primer shot from a gun. It wrinkles up under new catalyzed paints.

So I guess the final trick, the primary rule, for getting a good one-day-type paint job is to follow their rules…for the most part. Otherwise, do the disassembly and prep sanding they won't do, clean and detail the car afterwards yourself, and then wax it regularly and take care of it. If you do, nobody will know it was a cheap paint job.

Looking at the finished product, you'd never guess this was a $200 car with a 1-Day paint job. It looks great. And because it's high-quality DuPont Chromabase urethane paint, it'll stay looking good as long as Steve polishes it and keeps it up. Depending on what similar shops offer in your area (or even selecting a lower-price job from 1-Day), doing your own bodywork, prep, and (careful) rub out, you could get the same results for hundreds of dollars less. But this one is well worth the moderate price.

SCUFF AND SQUIRT

The whole paint job—sanding, masking, spraying pearl and clear, and drying time—took less than four hours. The only thing I did before taking this picture was reinstall the grille and the license plates.

This chapter is going to consist of more show than tell. The premise is pretty simple. It's like the one-day paint job, except that you do it at home, in your garage, with your own equipment. Of course there are a few twists.

The example we're going to show you, which we're pretty sure you couldn't get at any Uncle Earl's franchise, is how to add a classy pearl coat to an otherwise appliance-like, relatively new 4-door sedan. The vehicle in question happens to be my wife's recently acquired commuter car. It's an excellent car, and she got it for a very good price, with extremely low mileage, because it's nothing special—a utilitarian model. And since she bought it second-hand, she couldn't choose the color for it. Of course, it's refrigerator white. She doesn't like that. But it's new enough that–even though it came with a few dings and scratches—it doesn't warrant a complete repaint just to change it to a snappier color.

The simple solution, in this case, is to add a coat of white pearl over the existing white base. Pearl, or "pearlescent," paints used to be strictly the province of custom cars. They were tricky to mix and difficult to paint. The lore was that they were made of ground fish scales (from Sweden!). I don't think that's true. But today pearl is much more common and user-friendly. Many beautiful factory colors that used to be simple metallics now have pearls in them. They have a brighter, shimmering glow, and you can see the hue change slightly as the sun glints off it from different angles.

Pearl white was the first, basic pearlescent color (hence its name). Today you see it on several upscale car models like Lexus, Cadillac, Chrysler, and so on. A true pearl paint, such as pearl white, is translucent, so it must be painted over a straight base coat of the same, or similar, color—such as plain icebox white under a white pearl topcoat. Perfect!

A '93 Toyota Camry sedan in basic white looks like a refrigerator, so we don't need a "before" picture. Plus scuffing it and squirting it with pearl and clear isn't all that graphic, so we start with some amplification of prior subjects. First, we mentioned that it's a good idea to clean dirt and grease from areas such as the engine and suspension before starting the repaint process—especially on a white car. I washed the engine with Simple Green and rinsed with water. I also removed the grille, but left the headlights in place.

Now you're getting the idea. This is the quick and inexpensive way to an eye-catching custom paint job.

There is nothing wrong with the paint on our subject car other than a couple of dings that need to be filled and some scratches that need touching-up—and the fact it's a boring, dowdy color. It doesn't need to be stripped, block-sanded, primed, sealed, or anything else except cleaned well and thoroughly sanded with relatively fine paper (240 to 360 grit, probably wet). Touching-up the paint is really simple because (1) it's a plain, solid color that's simple to match, and (2) it doesn't need to be blended or buffed out, because it gets sanded along with the rest of the car.

If, by chance, the car needed some more extensive bodywork, this type of paint job could still apply. Do the bodywork yourself, block and prime the affected area, and spot-paint it the same color as the rest of the car. Then sand

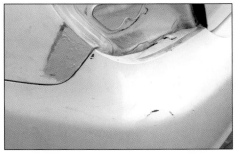

A previous owner had been rough on the car. A taillight was broken, the fender kinked, and the rubber bumper bonked and gouged. After some straightening, it called for a little filler.

this area along with the rest of the car before squirting the pearl coat.

What makes this paint process so simple, especially on newer cars that have little chrome trim or other removable outer-body parts, is that you simply close the doors, hood, and trunk, mask off the windows, peel off the few adhesive emblems it might have, mask off any other trim that shouldn't get paint on it (such as those black rubber/vinyl strips in the roof, or elsewhere, if your car has them), and spray the pearl coat. Since the existing paint is almost the same color, and the car is already completely painted with it, you don't have to worry about getting the pearl under body parts, into nooks and crannies you can't see, or—in this case—even in the doorjambs or under the hood or trunk. Most people see the car with the doors closed 99% of the time, and wouldn't notice the difference in the paint when the door's open, anyway. (If it makes a difference to you, it's not that much harder to paint in the doorjambs and other such areas, because the base coat is already there. It just takes a little more sanding, quite a bit more masking, and more work with the spray gun—not to mention the cost of the pearl paint, which isn't cheap. It's not that much more work. But the point of this chapter is how to do a quick, easy, and inexpensive paint job at home that is very effective.)

The taillight is replaced as a unit. Mounting holes from a bolted-on badge have been filled. We're leaving the chrome bar in place because it has lights and wires attached. So this is how it looked after a little filler and block sanding with 80-grit.

Pearls and Candies

That's about all we really need to tell you about this type of paint job. The photos walk you through the process.

But we need to tell you a little more about painting pearl and its older cousin, candy (originally candy apple, as in red). These are known as custom colors and, in their truest forms, require specific paint methods. This book is not about custom painting, per se. But if we're going to talk about, and show, pearl painting, we must mention a few guide points.

Several new factory colors have pearl in them. Most of these are formulated as two-stage paints, so they can be sprayed as a base coat over any color of primer and then clear-coated. Some of the new factory pearls, however, are three-step paints, which require a plain-color base coat, followed by a similar-color pearl coat, and then the clear. Check with your auto paint store to see which is which, but our real point is to look in the factory color chip books when shopping for a pearl color—the factory has some pretty good ones, mostly in easy-to-paint (and touch-up) two-step base coat/clear coat. The paint store should also have plenty of shades of

The next step was a coat of high-fill catalyzed primer (shown with masking removed).

I had a pint of touch-up paint mixed in single-stage gloss urethane to match the color code of the car. Since we're going to add pearl and clear, I could have used base-coat (instead of gloss) for this, but I wanted to demonstrate how you can do spot touch-up on your car even if you're not going to spray anything over it.

true pearl colors, which you find in "custom colors" paint chip books from PPG, DuPont, House of Kolor, and so on. They're nearly all three-step, and the company recommends specific base coat colors to use under them.

But here we're doing it the other way around. Your car already has a plain color on it. It could be white, or beige, or baby blue, or sea foam green—whatever. Most people wouldn't see a need to add pearl over a bright color like red or yellow (though it's perfectly okay to do so), and pearls generally don't work well over real dark colors, especially black. But whatever color your car is, your paint

Then came more block sanding with 180-grit dry paper, followed by pad-sanding with 360-grit. Here we've done selective masking—over the chrome bar, license, lower trunk edge, good taillight, and even the exhaust pipe. Note the holes in the taillight housing taped from inside to keep paint out of the trunk, plus masking over the rear window to keep over-spray off. The rear wheel/tire was also covered before spot painting.

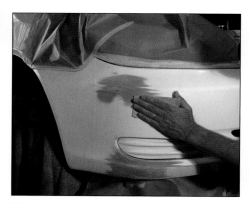

The front bumper had similar dings and gouges, as did the hood and other areas, so they got similar treatment.

store can probably find a pearl to complement it. In general, you want a pearl shade (other than white) that's just a tad darker than the existing color, because the pearl in the paint tends to lighten it slightly. But don't stray far from the existing color, or it is hard to spray an even coat of the pearl over it.

As we said, true pearls are translucent (and candies, though colored, are transparent). Therefore, whatever is underneath is going to show through. In our

Although it didn't break or scratch the paint, the driver's door had about a 3-inch shopping cart gonk in it that was deep enough to warrant plastic filler, not just spot putty. I started by stripping the paint with a 3M cleaning wheel on a drill, which is non-abrasive.

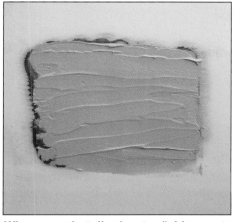

When people talk about a "skim coat of filler" this is what they should mean. This is about 1/8-inch thick at the deepest part of the dent.

Only mask at body-lines. In this case, we primarily wanted to keep overspray off the window and molding around it. We're only going to spray primer over the repaired area (plus maybe an inch or two around it) with a touch-up gun. But since overspray falls downward, we added the masking at the rub strip, just for insurance.

After a little sanding with 80-grit on a medium sanding block the filler is leveled, the edges of the paint are feathered a bit, and it's ready for a coat of high-fill primer. However, do not mask off a repaired area as shown for either primer or spot paint. We don't want a hard, taped edge in the middle of a paint panel.

case, this means that the base color (the existing color on the car), and any touch-up painting that you do, must all be exactly the same color and shade. If you leave any scratches or chips, they'll show through the pearl. If your touch-up paint isn't matched exactly to the existing color (say, if the car's paint has faded some), this difference shows as light or dark splotches under the pearl. If, by chance, you want to test a pearl color over the paint on your car to see how it looks, you must recoat that test spot with matching body color before shooting the complete car.

And spraying pearl is not like spraying non-translucent colors. The more pearl you put on, the more the color changes. Most pearl colors get darker at first, then start to turn milky as you add more paint. The point is you must spray the whole car evenly: do not overlap paint coats between panels. Different painters have different methods. It helps if you're not painting the doorjambs, because you won't have a layer of pearl overspray around each door opening (a common problem with neophyte pearl and candy painters). But you also must not paint the car panel-by-panel in the usual manner: a front fender, then the door, then the rear quarter, and so on. If you do, everywhere you overlap paint—the fender onto the door, then the door onto the fender, etc.—gets a darker or milkier "blush" in the pearl. Most custom painters avoid this by "walking" the length of the car while spraying. Others use a criss-cross pattern all over the car. Yes, it does take some practice and experience, but with pearl over a closely matching base color, it's not as hard as it might sound. The key is not to spray too much pearl. One even coat should do it—just enough to get that pearl, shimmering effect. The more you put on, the duller the pearl effect becomes, and the greater your chances for getting uneven splotches or streaks.

If this sounds a little scary or daunting, two things: First, since you're using

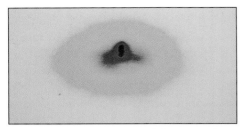

In Chapter 6 we showed featheredging chips or scratches. Here's a better example, that doesn't get down to bare metal, on a rear quarter. This was sanded with 180-grit on a small block.

This was actually a typical small, round door-ding, deep enough that it still needed a bit of spot putty even after a small coat of high-fill primer.

When it's hardened, sand both the putty and the primer level with 180-grit on a small block, as shown.

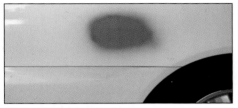

Even if it's sanded smooth, never paint directly over spot putty or body filler; always add another coat of primer or sealer. Otherwise the repair spot will "telegraph" back through the paint, even (in fact especially) if you color sand and rub out the paint.

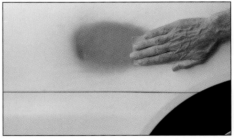

This is little-known, but important: After sanding the re-primed, spot-repaired area smooth with 360-grit paper on a pad, sand a much larger area (indicated by hands) with 600 or finer grit paper to remove all overspray all around the actual repair.

catalyzed paint, if it doesn't turn out right the first time, let it dry overnight, sand it down the next morning, and start over again. It's not that big a deal. With a true pearl, that probably means starting with a new base coat, then the pearl coat. However, the second option is to find a factory nontranslucent color, with pearl in it, that matches the existing paint on your car very closely. If you can find such a color, hopefully it is close enough that you don't have to paint the doorjambs, and you probably won't have to spot-in scratches and other touch-ups (though they should be primed in a shade close to body color).

Now just a brief word about candy paint for the more adventurous among you. To get the full, brilliant, candy-like effect, painters usually spray such colors over a special, highly metallic gold or silver base. Applying such a custom paint job takes the ultimate painter's

skill and experience. Only a few do it really well. However, in the last few years PPG and other companies have devised custom paint "systems" where a candy is sprayed over a similar-colored metallic base. It's not as brilliant, but it does have that deep, true-candy look, and it's much easier to paint (similar to a pearl color over a like-color base). I've tried it with success. So I'm—somewhat hesitatingly—suggesting that if your car has a metallic color on it to start with, and you'd like to "customize" it further, you *could* try spraying a coat of similar-color candy paint over it. The candy has to be sprayed evenly, like pearl, but adding more coats doesn't diminish its effect, it just makes it darker and deeper in color. Now, I've never tried this before and I don't know anybody who has, but I don't see why it wouldn't work. It could be, literally, brilliant. In either case, the pearl or candy should be

followed by one or more clear coats, specifically a "UV" clear, which blocks paint-fading ultraviolet light. Pearls and especially candies are quite susceptible to fading in the sun, particularly reds and lighter colors.

Totally Basic

What we've described is the quick trick to put a cool paint job on a plain-Jane car. But let's get totally basic. The only thing wrong with your car is that the paint is faded, scratched, or worn. Maybe it has some road-rash or shopping cart contusions or abrasions. You don't want or need to change the original color. You just want to make it look, once again, like the shiny car it once was. Simple. Find the color code for your year, make, and model car (it should be on a tag in a door jamb, or on your new-car receipt if you still have it),

Then you can spot-paint the area using paint color-matched to that on you car. If your car is single-stage catalyzed gloss (like this white), and you use similar paint for touch-up, you can color sand and rub out the spot-painted area and the repair will be nearly invisible. If you didn't sand off all primer overspray first, you will see a ring or halo of primer

around the spot paint. If your paint is base-coat/clear-coat (highly recommended with metallics), such repairs are even easier: do your repair and prime it; sand back the primer; spot paint the primed area with color-matched base coat; then (without any sanding) cover a larger area with clear, and then color sand and rub out the whole area.

But we're really talking about preparing a car with some nicks and bruises for a pearl-coat. So, after your spot painting, use a small brush and the leftover catalyzed paint in the spray gun cup to go around the whole car touching up any small chips or nicks still left.

and order up about a gallon (or less, depending on the size of your car) of that color at your auto paint store, along with necessary additives. Then sand the car, mask it, and shoot it. Since you're painting it the original color, you don't need to paint doorjambs, window frames, under the hood, or anything else (assuming they're all in decent condition). If the outside needs a little minor bodywork, spot putty, or just some high-fill primer and block sanding, that's covered elsewhere in this book. If you want to color-sand and rub it out after it's painted, we cover that, too. If it's a metallic color, you'd probably want to go base coat/clear coat, but you don't have to. These are all options.

The point of this chapter is that you can do the scuff-and-squirt job—whether it's a pearl coat or a respray of the car's original color—at home. But we took the spotted-in Camry to a body shop because (1) it's much easier to photograph someone else doing paint work and (2) they owed me a free paint job. They'll remain nameless because, like so many body shops these days, they don't offer complete paint jobs. Since I had to drive the car there, the only part I removed was the grille (plus the license plates, after I got there).

After a little protective taping, the crew started literally scuffing the car down with Scotchbrite pads as well as 1000-grit paper by hand and with a small orbital palm-sander.

I'm not sure it shows in the photo, but the entire car was sanded/scuffed satiny smooth, with no shiny paint showing anywhere.

If I were doing this myself, I would have masked some black weatherstrip moldings, such as those around the trunk, that were susceptible to overspray through seams.

There's a method of masking called "backtaping" you can use to seal door (or other) seams, and I understand 3M even makes a sort of tubular tape for this now. One good thing about newer cars is that they no longer have rubber gaskets around door handles. The only thing needing taping was the keyhole, which took a little cutting and prodding of tape with an X-Acto knife.

I personally don't see why any straight, non-metallic color needs a clear coat (other than, possibly, for UV protection if you're going to leave it out in the sun). Straight colors, metallics, and even metallics with pearls can all be ordered in one-stage paints that dry very glossy, like new-car paint from the factory. If that's all you need, sand the car, mask it, and shoot it (with the doors shut) in its original color, and you're done. Even if you choose base coat/clear coat, you don't *have* to rub out the clear if you can spray it on smooth and glossy enough. On the other hand, since you're using catalyzed paint, you *can* rub out either a clear coat or a one-stage color coat a day or two after you paint it, or maybe a year or two later, when the paint job needs a "tune-up." See how much you're learning from this book?

Even More Basic

Okay, let's say you've got an old bomb of some sort that you want to fix up some, or are in the process of fixing up, but you're not ready for (or maybe don't even want) a full, glossy paint job. The original color is immaterial—if you can even tell what it was. But you're not a fan of the "patina" or polka-dot look. You'd like the car at least all one color or shade. Why not do like the hot rodders in the old days did—primer it? It's an in look again, often referred to as "suede." But, unlike

But these guys, who usually do partial paint jobs (spot-ins) on newer cars, went to town masking off the trunk, engine, and all door seams so no overspray would get anywhere. I don't think that's necessary. A little rubbing compound usually quickly removes what overspray gets in doorjambs, etc. But I hate masking. It's up to you; you've only got yourself to please.

the old days when the basic choices were grey, black, or red-oxide lacquer primers, which happened to be water-absorbant, we have much better choices today.

The most practical, if you really are in the process of fixing up the car, is to spray the whole vehicle with a good, catalyzed, high-fill primer. Different brands come in different colors, usually some shade of gray. My advice here is don't put the primer over dirty, flaky, unsanded, or otherwise unstable paint, and especially not over rust, unless you fully intend to strip the car (and fix the rust) before painting it for real.

If you're not into shiny paint at all, I'd still recommend cleaning, sanding, and at least moderately prepping the surface. But choices of easy-to-paint suede finishes are now almost limitless, and are

Once all the sanding and masking was done (note they used masking paper and tape to cover the wheels), they cleaned the whole surface with a silicone-remover (notice the dry rag in one hand to wipe off the cleaner before it dries), followed by a thorough wiping with a tack cloth.

out adding a clear coat. Done! For even less-glossy blacks you can try an "anti-glare" black or something called "Trim Black," as used on hoods of '70s muscle cars and other areas of newer cars. Finally, the automotive paint shop can

with a clear coat. Since it's clear, how much you mask is your choice. Now, I must admit I've never done this, and I don't think I've seen anyone else do it. But why not? If the paint is just faded, scuffing it down and clearing it would

One problem I hadn't expected was that the color layer on many new cars is so thin that even this mild scuff-down went through to primer in a few areas, especially along body creases. So the painter mixed up a little base coat matched to the white on the car, and touched up any areas where primer was starting to show through. Since a pearl coat is translucent, the color you're painting it over must be uniform.

universally catalyzed-type paints that do not absorb water, and therefore protect the metal from further rust. The simplest way to suede paint is just to spray a base coat—in whatever color you want, from black to metallics or pearls—with-

Finally it was time to spray the white pearl over the white base. It must be sprayed very evenly over the whole body, and this painter pointed out that spraying pearl in dry, thin coats is best.

add a "flattener" or "flattening agent" to any paint you choose, including clears, and they can add more or less of it to "adjust" the gloss to the percentage you want. As I said, make friends with the people at your local automotive paint store. They can probably do things with paint you never thought of.

On the other hand, maybe you like glossy, but you're not too particular about the color. Whatever finish is on the vehicle now, you could always scuff it down, quickly mask it off, and shoot it

Spray just enough pearl to get a good, shimmery, pearlescent effect. Spraying too much makes it milky or splotchy. You don't want splotchy.

actually be easier (and longer lasting) than buffing it out as we show in Chapter 1—and you wouldn't have to worry about buffing through the color. Just remember that whatever is on the surface—including previous clear that is now peeling or chalky—shows through a new layer of clear. At the other extreme, if the vehicle is old and has a nice patina, and you want to keep it looking the way it is, you could squirt it with a coat of clear with flattener in it to "arrest the decay." These are just possibilities. They're not guaranteed.

Unlike pearls of old, which were mixed into clear lacquer, today's are usually mixed as base coats, which makes them easier to spray. It dries to a satin-like finish, which hopefully shows in this photo. Most paint companies offer various shades of pearl as custom colors, but several—especially whites—are used on new cars. I chose one from a new Lexus that was particularly bright and white—and gives me a specific color code for ordering more in the future if necessary, in any brand of paint.

If you're painting at home, it's best to let the car dry or "cure" overnight before you start unmasking, or driving, it. However, production body shops don't afford that luxury. Fortunately, the modern spray booth in this one included a heating cycle to speed up the curing of the catalyzed paint. After about an hour, we unmasked the car (again, note how tape and paper are pulled back at an angle, away from the paint).

The extra masking certainly kept doorjambs and similar areas clean, but this photo also demonstrates that a pearl coat matched to the original color of your car is close enough that you don't have to paint the jambs, under the hood, and so on. You don't really notice the difference when the door is opened—and it sure makes the whole paint job a lot easier. Plus it uses much less paint. I got three quarts of pearl, and we only used half of it for this entire car.

Pearlescent paint is very hard to show in printed photographs, but hopefully you can see the sparkle and glimmer. This car might still look a bit like a refrigerator—but a much prettier, classier one.

THE FULL JOB

The example for our complete paint job is a semi-rare 427 big-block, 4-speed, '67 Stingray Corvette that was essentially restored, but got painted a previous-year Milano Maroon instead of the correct Marlboro Maroon. John Harvey, who does custom bodywork and painting on a limited basis in a large shop he has built on his property South of Albuquerque, New Mexico, was therefore given the job of completely repainting a car that was already painted and "finished" by someone else. This is how it looked after he repainted it in the correct color.

After removing all external trim and the interior door panels, John started by wet sanding all painted areas of the body with 360-grit paper. Note in these photos that it is masked along the rockers and rear pan to keep the already detailed chassis clean.

In the previous chapters, we've laid a foundation covering the tools, skills and knowledge you needed to paint your own vehicle in your own garage. By now—or the second time you read this when you're ready to do the job—you have taken care of any dings, dents, or scrapes in the body; removed all readily accessible non-painted body parts like bumpers, badges, mirrors, handles, and so on; equipped your garage with the tools you need to do both bodywork and painting; cleaned and prepared your garage; sanded, primed, and otherwise prepped the body of your vehicle for paint; learned how to mask parts or areas that aren't easily removed, or can't be; made friends with your local automotive paint store employees; and figured out what types of paints, sealers, reducers, and so on you need to do the job you want to do on your car.

If you decided that your car's prior finish really needed to be removed, using a chemical stripper at home, you have also completed that step. If so, all the bare metal should be bodyworked, primed, blocked, and sanded down to 320 or 360 grit.

We've talked about things like detailing the undercarriage and engine now, or after the paint job. We assume you've decided one course or the other—but in any case for this stage of paint job you should have at least cleaned the under-

Note a few primer spots on the body. John found a few areas that needed a bit more priming and sanding to eliminate imperfections that showed up after the first paint job shrank a bit. He is wet sanding this area with 360 paper and a rubber pad.

In Chapter 6 we talked about the necessity and difficulty of sanding in hard-to-reach places, such as door-jambs and especially around hinges. Here is a pertinent example. Since this car had been fully sanded and prepped before the recent paint job, and since he was going to use an adhesion sealer, John decided that this was adequate sanding for this job in the hinge area. If you want it Concours-perfect, you have to remove the doors and hinges, as you see in the next chapter.

carriage and engine compartment of all grease, sludge and other assorted road grungies by having them steam-cleaned, pressure-washed, or by removing them yourself with a scraper, wire brush, and lots of Gunk, Simple Green, or other degreaser. You want to get all the grease and oil off the car (top, bottom, inside, out), *before* you put any new paint products on the sheetmetal.

By this point you must also know whether you are going to reupholster the car, and whether you need to replace some or all of the window glass. If you're going to do either, do it *after* you paint the car—in fact, we'd strongly suggest waiting until after you color sand and rub-out the car, if that's what you plan to do. There's always the chance that the upholsterer or glass man might put a

Optimally, you would have upholstery installed after painting is done, but this car was supposedly finished before the new owner decided to correct the color. So John protected the seats, dash, etc., with coverings during sanding and partial disassembly.

John removed the door panels to simplify masking and painting, but also to access outside door handles for removal. Of course door windows must be masked inside and out. You may notice some remnants of weather stripping on the door, which would usually be cleaned and sanded. But this car recently had new door rubbers installed. John removed (rather than trying to mask) them, but left these areas as-is so they would glue back exactly as they came off.

But before any painting, he sealed off both door openings completely with masking tape and paper, being sure to seal all seams in the paper with tape.

Of course the engine compartment was done and detailed, most of which was painted semi-flat black. So John covered or masked everything except the strip around the edges that had to be body color.

These cowl vents have chrome grilles that go over them, but they're a good example of an opening in the body that should be masked and sealed so that (1) paint or overspray won't enter the interior through it, and (2) no dirt or dust blows out of this cavity into your wet paint as you're spraying the car.

scratch or two in your new paint. Touching up some minor paint scratches is easier than trying to clean paint off of new upholstery or carpet; and, if you're going to take glass out, it's always best to repaint window openings before new rubber and glass is reinstalled.

Let's discuss glass first. If you're working on an older car that has rubber moldings around the windshield and other areas (i.e., back glass, wind wings), and (1) the glass is broken, pitted, foggy, or otherwise needs replacing, (2) the rubber molding is cracked or brittle, or (3) the windows leak water, anywhere, then you should remove the glass and either have it replaced, or at least replace the rubber moldings—which requires removal of the glass, either way. New rubber—not to mention new windshields—are now available for a surprisingly wide variety of older cars. Check with your

auto glass shop and peruse the ads in specialty car magazines. We talk more about glass removal and replacement in the next chapter. Read ahead if your vehicle needs this work.

Most people doing the typical in-the-garage do-it-yourself repaint job are not going to be pulling all the glass out of the car. Sanding down the existing paint, including the wet-sanding process, is a much easier and cleaner job if all the glass is still in the car and shut. That means you have to mask off the windows to start painting. On older cars that have rubber moldings, one trick is to lift up the lip of the rubber and slip a small piece of rope or cord (like clothesline) underneath it all the way around, to hold the rubber away from the metal so paint can get under it. This also makes masking the windows much easier. However, if this molding includes chrome or

stainless trim embedded in the rubber, do not try to remove this trim. Most types can only be removed/replaced in the loose rubber molding before it is installed on the glass. Then the entire glass/rubber/trim assembly is installed as a unit, and we recommend that you let a professional glass man do this after you paint the car. We're getting a bit ahead, but the point is if the glass has stainless

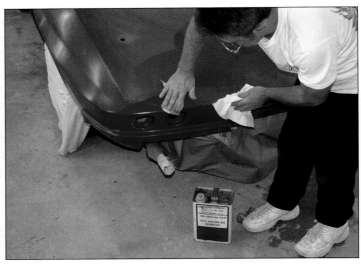

John of course used the air gun to blow sanding dust off the exterior and to blow out the interior, under the hood, in wheelwells, and so on, before starting the masking process. But once the car is all masked, it's time for a thorough cleaning with wax and grease remover, once again (you should have done this before sanding, too—remember?). John clearly demonstrates the wet-rag/dry-rag proper method of application.

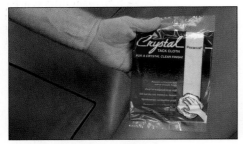

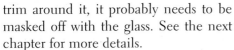

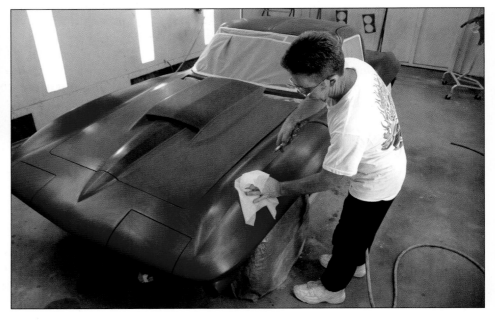

Although John has the luxury of a spray booth, we assume you've cleaned and sealed your garage as much as possible already (see Chapter 4), and turned on your exhaust fan. Right before you start spraying, it's best to open a fresh tack rag and use it, with your blow gun, to remove any remaining lint, dust, or dirt specs from the surface.

trim around it, it probably needs to be masked off with the glass. See the next chapter for more details.

Whether or not you'll be reupholstering the car, mask off the interior at the door openings. Depending on the age of the vehicle, there's a lot of stuff in there that's either metal or plastic that you don't want to get paint on. If your car happens to be of the pre-padded-dash era, and you need to repaint the dashboard as well as parts like the window frames, steering column, and so on (either because they *need* repainting, or because of a color change) then you've got a bunch of extra work to do. We don't need to tell you how. You can remove things like window frames and paint them outside the car, but in most cases you have to paint parts like the dash and steering column where they are; it's a tedious process of disassembly, sanding, and masking, and using a small touch-up gun to do the painting so you can get into tight quarters. As with everywhere else, be sure to mask carefully and thoroughly so paint doesn't go where you don't want it.

In all cases, the vehicle's age greatly affects your approach. Newer cars have lots of plastic, glue-in windows, and very little rubber molding. You must do lots of masking. On many older cars and pickups, even at this stage of paint, it's easier to rip everything out of the interior (if you're having it all redone)—headliner, windlace, carpet, sill strips, and so on—and not worry about masking off much inside. In some cases, glass has to be removed just to install a new headliner properly. Ask your upholsterer about this.

Jambing It

Any good-quality paint job should include fresh paint on the doorjambs, particularly, and any other visible painted surfaces. But if you're going to change the color of the car from what it was originally, you *must* paint all previously painted areas to do any decent kind of paint job on your vehicle.

One thing we haven't discussed in this book is how to choose a color for your car, and we won't, really. The simplest, quickest, easiest, and cheapest approach is to paint it the same color it was to start with. That way you can get by without painting the doorjambs, and you certainly don't have to paint under the hood and trunk, or in the interior. One twist on this that we have discussed is to spray a coat of similar-color pearl over the existing factory paint. You can do this without painting jambs and other such areas (as we showed in Chapter 8), or you can go the extra distance and shoot the pearl elsewhere, as we show here.

Otherwise, what can *we* tell you about what color to paint your car? Pick any color you want. There's virtually no limit. Look through the color chip books at the paint store. Look at all the vehicles on the freeway and streets. Look at the clothes in your closet. Look at the flowers in your garden. Choose any color you like. The only limitation is that if you change the color of the car from what it was originally, to do the job right, you've got to paint more than the outside of the car. Much more. One painter I knew long ago, who prided himself on the thoroughness of his work, used to bet people they

Be sure to blow out anything that might have settled in the masking paper, and tack-wipe all paint surfaces, including doorjambs, hood compartment, and so on.

Note John doesn't wet down the floor (which we also don't recommend), but he does take the extra precaution of grounding the car chassis to the floor with a piece of chain. All that wiping can create static electricity, which can magnetize dust and lint to the surface, especially in a dry climate like New Mexico.

Even if you're not taking the car all apart, there are bound to be some extraneous parts that need painting, and it's best to do them at the same time you're spraying base coats and clear coats on the vehicle. Pro shops have all sorts of stands and hangers for odd-shaped parts. At home you can use boxes, sawhorses, coat-hanger hooks from ceiling beams—whatever works. Just make sure they're clean and out of the way while you're spraying the car.

couldn't tell, by looking anywhere they wanted on the vehicle he had just painted, what color it was to start with. How far you want to go with your repaint depends on how important it is to you and how much work you want to do. You don't have to bet anybody. Satisfy yourself.

Let's start with the doorjambs. You could prepare, mask, and sand the

jambs—and under hood and trunk—first, as in the old days when painters did them in lacquer, let them dry for 20 minutes, then shut the doors and paint the outside of the car in enamel. If you're going to color sand and rub-out the paint, it doesn't make much difference if you get overspray from the jambs onto the body, or vice versa. Let's say you want to

Since the surface was all painted to start with, John didn't need an etching primer or a sealer, as such, but he wisely decided to start with a clear DuPont product appropriately called "Mid-Coat Adhesion Promoter." He started by spraying a thin layer inside the engine compartment and doorjambs.

Then he sprayed a similar thin coat over the whole car. Note the clean wheel/tire covers he has installed.

Since mixing paint with reducer/catalyst doesn't take long (especially with marked mixing cups, as shown), and you must throw away any unused mixed paint, most painters I've observed mix paint one spray gun cup-full (usually one quart) at a time. John is filling his gravity-feed HVLP gun through a strainer in his home-made stand.

Individual painters have their own methods for spraying a car, but most start at the top and then work down and around. Starting the base-coat color, John has sprayed the top, and is working down the right door.

Then he works around the car clockwise.

paint the doorjambs, under the hood, and in the trunk first. Fine. The first step, especially in the jambs, is to clean the area, particularly in the pockets around the hinges, of all dirt and oil. I'd recommend lacquer thinner here. Next, remove all rubber weatherstripping around the doors, around the trunk, wherever it might be. (If replacement weatherstrip is not available—which is rare—you must take the existing seals off very carefully, without cutting or tearing them, so you can glue them back on later.) It's usually glued on, and takes some work to get off.

Start with something like a putty knife or straight-edge razor blade in a holder. Get as much of the rubber off as you can this way. Once you get the rubber off, use a combination of 3M General Purpose Adhesive Cleaner (part no. 08984; every painter—every garage—should have a can of this stuff on hand at all times) and medium sandpaper to get all rubber and glue residue off the surface. Then, assuming you want to do a *good* paint job on your car, carefully sand the entire door jamb, as well as the areas under the hood and trunk, just as well and as thoroughly as you've sanded and prepped the outside of the car. Maybe you really don't care how your doorjambs look. Hardly any-

body sees them. But to those who look, it reveals the big difference between an okay paint job and a really good one. Also, since they're hard to get into and sand properly, especially around the hinge area which may have some paint-repelling lubricant on it, this is an area that is prone to improper preparation and the first place new paint will peel back off. If you care about such things, get in there and prepare it right.

Since you're painting the doorjambs, remove the interior door panels, window frames (if any), and possibly the door glass at this stage. On older cars, removing the upholstered door panels is pretty simple. On newer cars, with power windows, power mirrors, stereo speakers, power locks, and who knows what else in the doors, it can get quite complicated. In such cases—not to mention removal and replacement of

After one coat on the exterior, he opens the doors and hood and sprays inside, being sure to get down under the bottoms of the doors.

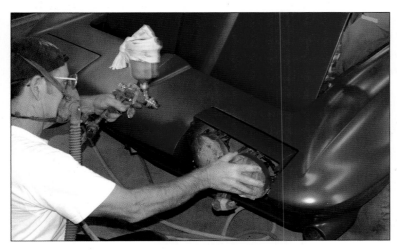

On the Stingray, he had to tilt up the pre-masked headlights and spray the otherwise hidden areas.

Areas that far too many painters miss or spray inadequately are inside the wheelwells and at the bottom of rocker panels. You really have to get down to see what you're doing here, and you need good side lighting to do so.

A basic rule of spray painting, especially with metallic colors (and definitely with an HVLP gun, as John is using), is that two even, thin coats are better than one thick one. The base coat dries quickly, and you can usually start your second go-around as soon as you have completed all the steps we have just shown for the first one. Note particularly how John is holding his gun parallel to the surface as he sprays, and how he holds the air hose (and his body) away from the freshly painted surface.

glass, body trim, "bumpers," and other components—we strongly suggest that you purchase a factory shop manual for your specific year, make, and model of car. They can be expensive, but are well worth the time and frustration saved in many otherwise stupefying procedures. (Besides, valuable repair information is included, too.) If your car isn't new enough to get one at your dealer's parts counter, at least one auto specialty bookstore—AutoBooks, 3524 W. Magnolia Bl., Burbank, CA 91505; 818/845-0707—carries many in stock, can order what's available new, and has sources for older volumes.

One way to proceed from here is to prepare and paint the doorjambs, hood and trunk areas first and let them dry a full day. Then close the doors, hood, and trunk, scuff any overspray off the outside surface around them, and paint the whole outside of the car. Some painters like to "backtape" the openings so overspray won't get into the jambs and other areas—in fact, there's a special "round" type of tape for this purpose. But if you're going to color sand the car, the overspray in these areas easily sands off in the process.

There are two alternatives for paint jobs that aren't getting rubbed out. One is to either paint the jambs, etc., first, let them dry, mask them off, then paint the outside of the car. Probably easier is to

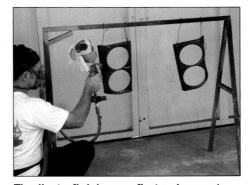

Finally, to finish your first color coat, don't forget the extra parts you have hanging or propped up nearby.

Another basic rule of paint spraying is not to add more paint than you need, especially for a color coat that will be clear coated. The color you're spraying and the color(s) you're spraying it over will determine how many coats you need for complete, even coverage (on the outer surface as well as in the jambs, etc.). In this case two coats were plenty before John started laying on the clear coat, which, as you can see, goes on very glossy compared to the matte-finish base coat.

Note the doors and hood are never fully closed in any of the photos. After a clear coat over the outside, John opens all hatches and sprays inside.

paint the outside of the car with everything shut; then sand any overspray off the jambs, etc., fully mask around them to keep overspray off the outside of the car, and paint them. But this leaves a tape edge around all the openings and door edges.

Here's one trick for semi-lazy painters: sand and prep the whole car, including jambs, etc. Then shut everything, mask off the windows, and paint the outside, either in a 1-stage color you intend to rub out, or in base coat/clear coat. Let this dry. Then open doors, trunk, and so on, scuff down any overspray in these areas, mask off the interior openings as necessary and the inside of the door glass (and whatever else needs masking), and spray the jambs, under the hood, and inside the trunk with a glossy, 1-stage paint the same color as the outside, that doesn't need to be rubbed out. After that dries, close everything again, and color-sand and rub out the exterior. Any overspray from painting the jambs gets sanded off in the process. When you're done and have cleaned up all the mess, you have a glossy outside, glossy jambs, and no tape lines.

The above method primarily pertains to metallic or metallic-with-pearl colors where you want a base coat/clear

Then he does it all again for a second full coat. With clear, it's especially important to get full coverage in hard-to-see places like the wheelwells and lower body panels. You may have also noticed John keeps a clean rag tied around the top of his paint gun cup as insurance against any drips from the lid or vent hole. It's a habit from siphon-cup days, but one drip can spoil a paint coat.

After spraying the hood stripe with gloss black, John finished the job by color sanding and rubbing out the car and then reassembling everything. Even though the owner essentially built this car for resale, after addition of the correct wheel trim rings, he had it judged by the National Corvette Restorers' Society, which gave it the prestigious Top Flight Award. Not bad, John!

coat/rub out on the outside, but just a single-stage gloss paint with no rub out in the "hidden" areas. Of course, you could very well follow the same process using a base coat and clear coat on the jambs and other "inside" areas, but just not rub out the clear in these areas.

The All-at-Once

With so many colors being base coat/clear coat these days, the method most painters are using for this level of paint job is the one we illustrate here. In fact, it works fine for 1-stage or 2-stage paints; and it works equally well if you're going to rub out just the outside, the outside and the jambs, or just leave the whole thing glossy-as-sprayed. What we're talking about, very simply (as you see in the photos) is to prep and sand everything, inside and out, mask everything that you don't want paint on — glass, interior, engine, etc. — and then paint everything at the same time: the outside, the doorjambs, under the hood, under the trunk, or wherever else you might need to paint. Paint as many stages as your chosen type of paint requires. Then let it all dry overnight, masked, with the doors and other parts at least partially open. The accompanying photos show how it's done.

With all bodywork finished and the whole vehicle sanded, the cleaning, masking, base coats, and clear coats all took less than half a day for our example. This particular Corvette restoration required some black stripes painted last — that's the way the factory did it. Then everything was rubbed out, all the weatherstrip rubber and stuff like under-hood insulation was glued back in place, parts such as outside door handles, emblems, and bumpers were bolted back on, the inside door panels and sill strips were replaced, and it was done. You can do the same in your garage, and save several thousand bucks.

How To Spray Paint

The only way to learn how to spray paint is to do it. Practice. Make runs and drips. Make orange peel. Make fisheyes. Keep practicing until you start to get a feel for the spraying process: how close or far away to hold the sprayer; how to move your hand to make even passes; how much to overlap; where to start and stop; how much paint to put on to make it smooth (without orange peel or dry spray), without letting it run or sag. You can practice with your spray gun and compressor, but I strongly suggest you start with spray cans. It's quicker and cheaper. Start small and work your way up. I mean literally small. I started with model cars and bicycle frames. Those are the kinds of things spray cans are made to paint. You won't learn much trying to paint big garbage cans with spray bombs; stick to things more the size of buckets. Or skinny things like wrought iron fences or chairs with rungs.

The first step is to clean the object (soap and water, wax and grease remover, or even cheap lacquer thinner on a rag). This should eliminate fisheye or separation problems. Second, sand the object to get rid of any scale, cracks, and crud, or just to scuff up the surface for adhesion. Paint doesn't like to adhere to a slick, shiny surface.

One of the best "tricks" to learn with spray cans is to start with a light, quick, dust coat. Don't try to put a layer of color on the surface with your first application. Move the can quickly, and waft it back and forth in several directions, just enough to get a very light, even, slightly sticky coat of paint all over

Turning the fan control knob in (clockwise) reduces the width of the fan pattern for spraying smaller areas. When you do this, you should also reduce the fluid flow rate by turning in the second knob down (on this gun), plus reduce air pressure slightly with the knob where the hose connects to the gun.

Most of the time you are spraying with the fan and fluid control adjusted wide open, and the nozzle turned so the fan sprays vertically, as shown.

Continued on page 122

How To Spray Paint CONTINUED

it. This is what's called a "tack coat." Let this dry for about five minutes. Then spray your first color coat over this. Keep it thin, and spray in smooth, long passes, overlapping each pass about 50% as you move from left-to-right, then right-to-left, but make this coat cover the object in color—just enough color to cover it. Let this dry 10 to 15 minutes, then spray another smooth, thin color coat. When it looks like the object is fully and evenly covered in the new color, after waiting another 15 minutes or so, make another pass, moving your hand a bit slower so you spray more paint (but not too much!), hopefully producing a smooth and glossy surface. This is, of course, called the "gloss coat." If the first full pass around the object being painted doesn't look shiny or smooth enough, try going around it once more, right away. This is where you learn to spray paint. Unfortunately the type of paint in the can (and other things, like the weather) affects it. But it either gets smooth and glossy, or it gets runs. Keep practicing until you get it smooth and glossy.

Mixing and "Adjusting" the Paint

Okay, let's move to the real stuff. Virtually all automotive paints, new and old, require thinning with what we now call "reducers" to make them the correct consistency for spraying. This is done for several reasons, beginning with the fact that it's easier to store and mix paint colors in smaller amounts. But the real reason for adding the reducer at the time of painting is to allow the painter to adjust not only the consistency of the paint, but also its drying rate, to match his own spraying preferences and weather conditions, specifically temperature. So automotive paint, itself, is "adjustable" in two ways: you can control its viscosity (how thick it is), and how quickly it dries. In the old days of straight enamels and lacquers, thinning allowed much more flexibility. The recommended reduction might be anywhere from one to two parts thinner to one part paint, and thinners came in at least fast, medium, and slow speeds. These variables affected only the paint's spraying viscosity and its drying rate, not how it "cured" or its long-term stability. The rule of thumb was that you didn't want the paint too thick—you wanted it to "lay out" rather than orange peel; and in most climates, especially with lacquer, you didn't want the paint to dry too fast, because that would lead to a condition called

"dry spray," which is a pebbly overspray on the surface. Painters who had to work in cold weather in non-heated shops needed to speed up drying times.

Who knows what the paint variables might be in the future when we get water-based or other types of paints perfected? But for now, with catalyzed paints, things are much more stringent than they used to be when it comes to mixing paints and their various additives. Some materials—certain sealers, primers, and clears—take no reducer at all. Add exactly the amount of catalyst, sometimes called "hardener," specified, and spray it. Several other types of paints—mostly base coat colors these days—use what's called a "reactive reducer," which has the chemical catalyzing agent in it. These should generally be mixed in the exact proportions specified, so you can't adjust viscosity much, but the reducers do come in different temperature ranges, usually denoted by the number on the can. For instance, PPG DRR-1185 is a reactive reducer (RR) meant to be sprayed in an 85-degree environment. If you find your paint drying too quickly, switch to a higher-number reducer, say 1195, which dries slower (the opposite, of course, pertains as well).

One important note: I don't know the chemical specifics, but these reactive reducers have a short shelf life once they're opened to air. Within a week or so, they go bad, and there is no way to test them or tell this, until you mix and spray some paint and it comes out splotchy and weird. Hopefully, in time, they'll improve on this.

A third type of current paint takes a specific, small amount of catalyst, and a reducer, which not only comes in different temperature ranges but can also be increased or decreased within limits to "adjust" paint viscosity. Again, unless you're painting in really cold weather (which is not generally advised, anyway), the rule of thumb—if your paint is "adjustable"—is to mix it a bit on the slower and thinner side, rather than vice versa.

Adjusting the Gun

Excluding pressure pots, which we're not considering, every type of automotive spray gun—siphon-feed, gravity-feed, HVLP, non-HVLP, touch-up, whatever—has three adjustments: air pressure, fan control, and fluid control. Most HVLP guns have an air pressure valve, and dial gauge, attached to the gun. Other types don't, but

122   HOW TO PAINT YOUR CAR ON A BUDGET

we strongly advise you add one, with or without a gauge, where the air hose attaches to the gun. It's air pressure at the gun that counts, and needs to be controlled steadily. The fan control knob on the gun widens or narrows the paint fan pattern, so the paint covers a larger or smaller area as you paint. Note that the gun's nozzle or spray tip can be loosened and turned for a vertical or horizontal fan. Most automotive painting is done with a wide fan in the vertical spray position, as you move the gun horizontally—left and right—while painting the body of the car. Certain smaller areas are easier to paint with the fan adjusted narrower, and vertical areas (such as door-jambs) where you're moving the gun up and down, are easiest to paint with the tip turned to a horizontal fan.

Most automotive painting is done with the fan and fluid controls wide open and the pressure set to what is compatible with the type of paint and type of gun you're using. When you narrow the fan pattern, you are still spraying the same amount of paint in a smaller area, and its velocity increases. That's what the fluid control is for: when you decrease the fan width, decrease the paint flow proportionally with the fluid control knob, so it covers properly without running. You do this by feel and experience. Likewise, you usually want to decrease the air pressure in the same manner, for the same reasons. That's really all there is to gun adjustment. However, if

When spraying, keep the gun the same distance from the surface at all times. The old rule was a hand's-width (6 to 8 inches) away, but painters using HVLP guns tend to hold it closer, which makes sense because the pressure is lower. In any case, holding the gun too close causes runs; holding it too far away causes orange peel or, worse, a rough, "pebbly" surface. Too much or too little air pressure and fluid flow produces the same problems.

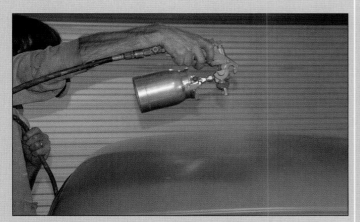

When using the wide, vertical fan pattern, you should hold the gun parallel to the surface as you spray. It's not as easy as it looks, especially in the middle of a roof. Keep a step stool handy, if necessary. This example is close, but not quite right as the bottom of the cup is too close—the gun is not parallel.

you're resetting adjustments on your gun, it's best to test it on something other than your car, to see if you've got it right. I use the side of a trash can.

On the other hand, you can't adjust a spray gun if it's not working properly. If the gun sprays more paint at the outer ends of the fan than in the middle or vice versa, or if it "spits" while you're spraying or sprays unevenly in any other way, you need to clean, fix, or replace the gun. This assumes that your air compressor is 1) functioning properly; 2) big enough to keep up with your gun, and 3) designed for an HVLP gun, if that's what you're using. Thoroughly clean every gun after each use by spraying lots of cheap hardware-store lacquer thinner through it and wiping it dry. Do not use sharp objects, such as wire, to clean the gun. And periodically add a few drops of light oil to (or replace) the packing around the needle so it doesn't leak air. A good gun that gets worn can be rebuilt; cheap ones can be replaced.

Continued on page 124

How To Spray Paint CONTINUED

Not only do you need to keep the gun parallel to the surface (viewed from the side) as you spray, but you also need to keep it perpendicular to it, as viewed from the top.

In other words, keep the gun the same distance from the surface throughout a full pass from side-to-side. Do not swing it in an arc, so that it's angled to the surface at the ends of the pass, like this.

Spraying Paint

Once you've got the paint mixed properly, and the gun adjusted, the only magic left to painting is the motion and operation of the gun. This, as we've said repeatedly, requires practice to develop the proper "feel" for spray painting. But the basic pointers are simple.

For most types of paint, hold the nozzle about eight inches (an outstretched hand-width) from the surface at all times—when making a pass, do not swing the gun in an arc. Most painters spray panels that are a full arm's width at a time, top to bottom, then step to the next panel, and repeat. If you need to step side-to-side as you're painting a wide panel, to keep the nozzle the same distance from the surface at all times, do so. Pull the trigger to start spraying paint as you begin the pass, and let go to stop spraying at the end of the pass. Then move halfway down the spray pattern, and start your pass back, pulling the trigger as you begin to move your hand the opposite direction. Do not pull the gun away, or move it down, while still spraying.

Keep the gun nozzle perpindicular to the surface at all times, whether you're spraying the roof, side, or in a wheelwell lip. Many painters are careless about this, and it leads to uneven coats.

Finally, most painters like to start painting at the top of the vehicle (i.e., roof) and work down, in a rotational pattern. This is so any overspray that falls on the surface gets painted over (and hopefully melted in), rather than falling on top of fresh paint. For similar reasons, you want to paint panels consecutively around the car, so that you are overlapping the wettest paint with new wet paint, allowing it to blend together. Most painters spray, for instance, the whole top, then the hood, then the left side, then the trunk, then the right side.

Your goal is to get an even color coat on the vehicle, without streaks, splotches, or darker areas where paint overlaps. Of secondary importance is minimizing dry overspray at the edges of panels. This is more important with clear coats or color gloss coats that won't be cleared. It's extremely important if you don't intend to rub out the finish. The trick is to spray your final gloss coat (color or clear) quickly and fairly heavily, so that it all stays wet from start to finish. This is easier said than done.

One last general rule of spray painting: the days of "40 hand-rubbed coats" are long gone, and were bad to begin with. Paint and metal have different coefficients of expansion, and cars are subjected to wide variations in temperature, especially going from the garage to the open, hot sun and back. You want the minimum amount of paint (including primers, etc.) on the car as possible. You must put on enough color to cover properly. And you've got to spray enough clear or color to allow for color-sanding and rub out without fear of rubbing through—and even, preferably, allowing for a second rub out later—if you're going to rub it out. But adding thick, multiple layers of paint (or primer, without sanding most of it back off), only leads to cracking, splitting, and checking as the paint ages and is subjected to the elements.

*G*OING *F*URTHER

Although this one isn't over-restored like so many, and it does get driven, Jim McNiel's historic Hirohata Merc custom is probably finished better now than it was the first time. It's even won a couple Concours trophies already. But the body still hasn't ever been off the frame.

The paint job outlined in the last chapter is by far the most common, whether in professional bodyshops or in home garages. It's the type I have done on the majority of my own cars.

Now we're going to take it further, by removing all glass, doors, trunk, interior, probably driveline, maybe even the body from the frame.

I did one paint job in which the car was completely stripped of interior, glass, driveline, and front-end sheetmetal, but the body was left on the frame and the doors and trunk were never removed. The reason these were left on (they were fully gutted of glass, handles, latches, etc.) was because they fit fine, had never been hit or removed since the

Despite the seemingly simple list of basic building/painting steps we presented in Chapter 1, we have already seen numerous cases where that sequence shouldn't, or couldn't, be followed. The restoration of the famous Hirohata '51 Mercury, built in the Barris Kustom shops in '52–'53, actually follows that recipe closer than it might appear. Longtime owner/keeper/restorer of the car, Jim McNiel, began by rebuilding the engine and mechanicals (painting and chroming parts as he did so). After removing all external trim, we showed the car being stripped to bare metal in Jim's garage in Chapter 2. After he did minor bodywork, Jim etched, sealed, and applied several coats of high-fill primer to the body, block sanding several times between coats. That was the state of the car in this photo, in Jim's garage, when time began running out for the car to be finished in time for a large museum exhibit.

That's when Hershel " Junior" Conway, who began his illustrious painting career at George Barris' shop as a teen, volunteered to paint the car, in original lacquers, in his shop in the short time available. With Junior steering and Jim helping, this is how the car looked as it left Jim's driveway.

car was built in 1953, and this vehicle was completely media-blasted, which removed all existing paint, primers, dirt, and so on, inside and out of all components. Removing the front sheetmetal and original driveline not only allowed easier installation of new front suspension and engine and transmission mounts, but also made it easy to modify, detail, and paint the firewall before anything else.

Naturally there was a lot of trial-fitting of components along the way, but

As soon as the car got to Junior's, he removed the doors, hood, trunk, all window glass, and then masked off the engine compartment, interior, and even most of the undercarriage. The front fenders and splash aprons couldn't be detached since they were welded and leaded to the body. Then, even though it had been blocked several times already, Junior added more primer and did lots more block sanding, with several helpers. Note the guide-coated door in the background.

generally the process went like this: the firewall and body (including jambs, inside trunk, etc.), were painted first, along with the hood, front fenders, splash aprons, and so on separately. The dash and window frames were painted a different color to match the upholstery. All the painted components were color

You can see that the rear window and side glass have been removed, with their custom moldings, but the headliner is still in place, so these areas had to be fully masked. Junior is carefully hand-sanding the side-window lip, especially in the tight corner where it meets the top.

All this preparation makes the actual spraying of paint onto the body relatively easy. The reason Junior is wearing a simple mask is because PPG provided old-style (non-toxic) lacquer for this restoration. How he lays it down so smooth and glossy, I have no idea (other than decades of practice).

A spray booth is not critical for lacquer, especially without clear, such as this. While he did the body and doors in the booth, he did the other parts in the shop, either propped on stands or hanging from racks.

Several things here: Removing the doors allows access to the otherwise impossible-to-reach area around the hinges and inside the front fender. It also allows easy and thorough sanding of the jamb areas of the doors (which Jim is doing), as well as in the body. And you can see Junior spends as much time and attention sanding down under the rocker moldings as he does on more visible body areas.

sanded and rubbed out. Then the frame was sanded and painted gloss black with spray cans, the underside of the floorboards were similarly sprayed with black undercoating, and certain under-car and under-hood parts, such as the gas tank, were sprayed body color. Meanwhile the engine and driveline parts were assembled, painted, and detailed separately, and then installed. Next came all new glass, including rubber gaskets, channels, and felt strips, at a glass shop. Then the front sheetmetal was very carefully reinstalled and aligned, and all chrome trim, grille, bumpers, and so on were added. Finally, new gauges were installed in the dash, along with accessories such as air conditioning and stereo system. The car was fully rewired, and, last, the interior was reupholstered. I mention all this to present the steps of "building" a car in

one real-case scenario. It can vary to some degree in other situations, as we shall see.

People often talk about "frame-off" restorations. That's an incorrect term. I have one car, a '32 Ford roadster, that will get a body-off-frame paint job when it's ready. I've already had the body off the frame a few times. It's no big deal with a car like an early roadster, and it's the type of car that deserves this kind of restoration and paint. But I am not at all a fan of taking big '50s-and–later car bodies off their frames just to paint them. It's usually a waste of time and a huge amount of effort. More importantly, that's not what this book is about. It's about painting your car at home in your garage, so that you can do the quality of job you want, and save a whole lot of dollars doing it yourself. I doubt that your garage is equipped for removing full-size

Besides blocking primer coats, another key to glass-like paint—just as in the old days—is sanding with 400 to 600-grit (or finer) paper between color coats, which Junior is doing here. Note that even the door hinges are painted separately.

We wanted to show Bill Larzelere buffing out the paint here to illustrate that it's easiest (and cleanest) to do the color sand and rub out at this stage, when everything is apart and all masked. Whether it's lacquer or catalyzed paint, however, it's always best to let it dry or cure at least overnight before starting the rub out.

auto bodies from their frames. Which is not to say that you can't do show-quality paint jobs, if you want to, right in your garage. Our example for this chapter is a perfect case in point. One of the most famous custom cars ever built, it won plenty of shows back in the '50s, and has won plenty more since being restored, and its body has never left its frame.

Jim McNiel acquired the once-famous Hirohata full-custom Barris '51 Mercury from the back of a used car lot for $500 in 1959, where it sat forlorn and forgotten. During the next three decades, he did all the restoration work on it himself, in his small, crowded, two-car garage, until an impending deadline for a big museum show convinced him to give it to Hershel "Junior" Conway for paint. Conway, a well-known and highly respected painter of concours-quality classics, who started out painting customs in Barris's Lynwood shop in the 1950s, volunteered his space—Junior's House of Color in Bell Gardens, California—to get the car painted in its original colors of hand-rubbed lacquer in time for the show.

Jim had kept the car indoors for more than 30 years, so it was actually in very good, if well-worn, condition. It did have four different paint jobs on it, but these actually protected the extensive custom bodywork, all done in lead.

Inside, the car still had its original Carson and Gaylord white and green tuck-and-roll upholstery, along with the original, delicate Von Dutch pinstriping on the dashboard. Although the upholstery was worn, Jim wanted to save as much of this as possible.

Jim had started by rebuilding and detailing the engine, running gear, and the chassis under the car. While he had the Cadillac engine out rebuilding it, he repaired cuts, dings, and dents in the firewall and inner fender panels, and painted them gloss black. He painted the frame with his regular spray gun in a semi-flattened black. Painting the engine the same pastel "ice green" as the upper body, which was an excellent contrast to the black engine bay, he reinstalled it and got the car running, and everything working properly, before turning to the external paint job. On a car like this, which was all still together in its historical original form to start with, this was a practical approach. At this point, the only things Jim had taken off the car were the hood, bumpers,

Junior had to mask-off the upper body to spray the darker green lower panel. But once that was done, dry, and unmasked, Bill could rub out both colors at the same time, including inside the doorjambs.

grille, and most of the chrome trim, to have it replated or polished.

Next it was time to strip the many layers of paint off the car, which about six of us did in Jim's garage, using "aircraft" liquid stripper with putty knives and small wire brushes, being very careful not to gouge any of the soft lead on the body (see Chapter 2). Jim

After being painted separately, each of the other parts of the car were also rubbed and buffed, including jambs and edges, before reinstallation. If you're using a power buffer, be sure smaller parts, such as the fender skirts, are held securely so they don't go flying across the room (don't laugh, it's happened far too often).

As we say in the text, putting all the pieces back on the car after they're painted (and especially after their rubbed out) requires extreme care, some helping hands, and preferably a good idea of how they reattach and adjust. If you took them off, you should be able to get them back on. Some protective tape around the edges helps, too.

spread cardboard on the floor to catch the drippings and flakes. Once the car was stripped, Jim prepped the bare metal with an acid etch solution (Metal-Prep), and then some layers of high-fill primer (PPG K200 at that time), and began block sanding. But that's when the show deadline began looming, and Junior said to bring the car over to his shop. Meanwhile, some tech experts at PPG in Detroit were matching carefully saved samples of the original two colors, and mixing them up in real old-style lacquer for this classic custom restoration.

When the car arrived at Junior's, the engine was in and running, the engine compartment was painted and detailed, and—though Jim had removed things like door panels, carpet, and all the trunk upholstery—much of the original interior was in place, such as the head-liner, pinstriped dash, steering wheel, seat, and even the windlace.

Now, you must understand that when a car comes into Junior's shop for a "paint job," (which costs well into five figures, total), it starts with a *complete* disassembly of the vehicle, stripping of the body to bare metal for metal-finishing (not filler bodywork), complete gutting of the interior, and so on. While Junior is prepping and painting all the sheetmetal, his helpers are doing things like having all the original nuts, bolts, and fasteners replated; all chassis and suspension components rebuilt and detailed; all rubber (or plastic) bushings, grommets, and so on replaced; all new wiring installed; things like steering wheels, gauges, and knobs rebuilt—everything.

Most of this Jim did in his garage. But once the car got to Junior's, the paint job itself began with the removal of the hood, doors, trunk, and other body parts such as fender skirts and similar small items. The front fenders, splash pans, and other components on this car couldn't be removed because they were molded into the body. But they also carefully removed the original glass and its custom-made chrome, rubber, or plastic frames. Removing the cut-down front and rear glass and moldings was particularly difficult, not only because these 50-year-old components were custom-made and delicate, but also because they wrapped around the original Carson headliner, which Jim kept in the car.

So the variables in this non-typical Junior paint job included much careful masking and sanding in and around the window-opening areas, both to prepare them for paint and to preserve the

This is how far apart it got. I masked off the interior, engine, and parts of the firewall to paint and rub out the cab. Then, after more cleaning and sanding, I used semi-gloss and gloss black spray cans to paint the frame and chassis parts before putting things back together.

This F-100 should have been stripped of several paint jobs when I got it 20-some years ago. This time it needed some rust holes patched in the lower doors and a new front fender. The plan was to fix and spot-paint these areas. As you can see, that plan has gone awry. Note that even for dry sanding I'm wearing gloves to save my hands.

The rear window stayed in because its rubber seal holds the headliner on the inside, which also didn't come out. The hood needed some serious sanding before getting repainted yellow inside and out.

non-removable portions of the upholstery (i.e., the headliner). Then, once the doors and hinges were removed, they fully masked the entire door openings to keep any paint out of the interior.

Fortunately, the design of the '51 Mercury firewall and inner fenders allows for relatively easy masking of the entire engine and engine compartment. Junior also masked off exposed parts of the already-detailed frame, including under the rocker moldings and in the wheelwells. The fact that this car was

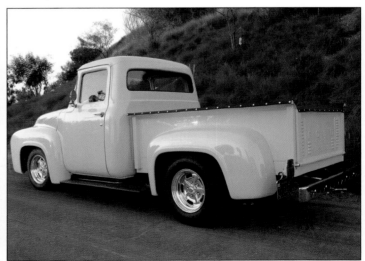

The doors were painted with everything out of them, as were the cab jambs. So not only are the jamb areas sanded and rubbed out smooth, but all the bolts, screws, latches, strikers, and weatherstrip are new or freshly plated. These small details take a lot of work, but make a big visual difference. At right is the finished truck.

being painted in lacquer, rather than catalyzed enamel or urethane, made a big difference in terms of reducing overspray problems.

The point of this chapter is to show that if you want the highest quality paint job *everywhere* on your car—meaning in the doorjambs, around windows, in the trunk, and so on—it's not only necessary, but actually easier in the long run, in terms of sanding, priming, blocking, spraying, and even rubbing out the finish, to remove the doors, trunk, hood, glass, and most everything else that comes off the main body of the car, including the front fenders in most cases. But you don't necessarily have to remove the body from the chassis to paint your car as well as this very famous show car.

Tips and Tricks

Most of this applies to older cars more than new ones, which not only have all sorts of electrical stuff in the doors, but really require a shop manual to tell you how to remove window glass and other such components. If you're doing a color change on a newer car,

you're going to have to paint areas such as doorjambs. But you have to decide whether the work involved makes taking the doors off and glass out worth it. On newer cars, the paint in these areas (i.e., doorjambs) should be in good shape, requiring primarily a good cleaning and scuffing and possibly a coat of a high-adhesion sealer before repainting. But on older cars paint is probably scratched and chipped, if not peeling or rusty, in such areas, and going the extra step of removing doors, etc., makes sense.

Taking off parts like doors and the hood requires some extra hands, and putting them back on after everything is painted really calls for some extra help and care. We could write a whole chapter on how to fit and align body panels. One of the first things the body and paint judges check at any car show is whether all the "gaps" (around doors, between hood and fender, etc.) are equal, and whether all body parts line up with each other.

Door, hood, and trunk hinges are all adjustable in several directions. Fenders and other bolt-on body panels are usually shimmed to fit properly when the car is first assembled. Depending on the age

and brand of vehicle, the assembly line guys might have gotten everything lined up well, or might not have. And if the car has been hit or worked on in its life, who knows who has shimmed or adjusted body parts since it left the factory?

Let's assume, to start with, that the panels on your car fit properly. After you remove and paint parts like doors, then you have to get them back on in exactly the same place. A simple trick most people won't notice is to drill about a 1/8-inch hole through each half of the door, hood, or trunk hinge, into the panel it bolts to, before removing them. When reinstalling a door, for instance, first bolt the hinge loosely to the doorpost (on the body), and insert a 1/8-inch drill bit in the hole, and move the hinge until the bit slips through the corresponding hole in the post. Do this with both hinges. Then (with at least one helper), attach the door to the other half of the hinges, and align them the same way. Snug up the bolts and carefully close the door to see if it fits properly in its opening. It should be pretty close if you've used the drill bit trick. But given the adjustability of most hinges, you can move the door forward or back, up or

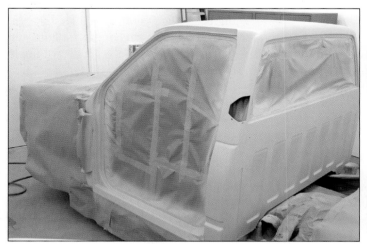 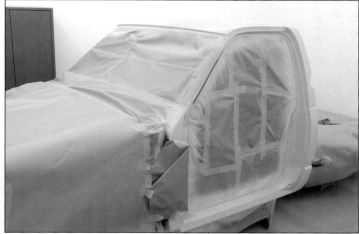

Here's another pickup undergoing a similar paint job, but to a greater degree and on purpose. Dave Crook has been working on this redesigned and customized SS-454 Chevy for a few years in his spotless home garage. While the cab is still on the frame, the dash is in it, and the running gear is all in place, Dave started this one by taking everything to bare metal with liquid stripper. After making modifications, doing bodywork, and lots of blocking with high-fill primer, these photos were taken just after his final primer coat before paint.

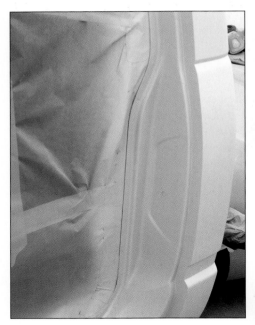

Here's a good look at how a well-finished doorjamb should be prepared.

Since this was a long-term project that required metalwork on most body panels, as well as blocking and painting, Dave built sturdy custom stands to hold the parts while he was working on them. It's a lot smarter, and ultimately easier, than chasing a loose fender around the garage floor.

In this photo, besides the easily accessible parts ready to paint on racks, note the exhaust fan Dave installed in the wall of his recently rebuilt backyard garage, plus the large pieces of masking paper he has taped to the wall next to it. Since he's now ready to shoot color, these are used to test his spray gun on as he adjusts the pattern. Smart.

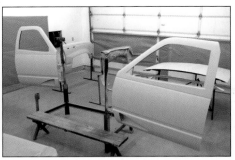

The doors are bolted (at the hinge locations) to an adjustable, roll-around rack of a type that used to be common in body-and-paint shops, though Dave built this one himself.

down, and in or out at the top, bottom, or both, until the gaps between it and the body are all equal. The same is true, more or less, of hoods and trunks, and in all cases the latches (strikers and dovetails, if they have them) must also be adjusted to hold these parts in the proper alignment when they're closed. If you've installed new rubber bumpers or weatherstrip seals, it might take a while for these to compress to get doors and other parts to close fully and properly. Or they might have to be trimmed or adjusted a little themselves.

When removing panels such as front fenders that have shims in them, save and mark the location of these so they can be reinstalled in the same place at the same thickness to start with. Shims can then be added or removed to fine tune the fit after the parts are painted and replaced.

Obviously, not scratching freshly painted body parts while reassembling them is paramount. A good precaution used by many painters is to run masking tape along the edges of both parts (such as the hood, cowl, and fenders), where they might touch. Just be sure

the paint is dry and cured enough that removing this tape won't pull off any fresh paint. This is where a less-sticky type of tape like the blue stuff is preferable.

Another old painters' trick is to use paint stirring sticks (or pieces of them) as wedges between doors and body, fenders and hood, and so on, to align them before tightening hinge bolts. They're made out of soft wood, and they're just the right thickness for most body gaps—about 1/8 inch.

But reassembling auto body components properly is something of an art that takes some practice and experience. Learning how to do it with all freshly

painted pieces is not a good idea. We strongly suggest that you do some practicing before you paint. At the least, loosen hinge bolts and fender attachments, and make sure that you can get everything to line up properly. Even if it all looks perfect to start with, loosen it all up, get it out of alignment (see which way things move), and then try to get it all straight again. Next, I'd suggest—assuming you plan to do the doors-off/glass-out level of paint job anyway— that you take the car apart before you start the sanding or stripping process. It's much easier to sand doorjambs when the doors aren't in the way. And it's easy to sand and prep the inside of a hood or trunk when it's loose and upside down—same with spraying paint, and even color sanding and rubbing out. That's the reason for this stage of paint job. It's ultimately more work,

 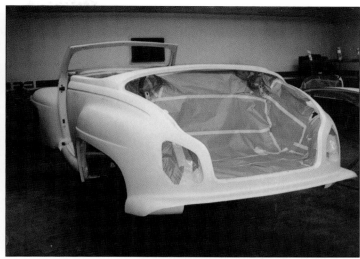

It'll be a while yet before Dave's done painting the pickup. But he did have some in-progress photos of his last, now-finished project: a full-custom '47 Ford convertible that you would have to see in person to fully appreciate. This one was built body-off-frame, with all parts initially chemical-stripped in submersion tanks. At this point Dave has welded and leaded the fenders, splash aprons, and other parts to the highly customized body, which has been metalworked and is now coated in high-fill primer for blocking.

As with the pickup, Dave made custom stands and racks from tubing to hold all the various body parts for working and, ultimately, painting. You can see that this work is being done in his home garage.

The body required a pretty hefty jig, which Dave mounted on a roll-around dolly for convenience. In this photo the body has been painted, color sanded, and rubbed-out, and is ready to be set on the completely finished and detailed chassis.

altogether, but it actually makes the job easier—and usually better.

As far as glass is concerned, this is one of those classic "it's a lot easier to take apart than to put back together" situations. On older vehicles that have rubber moldings around the windshield, back glass, and sometimes things like side quarter windows, we assume that you want to replace these with new, fresh rubber, which is available for most older vehicles these days. If so, the easiest way to get this glass out is to cut the lip off this rubber seal with a razor blade or X-Acto knife, all the way around, on the inside, and just pop the glass out. If, by any chance, new rubber isn't available and yours is reusable, you can carefully pry this lip, from the inside, over the metal edge of the window opening, with a dull putty knife, or preferably a similar tool made of plastic, being very careful not to cut or tear the rubber. On the other hand, if new glass seals aren't available, and yours is brittle and prone to cracking, maybe you should leave it and the glass in place and paint around it. Do this only as a last resort.

Taking roll-up side windows out is a more mechanical operation. When removing the glass on an older car, it's very wise to

The completed car—painted in many coats of jade green candy over a white pearl base—is incredible, not only in its many unique design features, but even more so in its flawless body fit and finish.

remove the felt channels and fuzz strips as well, because they should probably be replaced with new ones, and they're no fun to try to mask off.

Finally, once you get everything sanded, primed, painted, rubbed out, and fitted all back together, I strongly suggest you take the car to a good glass shop to have all the glass, rubber seals, channels, trim strips, and so on, replaced. You could do it at home—especially the side glass channels and so on—but we're not going to cover all that here. I've done it myself in the past many times, but it's taken me many years to realize it's so much easier (and not really that expen-

sive) to have a good professional auto glass guy do it, in his shop, with the proper tools and experience to fit things right the first time. The natural sequence is to have glass reinstalled once all the paint and rub out is finished, then the upholstery after the glass. However, on some vehicles there is some interface between upholstery and glass installation, especially in terms of headliners and sometimes with windlace or weatherstripping. So check with your upholsterer to see what should be done first on your vehicle.

When it comes to sanding, painting, rubbing, and detailing doorjambs, you're not going to find many better than this. And if it's this good here, imagine what the rest is like. This car has rightfully earned its share of show trophies and magazine covers. But it was built and painted by its owner in his backyard garage. Sure he's got years of experience now, but that's where he started. Have you been practicing?

COLOR SAND AND RUB OUT

Finally, let's take a look at this '60 Pontiac color sanded and rubbed-out by Bill Larzelere. The final rub out, done carefully and properly, is what takes any paint job—done by a pro or done by you at home—from the level of "as good as factory" to full-on custom paint. Anybody who knows cars and knows paint will immediately see the difference. And the best part about this final step is that it doesn't really cost anything other than a little polishing compound and a few sheets of sandpaper—plus your free time and effort. Yes, you can do all of this, and be proud of it.

There are at least as many ways to color sand and rub out your car as there are ways to put your pants on in the morning. And, given the title and scope of this book, you might think we'd want to show someone doing it at home. But why not show how one of the best does it, so you can learn some tricks? Bill Larzelere, who calls his business "Automotive Grooming" (Burbank, California), has detailed and rubbed out countless Pebble Beach classics and other well-known show winners over the past 30-plus years. Our demonstration subject is a cinnamon red '60 Pontiac.

In the old days of lacquer, you could color sand it with 600 paper, hand-rub it with paste compound, and you'd be ready for wax. Today's paints, either 1-stage or 2-stage, generally require color sanding in stages, beginning with 1000-grit and working up to 2500-grit or so. All color sanding should be done wet, and paper for it comes already cut in half-sheets, ready to fold in thirds. The best paper has the most uniform grit.

This low-mileage original needed little more than a new paint job, which the owner had resprayed in base coat/clear coat by a less-than-excellent painter. A good rub out person can save a mediocre paint job (to a point). But Bill had partially sanded this one when he realized the hood really needed to be resprayed. Unfortunately, as you can see, it still has plenty of orange-peel in the clear, but this is where we begin to follow the process.

This is finally it—the step that makes all that other work worthwhile. Many painters get real satisfaction from learning how to lay down a smooth, glossy, wet coat of paint with no orange peel or runs. But, even for a first-time amateur, seeing that glass-smooth gloss appear from the dull, color-sanded paint after a few passes with a buffer and compound is exhilarating. And it gets even better from there. The rub out with compound is good. But the polish step with a

good sealer/glaze is nearly miraculous. And adding a coat of your favorite car wax by hand is frosting on the cake—that you can continue doing for years to keep that shine just as good as new.

Even early brush-painted lacquer paint jobs, or those applied with bug sprayers or vacuum-cleaner attachments, can—and have been—color sanded and rubbed out to perfectly smooth and glossy finishes. Things have improved since then. In fact, the chances that you're

using lacquer paint are slim these days. If, by chance you have acquired and used lacquer paint, including clear, then you *must* finish the job by rubbing it out, because lacquer does not dry glossy. Lacquer, however, can be hand-rubbed, while most other paints these days can't be, easily.

Of course, you don't have to rub out your paint if it's not lacquer, or if it's base coat with the requisite clear coat. Nearly all types dry or harden very glossy, and you can leave it that way. Factory paint jobs are not rubbed out. Neither are most body shop jobs. But one thing that truly denotes a custom paint job is the rub out. Even on basic colors like black or red—in fact, *especially* on such colors—a glass-like rub out makes all the difference. Anybody who knows paint or cars, and most who don't, see it immediately.

But a couple of caveats: We cover all levels of paint jobs in this book. The color sand and rub out is for the top

Soak your wet-sanding paper at least 30 minutes, to soften it up, before use. Since he does this every day, Bill keeps various grits soaking in labeled, sealed containers in a cabinet in his shop, along with a variety of buffing compounds and polishes.

The entire rub out process can be quite messy. For color sanding, many painters keep a dribbling hose in one hand to continually rinse off sanding grit with clean water (if you do, a good tip is to tape around the metal hose end to avoid any paint scratches). I prefer a handy bucket of water to dip the paper in. Either method is best done outside, though hot sun doesn't help. Bill works inside, and prefers to apply small amounts of water directly to his pre-soaked paper from a squirt bottle.

Most color sanding should be done with some sort of block. Bill cuts a semi-hard rubber squeegee slightly smaller than the folded paper, so he can hold the paper by the edges as he sands in back-and-forth strokes, starting with 1000 grit on this fairly rough paint.

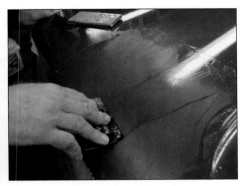

Color sanding is basically a visual process. The first step is to sand evenly until all the orange peel disappears. But to see what you're doing, you must continually clean the surface. Bill, like most, uses a small rubber squeegee to wipe off the water and grit. I like to use a chamois. Or you could even use a towel.

He also keeps a spray bottle of water handy to add more, if needed.

level. That means you have to do all the preliminary steps fully, and to equal quality, too. This refers primarily to bodywork and block sanding. If you're going to make the paint surface as smooth as glass, it immediately shows every ripple, dimple, sand-scratch, or any other imperfection that lies underneath it. If you don't rub out the paint, imperfect preparation won't show nearly as badly. As usual, it's your choice.

Rubbing out straight colors (red, yellow, black) is no problem. In fact, I see no reason to put clear coats over them, though people do. On the other hand, while you *can* rub out metallics, pearls, or candies, it is not recommended without adding a few liberal clear coats first. Paints with micro-particles in them (metallics, pearls) can do weird things when you rub on them, possibly flipping-over or "rearranging" those particles. Sanding and rubbing directly on transparent paints (candies) can possibly cause thin spots, which lightens the hue of the color. In both cases, it is much better to sand and rub on a clear coat on top of them, and it is imperative to put enough clear on so that you won't sand or rub through it at any time during these final steps.

On the other hand, the good part for amateur painters working in home garages, assuming you've done the **Continued on page 140**

Continued on page 140

Here you can see that some of the orange peel remains. The trick is to sand with the 1000-grit until all the shiny areas are gone, and the surface has a uniform satin finish, but not further.

In this concave area Bill is using a piece of small, round, pliable sponge rubber as his color-sanding block.

But in tight or delicate areas, he also uses his finger(s). Just be careful. Too little is always better than too much at any stage of this process. You can always sand or rub more later (other-wise you can spray more paint).

Never color sand directly on an edge, corner, or any raised/peaked surface. Sand up to it, as shown here and in the prior photo. If you sand on it, you will immediately go through the clear coat, if not through the paint—guaranteed.

For your first stage of color sanding, you can clearly see when orange peel disappears. But how can you tell how much to sand with 1500 or 2000 paper? The key through the whole sand/rub process is not to go too far at any one stage, so you don't go through the clear or color coats. One simple way to "see" your sanding progress with the next finer paper is to sand the opposite direction from the prior grit (90 degrees to it). Some use a light dusting of spray paint for a guide coat. Bill's secret is a thin coat of spray-on graphite, as shown, which not only gives a visual guide but also lubricates the paper at the same time. Ingenious.

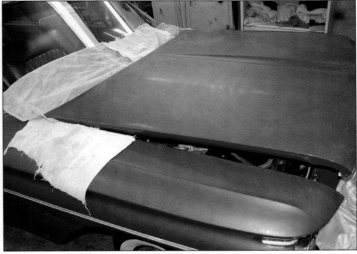

This is what a section of the hood looks like after a first round of color sanding with 1000-grit. All the orange peel is gone and it has a uniform satin finish. The towels and masking paper protect the already sanded areas and keep water and sanding sludge from getting in the engine compartment. If he were sanding the whole car at once, Bill would seal the seams with 3/4-inch tape.

This is the hood, finish-sanded to 2500-grit, ready for buffing (as is the previously sanded fender). As mentioned in the text, you should thoroughly rinse the surface between each sanding grit, and definitely before you start buffing.

With modern paints hand rubbing is impractical, if not impossible. Power buffing is at least a 2-stage process, consisting of buffing or "cutting" with an abrasive compound, followed by polishing (sometimes called "sealing") with a much less-abrasive glaze or polish. Either can be applied with a wool/yarn pad or the newer foam rubber style, and either of these is available in a bolt-on or Velcro attachment to a rubber or plastic backing pad. In either case, coarser pads are used for buffing/cutting, finer ones for polishing. Never use the same pad for both.

Although they look the same, metal grinders turn up to 6,000 rpm, while paint buffers should never turn more than about 2,500 (so you don't "burn" the paint). These days, a very practical style of buffer available from various manufacturers can be easily adjusted (with the orange rotary knob) from slow to faster speeds as you're working, to fit the application.

Bill begins the buffing process with an older-style wool-yarn pad that attaches to a hard rubber backing pad with a large screw-on nut.

It takes some practice to learn how much compound to apply (too much, a common problem, just clogs your pad). Bill starts by daubing abrasive rubbing compound on the surface with a brush. Most others squirt or dribble it from a squeeze bottle.

Although I readily admit that I've consistently had good results for years with Meguiar's and 3M products, it's my opinion that most automotive polishing products are snake oil. There's always some new latest, greatest thing and something else that claims to be better. Ask your paint store what the pros prefer. Test different products to see which work best for you. While most compounds and glazes come in (or can be put in) easy-to-apply pour bottles, as seen elsewhere in this book, Bill prefers to mix his own to a thick, brush-on consistency.

Start with your buffer on a low speed, so you don't fling the compound all over, holding it fairly level to the surface, to start working the compound into the paint. Then increase speed as you move the buffer back and forth. If you've done your color sanding adequately, the shine should come up quickly, as you can see.

Bill obviously knows what he's doing. Watching a deft rub-out guy do his thing is almost like watching a ballet. To a point, the more you buff, the more it shines. But you have to keep the pad moving constantly, cut with the leading edge, and know when to stop and add more compound to the next area. The cutting pad does generate heat, which can bubble or even burn the paint (turn it brown) if you stay in one area too long, press too hard, or run it too fast.

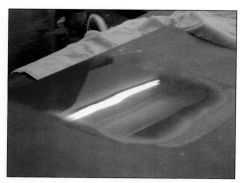

After a few passes back and forth one way, then the other, you should get a shine like this right away. Oh...this is what all that work was for!

preliminary steps well, is that the color sand and rub out not only removes sorange peel, it also removes small-dust, lint, or even minor surface dirt particles that inevitably get on your garage paint job. If you're careful, and use a block, you can even sand out minor runs or sags in your final coat.

Then again, if a big black bug lands in one of your clear coats, or some other nasty dirt somehow gets in it, you're not going to be able to just rub it out. You're going to have to sand it down, spray some more color in that area (if not the whole car), and reclear it. But we've said this all along: with lacquer or catalyzed paints, if

The buffer is even more dangerous than color sanding on or near peaks, ridges, or edges. Here Bill shows how to buff up to a painted peak, without buffing on it.

you screw something up, let it sit overnight, sand it the next morning, and start again where you left off. That's the thing about doing it yourself—if you do it once, you can do it again...and probably learn to do it better the second time.

The same goes for the rub out. It scares many amateur or first-time painters. People tell them, "You can ruin the whole paint job if you buff through it." Don't worry. We show you how to buff so you don't burn, blister, or bubble the paint.

Add compound and buff about a 4 to 6 sq. ft. section at a time, primarily so the compound doesn't dry out. But this is also good advice for beginners—take it slow and a little at a time until you start to feel comfortable with the buffer. And even then (maybe especially then) be careful—one bad "bite" from the buffer can ruin the paint.

Always remember that the buffer turns clockwise, and the outer edge moves the fastest. Here Bill demonstrates his axiom, "Buff off the edge"; meaning, the edge of the pad contacting the paint is moving away from (off) the lip of the hood. Another way he states it is, "Never cut towards, always away." That buffer has a lot of torque; if you ever "catch an edge" with it, you'll find out.

Here's another secret I'd never seen before: After adding compound to an area, Bill spritzes it with a little water from the spray bottle. This somehow keeps it from flying off in all directions when he starts buffing it. Also notice that he's put a liberal dose of compound on this slightly rougher area, and is using the outer edge of the buffing wheel, along with some pressure, to aggressively smooth down the paint. This is possible, but experience teaches you how aggressive you can be.

Your buffing wheel eventually loads up with rubbed-off paint and compound, and must be cleaned several times during a job. Bill is using a special spur-wheel made for this, as he spins the buffer; however, a wide screwdriver blade works nearly as well. On foam rubber pads, use a hair brush or your air nozzle to clean it.

With the hood buffed, Bill is going to start on the cowl and front fender. He's run one large piece of tape along the edge of the hood so he won't catch it with the buffer. Another smaller one covers the seam between hood and cowl, because he'll have to buff across both at once. When you're done power buffing, pull the tape and rub the edges by hand if they need it. But they probably won't need much.

You can power-buff areas like the concave dip in this hood if you do it carefully and gingerly, going slowly to start, and being very careful not to buff directly on the raised edge, on either side.

The sharp peak in the middle makes buffing the fender on this Pontiac difficult. Here Bill is buffing the fender up to the taped edge of the hood. Next he'll tip the buffer the other way and buff up to the fender peak, without getting on it.

This is a "don't do this at home" photo. Only a very experienced buffer should ever tip the pad on edge like this (Bill is buffing the hood edge closest to him, so the wheel is turning towards him, off the edge). If you don't know what you're doing, this trick could burn a hole through the paint in seconds.

But there's always a chance you might rub or sand through a paint layer, either because you rubbed too hard or too much, or because you didn't put enough paint on in the first place. No big deal. Put some more paint on (a little more than last time, right?), and start the buffing process again, with a more experienced hand this time.

In general, the rub out not only won't "ruin" your paint job, it allows you to turn out a top-quality paint job in your garage, at home, without needing a professional spray booth.

Here's a tip for beginners: since the color sand and rub out proceeds in steps, be conservative. It's easier to rub a little more paint off later than it is to put more paint back on. This also raises the issues of time and shrinkage. In the case of older lacquer paint jobs, you needed to let the paint sit and shrink for at least a couple of weeks before rubbing it out, and it usually needed another rub out about six months later because it would continue to shrink, including primer layers, at least that long. Modern catalyzed paints do not shrink nearly as much, though shrinkage is always a concern to some extent, especially after the painted vehicle has been out in the hot sun a few times. So this is another reason to make sure you put enough paint or clear on the car—you might very well want to rub it out again after six months or a year, or more.

On the other hand, some types of urethane clears chemically harden so much that they become very difficult to buff to a

In the text we say to thoroughly wash all surfaces to remove any traces of compound before starting the glaze step. That's best. But since he keeps things pretty clean as he goes, and he's working inside the shop, Bill wipes the surface of the hood with a static brush to remove any residue.

For the glaze/polish, Bill uses a foam pad on a Velcro backing. Whether foam or wool, polishing pads are finer and softer than cutting pads, so you need at least one of each. Whether you use foam or wool for either is your personal choice.

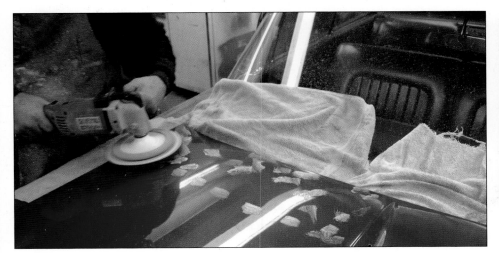

Again, Bill likes to apply his special-mixed glaze with a brush. The key here is to be sparing—it doesn't take much; using too much just gunks up the surface and the pad.

You might have thought the paint looked nice and shiny in the prior pictures, but I think even these photos show the magical difference the glaze makes.

shine, after color sanding, even with a power buffer and cutting pad. These clears must be sanded and buffed within two or three days of being sprayed, before they fully harden. Check with your paint dealer about this when selecting and purchasing the clear for your paint job.

In any case, most of the modern paints—especially clears—are nearly impossible to hand rub. They need to be sanded with successively finer grits of "ultra-fine" paper—from 1000 to as fine as 2500 grit—and then power-buffed with compound, followed by power-polishing with a glaze.

All color sanding should be done wet, preferably with a rubber pad behind the paper. It is imperative to keep the water, paper, and surface clean of any dirt or particles that can scratch the surface. Since you can't see what you're doing while the surface is wet, keep a squeegee or chamois handy to wipe the water off to see how your sanding is progressing. It's easy to see where you need to sand more once you wipe it dry; sand only enough to make the surface look uniform—don't oversand at any stage. When you progress from one grit of paper to another, and after each buffing session, thoroughly wash the surface with clean water to remove any traces of the rougher grit or compound.

Other tips and tricks are shown in the photos. But there really isn't a whole lot of science or magic to any of this whole process. It's mostly perspiration and patience. The magic is when you finally, after all this work, get to the stage when that amazing gloss comes up after a few passes with the polishing buffer. You might think the main reason you're doing this is to save a few thousand dollars. But that's not half as good as being able to lean back against that glass-smooth, deep-gloss paint on you car at the drive-in, gas station, or car show and say with well-deserved pride, "Yes, I did this myself."

Before we finish, anyone rubbing out paint should know about these relatively new mini-buffing pads, again available at your automotive paint store. They mount on a 1/4-inch drive mandrel, which can be used with a drill motor (variable speed is preferred) or with an air-drive right-angle die grinder to get into tighter spots (but be careful to limit RPM). The lighter colored pad is for compound buffing, while the yellowish one is for glaze polishing. They are excellent for buffing in small areas, such as between louvers (as shown) or on a dashboard, where a full-size buffing pad not only wouldn't fit, but could be dangerous.

You saw the orange peel in the clear coat in the opening photos. Now look at how clearly you can see the objects against the shop wall reflected in the hood. And this, believe it or not, is just the beginning of a Bill Larzelere rub-out. Now he'll spend considerably more time with even finer secret hand-rubbing glazes to make the finish "crisper." Like most steps in this book, all it takes is your time and patience, which is free. The satisfaction with a beautifully finished job is priceless. The best part about this final step is that it doesn't really cost anything other than a little polishing compound and a few sheets of sandpaper—plus your free time and effort. Yes, you can do all of this, and be proud of it.

HOW TO PAINT YOUR CAR ON A BUDGET